England for All Seasons

BY SUSAN ALLEN TOTH

*Blooming**

*Ivy Days**

*How to Prepare for Your High-School Reunion**

Reading Rooms
(editor, with John Coughlan)

A House of One's Own
(with James Stageberg)

*My Love Affair with England**

*England As You Like It**

*England for All Seasons**

*Published by Ballantine Books

ENGLAND
FOR ALL SEASONS

Susan Allen Toth

BALLANTINE BOOKS • *NEW YORK*

http://www.randomhouse.com

LIBRARY OF CONGRESS CATALOGING IN PUBLICATION DATA
Toth, Susan Allen.
    England for all seasons / Susan Allen Toth. — 1st ed.
        p.   cm.
    ISBN 0-345-40390-8
    1. England—Description and travel.   2. Toth, Susan Allen—
Journeys—England.   I. Title
DA632.T66   1997
914.204'859—dc21   96-44395
                                                              CIP

Manufactured in the United States of America

First Edition: March 1997

10   9   8   7   6   5   4   3   2   1

For James Stageberg, who is my beacon,
and for Molly Friedrich, who has kept me on course

Contents

III. AT THE WATER'S EDGE

IV. BEYOND PICCADILLY: FAVORITE PLACES

V. THE IMPERFECT TRAVELER

Acknowledgments

Some of these chapters originally appeared, under different titles, in slightly different form, in *The New York Times*, *The Washington Post*, the *Los Angeles Times*, the *Minneapolis Star Tribune*, and *Garden Design*.

England for All Seasons:
An Introduction

"What is the best time to go to England?" When I hear this familiar question, I have a short answer. Go when you can. Go for your summer vacation, for a week over Christmas, for as long as your mother will take the kids or the teenager next door will feed the cats. Go (as my husband and I do) when the airlines announce a fare war, when Uncle Sam gives you a tax refund, when your garden is past its peak, when it is too hot or cold at home, when you hear of a fairly inexpensive London hotel or rental apartment, when you just plain get lonely for England. (It is possible, readers tell me, to feel lonesome for England even if you've never been there.)

But the question, "When is the best time to go?," has another dimension, one that implies a certain understandable anxiety. For most travelers, a trip to England is a very big deal. It doesn't happen often, it costs a lot of money, and it requires some planning. People who ask about the best time for a trip are not harum-scarum, frantic, last-minute travelers. They are looking ahead, thinking about their vacation, wanting to make the most of it. When they return, they want to savor their experiences. This book is written for them.

England for All Seasons, like my earlier books, *My Love Affair with England* and *England As You Like It*, is a personal account of my independent, often idiosyncratic travels in England. It is intended as an encouraging guide and a friendly, if highly opinionated, companion for other independent-minded travelers. It will not tell you where or when to watch the Changing of the Guard at Buckingham Palace, how to find Madame Tussaud's, or which London restaurants serve the best roast beef and Yorkshire pudding. Such information is easily available in many all-purpose guidebooks.

England for All Seasons, on the other hand, may perhaps lure you to a Moorish-style Victorian artist's studio in Kensington, an early-morning meat market near St. Paul's, a modern grand castle on the edge of Dartmoor, a flowering churchyard beside a hidden Cornish estuary, a romantic beach in Anglesey, or a donkey sanctuary in Devon. It will take you through a pedestrian tunnel across the Thames, into the driver's seat of a London double-decker bus, across a remote burn on the Isle of Mull—and more.

In Section I, "England's Special Pleasures," I deal immediately with England's famous weather. (See Chapter 1, "In Praise of English Rain," to see how I can possibly think of it with pleasure.) Since few Americans know about the popular English pastime of garden visiting, I want to urge readers to set foot on the nearest garden path (Chapter 2, "The Art of Garden Visiting"). For travelers who are book lovers, I offer a kind of miniguide to literary England (Chapter 4, "Looking for Literary Landscapes"). In other chapters, I reveal my predilections for English desserts (Chapter 3, "Hitching a Ride on the Sweet Trolley"), for quirky English books as souvenirs (Chapter 5, "A Suitcase Full of Books"), and for one of the world's great cities (Chapter 6, "Lolloping Around London").

In Section II, "Meandering Through Museums," I describe several intriguing galleries and museums. Most of my choices are in London, but one, the Barbara Hepworth Museum and Sculpture Garden, is tucked away on a side street in the charming little resort of St. Ives.

In *England As You Like It*, I proposed my "thumbprint theory of travel," which suggests staying for a week at a time in one out-of-the-way place. Section III, "At the Water's Edge," includes three such "thumbprints," one at the tip of a cape near Falmouth, another on the Isle of Mull in Scotland's Hebrides, and the third on the Welsh peninsula of Anglesey. (Scotland and Wales, though part of the United Kingdom, are ancient lands with distinct histories and cultures of their own. I have sneakily included them in this book because so many travelers, once in England, do continue beyond the strictly English borders to Scotland and Wales.) For those travelers who choose to remain in London, I suggest Chapter 14, "New Views on An Ancient River."

Section IV, "Beyond Piccadilly: Favorite Places," adds some new entries to my continuing list of personal favorites. (For others, see *My Love Affair with England* and *England·As You Like It.*) These are places most first-time travelers to England might easily miss; some I didn't discover myself for years.

I am not an ideal traveler. I worry, fuss, second-guess myself, and sometimes wonder, tossing on an unfamiliar bed in a strange room, why I'm doing this at all. In Section V, "The Imperfect Traveler," I include a few observations on the ways I've learned to cope.

Yes, But When Should We Go?

England for All Seasons is intended to inspire readers to go to England whenever they can. As I've learned from meeting them and reading their letters, my readers are usually both curious and determined. So when I say, "Go any time," they often insist, "Yes, but when? What is the best month?" If you can indeed choose from all seasons, I have a longer answer—though in the end, it sounds a lot like the shorter one.

In March, April, and May, an English spring (though sometimes gray and damp) can be spectacularly green, fresh, and flowery. At the edge of some woodlands, daffodils still linger, and rhododendrons, azaleas, and magnolias blaze across the countryside in swirls of white, pink, yellow, and red like an Impressionist painting. Remember Robert Browning's pang of homesickness in his poem, "Oh, to be in England now that April's there"? He knew precisely what he was missing.

In June, England's famed roses burst into full bloom, the weather is often especially fine, and daylight lasts late into the evening. You can walk along a country lane after supper, watch the slow, gentle dusk beginning to shadow the hillside, and perhaps startle a few rabbits that are nibbling at the edges of blossoming hedgerows. In London, you can stroll in a pleasant twilight across one of the parks on your way to the theatre or take in one of the many other beguiling entertainments of the season.

In July and August, tourists do increase to a flood. But not all Americans realize that the real crush only begins around the middle of July, when British (and European) schools let out for a long break and families head for the roads. Don't be afraid to go in early July. Everything is open, often until late hours, and parks and gardens are in showoff shape.

Don't be afraid of the rest of the summer, either. If you plan carefully, you can often escape the crowds. Get started quite early in the morning, while slowpokes are still weighed down with bacon, eggs, and fried tomatoes and tour-bus operators haven't yet revved up their engines. Plan to eat at unfashionable times, like eleven-thirty A.M. or six P.M. You might even evade busy restaurants entirely by packing a lunch or supper from a grocery store or deli and dining outdoors in splendor (well, maybe under an umbrella), perhaps on a bench in Kensington Gardens or Green Park.

Avoid, if possible, the jam-packed lanes of Cornwall, the Lake District, or the Cotswolds on a high-summer weekend. But even at the most popular tourist destinations, you can almost always find some breathing space. Many people do not know about the pleasures of walking in England. If you have provided yourself with sturdy shoes and proper maps, you can head for the nearest footpath. (Ask for a Pathfinder map at a local bookstore; for a full discussion of British maps, see "Draw Me a Map!" in *England As You Like It*.) In a few minutes, the only other traveler you'll meet will probably be a British rambler.

In the fall, English summer can sometimes defer its departure for months. September and October may be sunny and mild—or cool, rainy, and windy, the kind of weather BBC announcers portentously describe as "equinoctial." Accommodations are easier to find. (Don't expect prices or availability to change right after our Labor Day. English schools often don't begin their fall terms until mid-September.) By late September, most visitors to the countryside have gone home, but many major tourist attractions—castles, country houses, gardens, seasonal museums, monuments, amusement parks—remain open until about the end of October.

By mid-November, some attractions outside of London close for the winter, reopening only in late March or early April. Don't plan on a late-fall visit to Hever Castle, Blenheim Palace, Chartwell, Beatrix Potter's Hill Top, or Sissinghurst, for example. In and around London, some places, like Hampton Court, Kew Gardens, the Banqueting House, and Sir John Soane's Museum, as well as major palaces and museums, stay open year-round. Others, like Carlyle's House, the Museum of Garden History, and Osterley Park, do not. Check before you go to avoid disappointment.

Since the sun can sometimes shine brightly enough to make up for drastically shortened days, November can still be a pleasant month for country excursions. A selection of gardens and country houses outside London do remain open, occasionally with reduced hours or only over weekends. Dover Castle, Stourhead Landscape Garden, Stonehenge, Tintagel Castle, St. Michael's Mount, and Anne Hathaway's Cottage, among others, welcome year-round visitors.

Anyone who has ever read much of Dickens knows about Christmas in England. By early December, Christmas is already lighting up London, with concerts, pantomimes, special family-oriented theatrical productions like *Treasure Island* or *The Wind in the Willows*, and carol services in Westminster Abbey. Many country-house hotels offer special (and expensive) packages over the holidays, complete with midnight wassail, plum pudding, and presents from St. Nick.

You don't need a package tour to spend Christmas in the country. The owner of a small bed-and-breakfast near Penzance once told me that he thought the holiday season was a marvelous time to be in

Cornwall. The climate was usually so mild—many Cornish gardens shelter semitropical plants—that he often only needed a light (waterproof) jacket for his walks. On fine days, he tramped the beach, and on blustery or stormy days, he sat by the fireside and read. It sounded so peaceful that I've been waiting for just the right Christmas to try it.

In late December and early January, the after-Christmas sales explode, with bargains like fireworks lighting up the streets, attracting shoppers who have a fierce fervor that startles many Americans. (Want to try queuing in a sleeping bag outside Harrods the night before?) The dead-of-winter months, January and February, can be dark, wet, and cold. Dramatic storms sometimes roar inland from the sea, smashing trees and closing country roads, and coastal resorts shutter their windows. (London, of course, never shuts down.) Snow puts a chilly cap on higher hills and mountains, especially in the north. But these months can also be seductively free of tourists, and in a mild winter, crocuses and daffodils will begin to glow by February, or even earlier, in meadows and gardens across much of England.

If England can be wonderful in all seasons, when should you go? How soon can you clean out your refrigerator, stop your mail, find your passport, and pack a bag? Maybe the best time to go to England is tomorrow.

Who's Who in England for All Seasons

Readers of my earlier books already know my cast of characters, mainly myself and James, a.k.a. James Stageberg—husband, chauffeur, adviser, and architectural critic. As we slog along a muddy footpath, with a driving rain seeping down our necks, James is apt to burst, unexpectedly, loudly, and with great cheer, into an off-key refrain of "Side by Side," "It's a Long Way to Tipperary," or "Don't Fence Me In." He confidently drives on the left side of British motorways and country lanes. At celebratory moments, he also knows how to jump up in the air and click his heels. Speaking as his fellow traveler, I find these no small talents.

Notes on a Few Floating Facts

At the end of many chapters, I include a few relevant facts—addresses, phone numbers, and other topical information. (To call England from most telephones in the U.S., dial 0-11-44 and then the English number. When dialing in England, use a "0" before the local number. Drop the "0" when calling from the U.S.) But facts change rapidly, just as currency, varying with the daily tremors of international finance, is sometimes said to "float." So I call these afterwords "A Few Floating Facts" to remind readers to recheck these facts carefully before leaving for England and check them again once they've arrived. Stay abreast—and afloat.

I

England's Special Pleasures

One reader's passion for antique trucks takes him to England for the annual London-to-Brighton antique-truck run. Others have reported their fascination with prehistoric standing stones, medieval castles, haunted country houses, London antiques markets, thatched-roof cottages, Beatles landmarks, canal boats, maritime museums, cream teas, James Herriot's Yorkshire, D-Day launching beaches, and the vagaries of the British royal family. Traveling around England, everyone discovers his or her own favorite—and often distinctly different—pleasures. Here are a few of mine.

1

In Praise of English Rain

Everyone knows it rains in England. Friends who always take their holidays in sunny climes ask me in kindly but puzzled tones, "How can you keep returning to a country where the weather is so dreadful?" What they really mean by *dreadful* is rain—chilly rain, frequent rain, sometimes constant rain, not to mention mist, fog, damp, and the gray skies that continually promise rain.

Yet those who love England can also sometimes come to love its rain. One of England's early anonymous poems is a marvel of intense longing: "Western wind, when wilt thou blow, / The small rain down can rain? / Christ, if my love were in my arms / And I in my bed again!" Whenever I read that short lyric, I picture myself snuggled into a warm bed, listening to wind whistling down a chimney and rain beating a lulling rhythm on an English roof.

My first view of England was through a gentle, drizzly rain. Eagerly staring out my airplane window more than thirty years ago, I gazed into a kaleidoscope of brilliant greens, softened by a kind of gray filter. It was a dreamy and almost unreal landscape. To someone raised on the midwestern plains—accustomed to the sharp clarity of blazing sunshine, the clean brilliance of snow, and brief, dark, dramatic thunderstorms—English rain seemed part of the romance upon which I had just embarked.

As my romance eventually became tempered by familiarity, I realized that English rain was not, alas, always or entirely wonderful. It could blur the passing landscape beyond recognition. It could turn a long hike unpleasant, if not impracticable. It could make me (and everyone else on a train or bus or Underground) smell of old wool and new vinyl. It could turn pocket tissues into soggy wads and dissolve the ink on my postcards. It could seep between my shoulder blades, somehow trickle up my sleeves, and soak mercilessly into my socks.

But over the years, I came to an accommodation with English rain. I even began to distinguish among its myriad varieties. Now I can cope with some, endure others, and, under the right conditions, cherish a few.

The best kind of rain, of course, is a cozy rain. This is the kind the anonymous medieval poet makes me remember, the rain that falls on a day when you'd just as soon stay in bed a little longer, write letters or read a good book by the fire, take early tea with hot scones and jam, and look out the streaked window with complacency. I also like a fresh rain, following a day or two of fairly hot sunshine, so that next morning the grass has a tender, vibrant springiness and gardens are dripping with dew.

I also appreciate a convenient rain. This rain occurs on a day when you have reluctantly agreed to an expedition you really don't want to undertake. A heavy rain means you can probably bow out of your three-hour boat trip to Puffin Island, your guided walking tour of Jack the Ripper sites, perhaps even (if the rain is heavy enough) your lunch with not-very-good-friends-from-home because, you assure them, you'll never be able to get a taxi.

A teasing rain is more problematical. This is the light rain that falls in a faint shower, then subsides into a bit of drizzle here, another drizzle there. Umbrellas open and close more often than tourists' camera shutters, and the tourists themselves can begin to snap. Once, as my husband and I were descending the steps at Castle Drogo, a family just ahead of us was trying to assess a teasing rain. The daughter (whose umbrella was down) said to her mother (whose umbrella was up), "See, it's not raining anymore."

"Yes, it is," said the mother.

"No, it's not," said the daughter more insistently. She held her hand palm-up to the sky to prove her point.

"Yes, it *is*," returned the mother, not bothering to look at her daughter's hand, "*and* I'm going to keep my umbrella up!" They both marched on in silence.

"It *is* raining, you know," I turned and muttered quietly to my husband. My umbrella was up.

"No, it's not," said James, just as firmly. His umbrella was down.

Rain in England can be very sneaky. That is why I am always prepared for rain at unlikely times and places. One bright, sunny June morning in Cornwall, when I tucked my umbrella into the car trunk, James hooted. "Boy, I wish I had a picture of you now!" he said, not unkindly. "What a pessimist you are! Imagine taking an umbrella on such a beautiful day!"

Of course, when a heavy afternoon shower caught us at an outdoor seal sanctuary, I hooted (umbrella up) as James, drenched, finally sprang for a ride in the motorized miniature tram back to the parking lot. I was sorry that the tram moved too quickly for me to take his picture.

English weather forecasters know all about the unpredictability of rain. In the "Travel and Weather Outlook" section of the London *Times*, a small masterpiece of obfuscation, they usually manage to keep their umbrellas up and down at the same time. I sometimes wonder if they smile secretively to themselves as they write: "Mostly dry, with patchy rain possible later. Some sunny spells"—or "Cloudy with outbreaks of rain at times. However, there will be drier interludes."

Sometimes an unpredictable rain can be rather exciting. During the months I prefer to travel in England, thunder showers are rare, but when they occur—usually without warning—they can have spectacular effects. Last summer in Cornwall, on what had begun as a sunny day, from inside our rented cottage I suddenly heard distant roaring sounds. Startled, I looked at James. "Just airplanes taking off," he assured me. "Maybe an air show over Falmouth." But the show was not manmade, and a few thunderclaps later, our lights, refrigerator, stove, and hot-water heater all went off in a flash, not to be revived for many long hours. It all seemed far too dramatic, too definite, too light-and-dark for true English weather.

The aftermath of that thunder shower introduced me to another kind of rain, a Mediterranean interlude. Rain kept falling on and off all day, yet the temperature was warm, so that everything felt uncharacteristically hot and steamy. We might have suddenly turned a corner and found ourselves on a summer street in Venice. We ate that noon in a large teashop, filled with other storm-tossed tourists looking for someone cooking on a gas stove. The room was so overheated and stuffy that I finally walked to a latched window—sensing many eyes upon me—and threw it open. As I sheepishly sat down again, a woman at a nearby table spoke up and said heartily, "Well done!"

Thinking later about her very British accolade, I realized that she, and probably many other diners in that very proper room, had also been uncomfortable in the damp heat. But no one had moved to open a window. Why? Perhaps, I decided, because to open a window would have been to acknowledge something about the weather, to notice and comment upon it, to actually try to *do* something about it. I had behaved, I now considered, in a very American way. Paying close attention to English rain was clearly only a stage on the path. I was evidently still a long way from true acceptance.

2

The Art of Garden Visiting

Perhaps I'm happiest in an English garden. As soon as I start down the path—maybe winding among sculptured dark green hedges, or luminous pale pink magnolias, or blazingly blue delphiniums mixed with white daisies—I leave the ordinary world. I forget the churning traffic along the M25, lingering jet lag, and the jagged rip in my new parka. I don't plan ahead for dinner. I don't wonder what we'll do tomorrow. I don't examine my life. While I am in the garden, I am joyously immersed in here-and-now. Sometimes subtly and sometimes with bravado, a good garden demands my full attention.

I'm not always sure where to focus first. Should I look around and try to understand its "bones," the garden's underlying structure and design? Should I walk all the paths, investigate every "room" or enclosure, circle the small lake, and follow the woodland walk—and then return to luxuriate in the color and fragrance of the perennial borders? Or should I stop right here, where the scarlet shrub roses crowd into red, pink, and white hollyhocks against a faded redbrick wall, and bend down to sniff the sweet white nicotiana brushing my knee?

I can't remember when I saw my first English garden. When I think back to my first student trip in 1960, my memories are suffused with flowers. Perhaps Queen Mary's Rose Garden in Regent's Park? Its midsummer color, from thousands of perfect roses in precisely arranged beds, still glows on a slide from that long-ago July. Or should I count the wavy green fronds of vegetable gardens, each with its own ramshackle potting shed, that seemed to line all the backyards on the way into London? What about the fancy wrought-iron window boxes in Mayfair, overflowing with primrose, viola, and verbena? Or the geometric floral patterns in the centers of residential London squares?

"Our England is a garden," wrote Kipling in a beloved poem that usually manages to appear on a tea towel, ceramic plaque, postcard, or decorated poster in almost every garden souvenir shop. Gardens are everywhere. They bloom and burgeon in front of country cottages, on landscaped rural acres, around castles and manors, on seaside promenades, and in town parks. On the forbidding slope of St. Michael's Mount in Cornwall, a rocky island battered by fierce salt spray, an exuberant garden tumbles down to the sea. Not far away, at the isolated medieval church of St. Just-in-Roseland on a tidal estuary, a semitropical garden shaded by palm trees flourishes among the gravestones (see Chapter 15, "A Beacon on the Cornish Coast"). A few miles in the other direction, in the middle of the seaside resort of St. Ives, Barbara Hepworth's polished marble and bronze sculptures gleam among the foliage of a small walled garden that is also a museum (see Chapter 13).

Some extensive gardens like Wakehurst Place, Wisley, or Kew, have miles of paths to explore. Margery Fish's intimate dense garden at East Lambrook Manor in Somerset is not larger than an acre. At Hever Castle, the theatrical grounds include a maze, ornate gardens with classical sculpture, grottos, an orchard, and a large, tree-lined lake. At Minterne, near Minterne Magna in Dorset, the garden simply consists of a meandering mile-and-a-half walk among spring-flowering shrubs. Port Lympne's garden, on the Kentish coast, stands in the midst of a wild animal park. Scotney Castle Garden encircles a calculatedly romantic ruin. No one garden is like any other.

I do not think anyone has ever tried to count the number of gardens in the United Kingdom. My most recent *Good Gardens Guide* rates more than a thousand, and *Gardens of England & Wales* lists almost thirty-five hundred (see below, "How to Find English Gardens"). Only in England do I sometimes think of our vacation as a series of stops at different gardens. In between, James and I may take long walks, tour country houses and castles, and visit historical monuments. But we always look forward to the next garden.

"Garden visiting" is a peculiarly British pastime, an increasingly popular hobby for an occasional weekend or a two-week holiday. I grew up knowing nothing about it. In my Midwest, most people take their local gardens rather for granted, as pleasant but not very exciting. Who would make a special trip to admire a rectangular bed with zinnias and marigolds in military formation, a modest assortment of lilacs and bridal-wreath clumped alongside a garage, or dusty circles of petunias in a nearby park? Few of the more imaginative gardens are ever open to public view, and only the largest cities or universities can afford arboreta and botanical gardens.

My passion for garden visiting developed slowly. For many years on my trips to England, I was much more attracted to cathedrals, castles, historic sites, and ancient monuments. Gardens somehow did not seem very significant. Then, after I married James, who, as an architect, wanted to explore country houses and volunteered to drive us to them, I began to observe that almost every country house had a landscaped setting—lawns with pebble paths, terraces, lakes, woodland trails, or perhaps a deer park. Both James and I love to walk, and the grounds of these houses offered spectacular possibilities. Although I was reasonably intrigued by Tudor linenfold paneling, coffered plaster ceilings, and carved mantelpieces, I became increasingly drawn to what awaited outside. Would the sun still be shining, I wondered uneasily, when we finally escape these Louis XIV chairs to stroll among the roses, catmint, and geraniums?

As I have grown older, I have tried—not always successfully—to rush less and savor more. When I was twenty, I do not think I could have lingered very long in any garden, no matter how seductive. But gradually I began to look forward to those suspended hours in gardens when I wasn't in a hurry, didn't need to talk to anyone, and couldn't do anything much except walk slowly, sit for a while on a well-placed bench, and quietly look around. Nor did the weather really matter. Except in a downpour, I could simply raise my umbrella and walk on. Flowers still sparkle in the rain.

A Short Potted Guide to Garden History

Just as enjoying an art museum is easier if one knows something about paintings, it is more fun to visit English gardens if you know something about their history, styles, and different features. For me, a bit of background often makes the foreground come more sharply into focus, and I tend to zoom in on what I might otherwise miss.

Anyone wanting to learn about English gardens can devote long, satisfying hours to all kinds of preparatory study. Most good-size libraries and bookstores provide wide-ranging reading on what many consider England's great art form. On my own shelves I now have books on cottage gardens, topiary gardens, water gardens, country-house gardens, royal gardens, vicarage gardens, gentlewomen's gardens, eccentric gardens, individual gardens, and illustrated advice from contemporary gardeners like John Brookes, Penelope Hobhouse, Christopher Lloyd, and Rosemary Verey on designing and planting shade gardens, country gardens, flower-arrangers' gardens, and more. In a long, cold Minnesota winter, I can never look at too many pictures of roses.

But not everyone wants to flip through dozens of books, or even one book, before heading off to England and its gardens. So, in the hope of encouraging novice garden visitors, I offer here a few short notes, which recklessly generalize, omit much, and leap over centuries in a line or two. Garden history is a highly speculative subject, for unlike stone houses, castles, and fortifications, gardens are perishable, seldom lasting even fifty years, at least in their original states. No true medieval garden has entirely survived.

Among the earliest gardens you will see in your travels are probably versions of the Renaissance *knot garden*. These are made of low, closely clipped hedging, either dwarf box (short for *boxwood*) or yew, whose lines form knotlike geometric patterns, like diamonds, circles, or trefoils, often contained within a square. (You'll also see lots of these spiky green hedges in other kinds of gardens. Box thrives in England's mild damp climate and so does yew, though more slowly.) Paths, usually of gravel, wind among these knots. In "open knots," the intervening spaces are filled with gravel, colored earth, sand, or grass. "Closed knots" are filled with flowers or herbs.

Lords and ladies in manor houses liked to look down from their windows at *parterres*, geometric designs of cut turf or low box hedges or flower beds laid out in highly formal arrangements. Paths some-times led to a fountain in the middle. Parterres became popular in the seventeenth century, fell out of favor, and returned to Victorian landscape schemes. They still linger in many municipal gardens, where primroses, petunias, snapdragons, and other sturdy bright flowers are arranged in predetermined patterns. (Watch for the occasional fanciful gardener who blithely plants in the shape of a cloverleaf, heart, swan, or even, ostentatiously, the letters of the town's name.)

Various European influences affected English garden design over the centuries. When a garden is composed mainly of parterres, artifi-cial pools, fountains, sculptured topiary (see below), and classical statuary, it is often said to be vaguely *Italianate*, though in fact it may be French and Dutch as well. Still, if you find yourself looking at a garden that is short on flowers but long on carefully cut shapes and rigid lines, and then you spy a statue of a revealingly draped, blank-faced young woman, perhaps a Diana clutching her bow and arrows, you can probably safely mutter, "Ah, yes. How Italianate." Unless a garden expert is standing next to you, you are on secure (and probably gravel-packed) ground.

If you are looking instead at rolling hills, a distant lake, and sheep grazing peacefully among magnificent trees, you might muse aloud, "Looks like Capability Brown was here." You have a very good chance of being right. Lancelot Brown, known as "Capability" because of his references to the *capabilities* of a setting, arrived with great éclat on the mid-eighteenth-century gardening scene. Away with parterres, straight lines, circles, and knots. Farewell to fountains, rigid avenues, and marble nymphs. No more fancy flower gardens. Often no more flowers, period. What Capability wanted was a broad landscape canvas upon which to create natural effects.

For thirty-five years, until his death in 1783, Capability Brown practiced a style of garden design that became known as "picturesque." His clients, who usually had enough wealth to hire infinite hours of labor, transformed their estates. They created new hills, dammed streams, and dug lakes. They often had to plant hundreds, sometimes thousands, of trees. Eventually they were able to look from the windows and terraces of their grand country houses into an idealized bucolic world, as much a planned composition as any painting.

Anyone who travels much in England gets to know Capability Brown and his followers. If you praise the curving lake in the park at Petworth House in West Sussex, you are paying homage to Capability. At Blenheim, when you gaze over placid hills to two large lakes and eye-catching groves of trees, you are looking at one of Capability's triumphs. At Stowe, Burghley House, Warwick Castle, Longleat, Hampton Court, Kew Gardens, Holkham Hall, Chatsworth, Milton Abbey, Castle Ashby, and Claremont Landscape Garden, among others, you are in the (sometimes diluted) presence of the master.

When you are observing, rather impressively, that you've just identified Capability's work, you might inquire if anyone has happened to notice the *ha-ha*. This is a little tricky. If your audience has never heard of a ha-ha, he or she may look at you as if you had unexpectedly hiccuped. A ha-ha is simply a dry ditch, usually constructed with retaining walls, that separates parkland from the house. Looking across the ha-ha, an observer sees only a seamless vista, as if the grassy pastures or lawns rolled right up to the terrace or front door. But the ha-ha keeps the horses, cows, deer, or sheep at a comfortably safe distance.

Animals, incidentally, were often an important part of Capability's overall strategy. Not only does a flock of sheep, slowly browsing under beech and oak trees, look very pastoral, but they are nonstop mowing machines. Landscape on such a large scale requires a certain amount of upkeep, though not nearly as much as a showy Italianate garden. That is another reason why landowners loved Capability.

Besides picturesque and calculatedly pastoral landscapes, the other quintessentially English garden style is known as a *cottage garden*. If, when you say the words "English garden," you immediately envision a thatched-roof cottage whose front yard is a riotous mass of old-fashioned flowers like roses, peonies, pinks, wallflowers, marigolds, foxglove, and hollyhocks, you are thinking of one of the most beloved English scenes, memorialized in countless postcards and snapshots.

Cottage gardens abound in England, endlessly varied examples of small-scale domestic gardening at its very best. Often you must marvel at them from the street. Sometimes the whole front of a half-timbered house is buried under a tapestry of flowers, perhaps pink climbing roses seductively tangled with white clematis, and a flourish of sky-blue cranesbill geraniums and white daisies crowding below. Or a meandering brick walk, its edges muffled by a low blanket of creeping thyme, may be lined with rows of deep blue, yellow, and purple lupine, with velvety purple pansies at their feet.

If you yourself are a gardener, you quickly realize that these seemingly casual, even random swirls of color and fragrance actually require judicious planning. In the best cottage gardens, something is always in bloom, with no gaps or bare spaces, and different shades and colors balance or play off each other.

I envy English cottage gardens. As a somewhat haphazard gardener, doomed to the short, frantic growing season of the upper Midwest, I eye those rampant roses, clematis, and delphiniums with delight tempered by fruitless despair. Even the English soil in such gardens, friable and rich with mulch and manure, often looks like it came out of an aristocratic catalogue. Peering under leaves, I sometimes look hopefully in cottage gardens for signs of a few telltale weeds, but they almost seem to have vanished magically. (The magic, naturally, is in the hands of all the devoted gardeners you'll see working in their plots morning, noon, and night.)

Related to the cottage garden is the extravagant bloom of a traditional *herbaceous border*, a prized feature of most larger English gardens. When you hear this mouthful of a phrase, perhaps from someone who may have heard you showing off about Capability Brown, don't panic. Just remember that *herbaceous* only means perennial plants. These are flowers like delphinium, daisies, iris, primrose, and daylilies that bloom for a certain length of time, die back, and return to bloom next season. (Annuals, on the other hand, are flowers like petunias, impatiens, or marigolds that bloom all summer and then die. They have to be grown next season from seed, unless they helpfully reseed themselves.)

That's it. You don't need to know anything more. If you purchase a guidebook at any of the larger public gardens, it will provide a short history of the setting, a map of the garden, and some information about plants. In private gardens open under the National Gardens Scheme (see below, "Opening Days at Private Gardens"), the owner is usually very pleased to answer questions, and some print up little pamphlets for the occasion. If you become avid for more, stop in at any bookstore in Britain and ask for the gardening section. You may be there for hours. In a nation whose television hits include the long-running *Gardeners' World* and whose chic galas include the annual Chelsea Flower Show, your obsession will fit right in.

A Short Walk Down a Garden Path

Of course you don't even need this smattering of data to enjoy an English garden. You can just start walking down a garden path, very, very slowly. Take in the colors—a drift of lavender, hovering in the air like a faint purple haze; a lemon-yellow daylily whose ruffled edges liquefy into a green center; a creamy-white rose tinged with the slightest blush of pink. Pay attention to forms and shapes, too:

the broad, heart-shaped leaves of hosta, the spiky spears of Asiatic lilies, the gigantic rippling umbrellas of gunnera. Notice the waxy fragility of camellia petals, the ragged fierceness of Scotch thistles, the gray wooliness of verbascum leaves. Bend down to smell the deep, rich perfume of old shrub roses, the spiciness of pinks, the almost cloying sweetness of peonies.

As I walk through a garden, I often wish I could look everywhere at once. And perhaps, at least subconsciously, I do. When I remember Kiftsgate Court, near Chipping Camden, I think of a zigzag path careening down a steep hill, ending on a lawn as lush as a putting green, encircling an aquamarine swimming pool. Views from the lawn stretched far into the Gloucestershire countryside. But in the same moment, I recall an upper terrace with the famous Kiftsgate Rose, a surprisingly old (planted 1938) but vigorous white climber so prolific that it has now almost overcome the large copper beech around which it continues to wreath and twine. Claimed by Kiftsgate's owners as perhaps the largest rose in England, it explodes with flowers.

Absorb the panorama of an English garden, if you can, while celebrating its detail. At Hidcote Garden, almost next door to Kiftsgate, let your eye follow a long avenue of pleached hornbeams until they end at a wrought-iron gate that teasingly reveals a glimpse of a stunning Cotswolds landscape. (Pleached, another insider's word, refers to pruned trees whose adjacent branches are interwoven so that they grow together, with a striking visual result often called a "hedge on stilts." Hornbeam, a smallish tree, is frequently pleached.) But savoring the long view isn't enough. Pause at Hidcote's renowned "tapestry hedges," which mix different hues of yew, holly, box, and copper beech, as if an abstract painter had splashed streaks of color on a glistening green wall.

Only someone there on the path can truly experience an English garden. When I look at my snapshots, I find I have never captured the total effect. Who could ever re-create the damp freshness of a late spring morning, lingering gray clouds broken by sudden bolts of golden sunshine, honey-colored stone walls covered with lustrous ivy, shadowy ornamental pools or a wandering little stream with banks of furry green moss, swatches of emerald grass, and the sound of a cuckoo in a nearby copse?

One blink, one turn of the head, one step in another direction, and the whole scene instantly changes. The best I can hope to record in any garden are moments: the lacy yellow flowers of alchemilla, left free to seed itself and grow where it wishes, spilling from cracks over gray lichen-covered paving stones; a regally purple clematis clinging to a gnarled old apple tree; an arbor of yellow laburnum dripping its ripe blossoms like overburdened grapes.

Somewhere in the garden, a perceptive visitor registers an impression of structure. Structure, or the *bones* of the garden (another handy term), involves the permanent features that give the garden its basic design. If you were to try to sketch the plan of a garden, the lines and shapes would be its bones. Dazzled by the monochromatic brilliance of Sissinghurst's fabled White Garden, all of whose plantings have shadings of white or silver, you don't think of structure. But climb the fifteenth-century tower and look over the garden from above. Suddenly you see its ingenious and complex plan, a series of skillfully designed paths and hedges arranged around buildings and viewpoints, linking the different areas and enclosures into a whole.

Although *bones* is a rather cold and skeletal word, structural elements are among my favorite parts of an English garden. When you're on a garden path, take a good look at the path itself. It is not likely to be a straight cement sidewalk. Winding, meandering, turning sharply, curving, paths are like friendly invitations, drawing the visitor farther into the garden. Paths ask you, often irresistibly, to wander and explore. Where does that woodland path lead? What happens around the next corner? Why not follow those stepping-stones across the fish pond? Enjoy the tactile sensations of garden paths, from the slightly intrusive crunch of pea-size pebbles to the softer springiness of wood chips or slivered bark. Look at the surface, too, to appreciate the gray-mottled smoothness of old cobblestones or pitted red brick in tidy geometric arrangements. Brick walks somehow suggest permanence and security. Remember how happily Dorothy sets out for Oz by following a yellow brick road?

Stone and brick walls also add to the charm of many English gardens. Hanging above our dining-room table is a framed blowup of a snapshot I once took of a section of an old brick garden wall. That's all it is: a sequence of red bricks laid on top of each other. But the different reds have transmuted with time—not over just years or decades, but, I like to think, over centuries—so that some are orange, others rosy-red, still others a kind of pale reddish-purple. Together they form a compelling study in harmonious color and texture. I want to reach out and touch that rough, cratered surface. But I also like the snapshot for another reason. It quietly says "English garden" to me, with undertones about history, survival, and even an ability to age gracefully.

Special Kinds of Gardens

Because English garden walls are so evocative, I treasure *walled gardens*. This kind of garden, clearly defined and enclosed by its high walls, offers some protection from wind and weather, so it is often used for growing tender fruits and vegetables (a "kitchen garden") or for providing sheltered walks and benches in sunny corners. Here is where you may find apple trees espaliered (trained flat) against a wall, or old-fashioned pink and white sweet peas secured to hazel-stick poles between rows of purple cabbages. Walled gardens are often the oldest part of a garden, dating back to medieval manors, when stone walls, higher than a man could climb, served as protection from more than the weather.

Don't assume that a walled garden is small. (England takes its walls seriously; one of its great sights, the Roman remnants of Hadrian's Wall, once marched defiantly across the width of the country.) At Wallington, the ancestral home of the Trevelyans near Morpeth in Northumberland, the glory of the 13,000-acre estate is (perhaps appropriately, given the estate's name) the walled garden. It is so big that I had to walk around its inside perimeter to assure myself that it did indeed have walls, because they disappeared in the distance, obscured by flowering shrubs. Walks on different levels connected miniature gardens-within-a-garden, which included statuary, a conservatory, and a Tuscan-style summerhouse, designed by the ubiquitous Capability Brown, who was born near Wallington. The walled garden was an enchanting world of its own.

Like a path, a gate or a door in a wall beckons alluringly. Who can resist wanting to open it and find out what is on the other side? That sense of entering a hidden world is part of the appeal of many English gardens. Perhaps that is why a few gardens actually embody mystery in mazes. These labyrinthine tunnels of clipped hedging (yew, box, or, more rarely, laurel) are popular attractions at places like Hampton Court in Surrey, Hever Castle in Kent, Longleat in Wiltshire, or Glendurgan, near Falmouth, Cornwall.

I am surprisingly unnerved in mazes. Although I'm not exactly afraid of getting lost—especially in the summer months at the most famous mazes, when giggling and shrieking tourists jostle together along the narrow tunnels—I still don't like the feeling of not knowing where to turn. I breathe a little faster as I feel my way along the tall impenetrable hedges, and I am relieved when I emerge again into the open lawn.

I also find *topiary* rather spooky. Topiary, the name for shrubs (usually box or yew) clipped into rigidly defined shapes, lurks in all kinds of gardens. Some of these shapes—cones, pyramids, globes, rectangular boxes—are geometrical. Others, determinedly representational, are drawn from a venerable inventory, dating back to some long-ago day when a fanatic clipper discovered that the yew under his or her hands was turning into a teapot, wedding cake, dog, swan, chesspiece, or teddy bear. (Possibilities are not infinite, of course. Topiary needs volume and a fairly simple outline; it is hard to imagine a yew as a giraffe or a Ferris wheel.)

As you travel around England, watch for topiary. Some are slyly whimsical, like the two enormous peacocks, green and bristly, who hover above a small front-yard garden in Somerset as if they were about to deposit giant eggs in a neighboring rosebush. Fat topiary hens might perch among cake stands in one garden; in another, a racing hound, frozen forever in its pursuit, leaps toward a fox several feet away.

Topiary is not always humorous. Quite uncannily, its living shapes can sometimes create an oddly haunting atmosphere. If you walk alone among the tall brooding pyramids of Athelhampton, especially if the light is failing at the end of a gray, cloudy afternoon, you may suddenly feel surrounded. Have those silent pyramids inexplicably inched closer? Where has everyone gone? Which way is the exit? When I looked down from the bedroom window of Parnham House at a grass terrace outlined by sternly clipped cone-shaped yews, I felt as if the cones—I think I counted fifty—were marshaled like sentinels. At night, if I lived there, I might easily convince myself that those dark forms were changing position behind my back, as they marched in military formation around the terrace, keeping guard.

At the oldest topiary garden in England, Levens Hall in Cumbria, which dates back to the late seventeenth century, some of the clipped yews have gradually assumed almost monstrous proportions. They loom over the garden like shapes from a child's nightmare: swollen loaves, waddling giant women, crazy spirals. In *Topiary Gardens*, garden writer Ethne Clark asserts that walking into Levens "is one of the most heart-stopping moments a visitor to topiary collections is likely to experience." But the effect is also exhilarating, as if you had joined Alice in Wonderland.

If topiary gardens can be unsettling, *water gardens*, happily, are very serene. Fittingly for a climate where water often seems to hang in the air, English gardens often include features like a small lake, an ornamental fishpond, a carefully channeled stream, a fountain, or a miniature waterfall among rocks. I treasure those gardens whose very heart is water, for they offer, quite literally, a rare opportunity for reflection.

One peaceful morning at Westbury Court, a seventeenth-century

Dutch garden in Gloucestershire, I watched shadows move across the surface of two long parallel canals that seemed almost like enormous pier glasses upended toward the sky. Designed as a formal garden, its canals outlined by severely classical hedges topped with tiny topiaries, Westbury was meant for gently pacing back and forth. Not a flower garden, it holds little to distract the eye but the luxuriant sheen of water. Walking along those glassy canals, I could feel my pulse gradually slow, taking its rhythm from the measured pace of the garden. On a two-week trip filled with plans, excursions, and a sometimes frantic desire to see and do still more, I am always grateful for time in a water garden.

Anyone hoping to find such a haven never has to go far. Longing to escape the endless tour groups inside Hampton Court? Just stroll outside to the edge of the Long Water, a shining stretch that seems to reach to the horizon. Visit Minterne in a Dorset spring and follow a woodland brook, overhung with irises and azaleas, for more than a mile along a primrose-studded path. Stop at Hodnet Hall in Shropshire, where rare flowers cluster around a chain of lakes, and allow plenty of time to sit on a bank and admire the ducks and black swans floating gracefully by. Peer into the clear shallow waters of a wide stream as it flows through Heale House Gardens in Wiltshire and you may find yourself mesmerized by the long, swaying tendrils of the submerged watergrasses as they bend to the swiftly moving current. You too may begin searching, as I do, for yet another oasis.

Landscape Gardens and Arboreta

Some gardens are ideal for rambling, walking up and down gentle hills, through meadows and woods, and around lakes often roomy enough for small boats. These are *landscape gardens* and *arboreta*, whose effect depends on judiciously planted shrubs and mature trees. Eased into forgetful complacency by the size and seemingly inexhaustible nature of our countryside, we Americans tend to take our trees for granted. According to Linda Proud in *Consider England*, the English emphatically do not: "Forests, parks, woodlands: all depend on that which is most beloved of the English, the tree. The very names of trees are music to the English ear: rowan, alder, elm, service, beech, birch, holly, hornbeam; but the king of them all is oak."

All these, and many uncommon species, appear in the great landscape gardens. To appreciate these places, a visitor needs to adjust his or her line of sight. In other kinds of gardens, I look most of the time at what lies at my feet—a short gaudy group of black-eyed red anemones, a peony bush almost sinking to the ground under the weight of its heady perfume, a threatening gunnera spreading its gigantic leaves. But in a landscape garden I try to keep looking up, out, and around, as if I were scanning the horizon with a short-range telescope. How else can I notice the dramatic effect of an acer's dark red leaves against the tall green ferns at the next bend of the lake, or the almost infinite shadings of green foliage that climb the hill? In a landscape garden, I have to pay attention to grand effects. I see these effects as extravagant swaths from a painter's brush, yards and yards of cutwork fabric flung against the sky, sculptures too monumental for any merely mortal hands.

Landscape gardens are seldom small. At Wakehurst Place Garden, not far from London's Gatwick Airport, various paths lead past flower gardens, rockeries, giant redwood trees, meadows, bogs, a lake, and a Himalayan glade, planted with species that grow at ten thousand feet. James and I can easily spend a whole morning exploring Wakehurst (and we have). At Stourhead in Wiltshire, an eighteenth-century survival of a picturesque garden, small classical buildings and mock ruins are carefully placed as "eye-catchers" around a lake. An amble around Stourhead's main path, which circles the lake, takes about an hour, although we often linger here and there—on a grassy bank, on the hill outside the pantheon, inside the grotto, on the bridge looking down the valley.

Landscape gardens never seem crowded. Even at Blenheim, one of England's most popular tourist attractions, where unending tour buses rumble up to the doors, the vast park has enough space to roam so that no one has to hear a clicking camera for hours. Although the Royal Botanic Gardens at Kew, just outside central London, are well known, Kew's three hundred acres offer opportunities to wander among rose gardens, a heath garden, a bluebell wood, an orangery, conservatories—and walks under specimen trees, the true glory of a landscape garden. Sheffield Park, more than one hundred acres in East Sussex, includes waterfalls and a chain of lakes. Walks at Dawyck Botanic Garden, in the Borders county of Peebleshire, wind among the woods and follow a lovely Scottish burn.

One early spring afternoon, we stopped at Claremont in Surrey, once a favorite retreat of Queen Victoria. A guidebook had warned us that this park was often busy, since families from the surrounding London suburbs take refuge there for outings and picnics. But on this cool, rainy day in March, we saw only one other couple who, like us, were wandering the paths under flowering magnolia trees and climbing the grassy steps of an outdoor amphitheatre carved into a hillside overlooking a lake.

Travelers tend not to seek out less famous gardens, especially those that don't feature flowers. So they miss gems like the Bedgebury National Pinetum in Kent, where we surveyed an astonishing variety of conifers, many of which I had never seen before. A pinetum, devoted to what I inexactly call "evergreens," can be dark and monotonous, as are most of the unimaginative plantations plunked down by the Forestry Commission on slopes all over Britain. But at Bedgebury, to my gratifying surprise, I soon began distinguishing different sizes, shapes, colors, and textures—trees with long spiky needles, others with prickly bristles, some branches light and feathery, others thickly compact, light green to grayish-green to greenish-black shades, trees that soared to the sky and spreading conifers that crept along the ground. As James and I wandered over the sandy hillsides, we became, very briefly, amateur botanists who excitedly called out new discoveries to each other.

National Collections and Other Specialties

Just as Bedgebury Pinetum has a comprehensive range of all the conifers that can be grown in Britain, other gardens throughout England claim the honor of maintaining specific "national collections." This means that the garden is responsible for growing and displaying as many varieties as possible of a certain kind of plant: jasmine, for example, or tree bamboo, or daylilies. Sometimes a garden guide will alert you in advance of what to look for. (And sometimes it won't. Reading the Wakehurst had national collections of *betula, hypericum, nothofagus,* and *skimmia* didn't help, since I didn't know until I looked in a garden dictionary that a betula was a birch and a nothofagus a beech.) Or you may simply come upon a mountainous pincushion of assorted heather in bloom, all different shades of white, rose, and purple, each plant carefully labeled, and you will know. I have never planned a trip to any particular garden to study a national collection, but I am properly impressed when I see one.

England shelters many kinds of specialists' gardens. At the back of one edition of the *Good Gardens Guide,* its editors listed separate divisions of arboreta, herb gardens, Japanese and Chinese gardens, rose gardens, rock gardens, water and bog gardens, and wild gardens and wildernesses. "Wilderness," of course, does not mean to the English gardener what it suggests to an American. An English "wilderness," usually an informal or uncultivated area next to more formal plantings, has been planned as a deliberately rustic or "wild" contrast.

How to Find English Gardens

At first I discovered English gardens mainly by chance, either when they were attached to a country house or when they were unexpectedly signposted along the road. When I acquired my first garden booklet, a thin publication issued by the English Tourist Board, it was a revelation. Now I didn't have to depend on fate to lead me to gardens: I could actually search them out myself. There they were, sprinkled all over a map. With that booklet I instantly became a dedicated garden visitor.

Soon I added *The Ordnance Survey Guide to Gardens in Britain*, a list of about two hundred, and then the opinionated but knowledgeable *Good Gardens Guide*. (See *My Love Affair with England* for further discussion of these guides.) But the true addict's constant companion is the annual edition of *Gardens of England & Wales*, revealing nearly thirty-five hundred private gardens open to the public on one or more designated days each year, with proceeds from their modest admission fees donated to charities. This inexpensive paperback, known familiarly in England as "the Yellow Book," is the key to thousands of unusual and very personal gardens.

OPENING DAYS AT PRIVATE GARDENS

Reading the Yellow Book is like being invited to a garden party. You simply show up on the right day, buy a ticket, and go in. Then you drift casually through the garden, sometimes following a short printed description, sometimes just wandering here and there. The owner is often nearby, chatting with friends or politely answering questions from both novices and fellow aficionados. ("What is that big yellow bush in the corner?" "Do you find that *Lavatera barnsley* tolerates the heat well?") Everyone seems to be in a good humor. Somewhere on the grounds, frequently with fair-weather seating scattered on a lawn or a terrace, smiling ladies serve tea and delicious homemade treats—cakes, scones, cookies, even dainty sandwiches. As we sit sedately sipping our tea, listening to the subdued murmur around us, James and I both often think of the ice cream socials we remember from long ago in our separate midwestern small towns.

Sometimes the party turns into a nonstop gala. In several parts of England that are crammed with gardens, like Cornwall, Kent, and the Cotswolds, gardeners in a particular area frequently arrange to open on the same spring or summer Saturday or Sunday. Consulting the Yellow Book, fervent garden lovers can dash from one delight to another, although, given the limits of open hours (usually two to five in the afternoon) and the perils of navigating narrow country roads, something of the tranquil spirit of true garden visiting tends to dissipate.

One mid-April Sunday afternoon a few years ago, James and I looked up at the sunny sky, grabbed the Yellow Book, and set out for three gardens in nearby Kent, a county close to our rented flat in West Sussex. As we approached Egypt Farm, near Plaxtol, we could see two distinctive conical roofs, like tiled hoods with metallic tassels. These were emblems of the oast houses, once used for drying hops, that still punctuate the Kent countryside.

Americans soon learn that today's "farm" in England does not necessarily mean humble, utilitarian, or even currently agricultural. The house at Egypt Farm was a two-story brick building, with a traditional Kentish tiled roof. It looked very inviting, with large windows, a terrace, jutting angles, and the oast houses attached like stumpy towers at one end of the house. Although owners seldom open their houses to public view as part of the National Gardens Scheme, guests can walk around, peer through windows from a discreet distance, and imagine themselves brewing a pot of tea in a kitchen whose old stone fireplace visibly looms against an interior fieldstone wall.

The charm of the garden at Egypt Farm was partly its setting. Nestled into a hill with long views over miles of Kent's gently rolling fields, pastures, and flowering orchards, the house was surrounded by carpet rolls of closely clipped lawn. The grass seemed so soft and tender that anyone like me with giddy childhood memories would want to throw himself or herself on the ground and roll over and over. (Garden visitors, however, observe a certain decorum.) The sun glinted on densely packed daffodils that waved here and there in the grass. Everything smelled fresh and green. Few people had arrived yet at Egypt Farm, so we walked almost alone over the lawn, circled each patch of daffodils, walked every path, considered the view from several perspectives, and decided to pause for tea.

On open garden days, almost everyone feels sociable. In a nearby low building, once a hop-pickers' barn, we talked briefly with the gracious older woman who served us. Years ago, when she was young, she told us, she had worked as a nanny in northern California for more than two years. Then her mother had asked her to come home, and so she had. She had married and remained there in Kent. Now a widow, she still corresponded with her old friends in California. She dreamed of returning for a visit—she had once hoped to live there permanently—but the trip would be too expensive. I mentioned the occasional bargains in overseas flights, but she smiled and shook her head. "One gets by as best one can," she said.

As we walked down the lane from Egypt Farm to Hamptons Farm House, our next garden, I thought about how often, when we travel, we are given tantalizing glimpses of others' lives: brief notes, edited selections from longer stories, condensed endings. Gardens make people generous—look how the owners of Egypt Farm had let us ramble unattended all over their property—and the lady in the tearoom had offered us a brief outline of her life. I wondered how, given time and friendship, she might have filled it in.

Hamptons Farm House looked out over the same glorious spring countryside. From a high-roofed pavilion, creatively salvaged from the skeleton of an old red-tiled barn, we could see apple and cherry trees blooming into the far distance, and at our feet fallen white petals covered much of the green lawn. As at Egypt Farm, the green also rippled with waves of daffodils, tulips, and hyacinth. The gardens led downward in a series of grassy terraces, following a tiny stream to flower-edged ponds, ending in a larger pond with a little wooden duck house in its center.

Yet what I remember best from Hamptons Farm is its trees. A wooded copse bordered the garden. Looking up at the clear sky, I could see the etched lines of still-bare branches. In two of the tallest trees I counted more than twenty rooks' nests, looking like unkempt baskets precariously held at the tips of ancient webbed fingers. I had never seen so many nests in so few trees. The rooks were circling and cawing, a raucous, disturbing sound. The stark trees, and those startling black blots against the sky, provided an eerie contrast to the well-groomed garden below.

When I checked my watch, not something I ordinarily do in a garden, I saw it was almost four P.M. We would barely have time for one more. From April through June, reading any weekend's entries in the Yellow Book for Kent—listings are arranged by county—can be maddening, for not even the most determined garden visitor could manage them all in one afternoon. Having chosen Egypt Farm and Hamptons Farm, I knew I might never see the dwarf rhododendrons and flowering cherries at Collingwood Grange, southeast of Cranbrook; or the 1920s garden at Meadow Wood, near Penshurst; or the more than two hundred shrub and climbing roses, intertwined with clematis, at Kypp Cottage, Biddenden. But we could just make Edenbridge House, near Marlpit Hill.

Careening with controlled haste along country roads, we arrived just before closing at Edenbridge House. Although the surrounding houses on its suburban street were not especially noteworthy, Edenbridge House might have respectably appeared in *Country Life*, a coolly upscale magazine. The redbrick walls and tile roof of the stately Kentish manor—any midwesterner would hesitate to call it a mere house—were set off by bright green lawns. The lawns in turn blended into long garden borders, filled in April by yellow and white daffodils.

Edenbridge House had more than one garden. Protected by a brick wall next to the house was a knot garden, low box hedges forming patterns whose centers held red and yellow wallflowers. Around a corner, another side of the house overlooked masses of mixed multicolored tulips, so bright and jarring—red, yellow, apricot, coral, white—that, even motionless, they seemed to dance in a kind of gay staccato. On another flowering terrace, a pink magnolia hung over a blanketed swimming pool. Except for the cool

April air and fading sun, I could have imagined myself in a long, floating dress, holding a glass of champagne in my hand, and nibbling on cucumber sandwiches.

GARDENS BY APPOINTMENT ONLY

Although entry into a garden under the National Gardens Scheme is certainly a privilege, it is shared with others. What garden visitor doesn't sometimes dream of a uniquely private tour? Only recently did I learn that this fantasy is often possible. For years I used to turn with a slight sigh of regret from guidebook entries for houses and gardens followed by the dismissive words *by appointment only*. What did that mean? How did one *make* an appointment? Who should one call, and what should one say? Wouldn't I need to be escorting a group, or announce myself as a garden expert, or at least flaunt an imposing credential on my letterhead?

But one late summer, as I was planning ahead for a September week in north Norfolk, I read wistfully about a fifteenth-century house, Mannington Hall, near Saxthorpe, known not only for its fine brick-and-flint architecture, unusually well preserved, but also for its moat garden, shrubs, roses, and woodland walks. Although the garden was regularly open in summer, it closed at the end of August, and the house was open—those dispiriting words—*by appointment only*. The more I studied a photograph of the handsome house, part medieval and part Renaissance, with a salt-and-pepper facade accented by rosy-red brick mullioned windows, the more intensely I wanted to be able to see it in person. The house, striking but understated and a little worn, *looked* like a person; as if, after a rich long life, it had now entered a robust old age.

So I wrote to the owner, listed as The Hon. Robin Walpole. The hardest part of my letter was its salutation. Dear Who? Dear Hon. Robin Walpole? Dear Sir? I couldn't remember who Honorables were, exactly. Nothing sounded quite right. Blundering forward with a resolutely American *Mr.*, I explained that we had read about

Mannington Hall, my husband was an architect and so was a friend we were traveling with, and we wondered if we could possibly arrange a brief visit. I named the week. When I walked to my Minneapolis corner mailbox and sent my letter on its journey, I couldn't quite imagine it ever being read by an Honorable Anybody in East Anglia.

But quite quickly I received a courteous handwritten note in reply. We were welcome to visit; the time was set for ten o'clock on a Tuesday. When we arrived at Mannington Hall a few weeks later, we approached a woman seated in a small gatehouse near an entrance into the garden. She checked our names in a little book, took our modest price of admission (a few dollars each), and said, pointing toward the house, "Ah, here comes Lord Walpole now." Walking toward us from the house was a pleasant-looking man, middle-aged with silvery gray hair, and dressed in a rough tweed jacket.

No one could have had a more charming or knowledgeable host. Lord Walpole (as part of polite conversation, I hazarded his title once or twice) took us slowly through Mannington Hall. He knew his house intimately, as one knows a member of the family, and he commented affectionately on its history, its alterations, and its distinctive details. He never tried to hurry us; in fact, concerned that we were taking too much of his morning, I kept nudging James onward. When we said good-bye to Lord Walpole, who amiably urged us to acquaint ourselves with the extensive gardens, he had spent an hour and a half with us.

So now I know that *by appointment only* offers its own kind of invitation. It does *not* mean "stay away" or "important credentials required." In the National Gardens Scheme handbook, an even friendlier caveat is appended to many listings: "Private visits welcome, please tel. 01234," or "Private visits also welcome April to October," or "Private visits welcome mornings June 25 to July 9." Although I seldom organize my plans far enough in advance to arrange such visits, once in a while I do. That is how, not long ago, we took tea with Mr. Leonard Stocks of Castle Tor.

Castle Tor, a private house and garden in the Devon seaside town of Torquay, is not on any standard itinerary. But, glancing through the Devon entries in the *Good Gardens Guide*, as I pondered possibilities for our two-day drive from Cornwall back to London, I was suddenly snagged by a captivating opening line. "Half a century ago the then owner of Castle Tor approached Sir Edwin Lutyens and asked him to design a smaller version of Castle Drogo; being too busy Sir Edwin nominated a pupil of his, Frederick Harrild, and the result is this fascinating architectural garden with magnificent views of Lyme Bay and Tor Bay." The garden, which the editor enthusiastically described at length, was "open by appointment." Entrance fee was a mere pound.

I knew we had to try to see Castle Tor. Years before, on our first visit to the West Country, James and I had become instantly enamored of Castle Drogo, a modernist masterpiece by an architect considered one of England's finest. We had eagerly returned several times to this massive yet almost impossibly elegant house and garden (see Chapter 18, "A Modernist Castle in Dartmoor"). Since then, whenever we have had the chance to see the work of Edwin Lutyens, we have made a detour—to Lindisfarne Castle, for example, an Edwardian summer retreat inside a Tudor fort on Northumberland's Holy Island, and to Little Thakeham, a sumptuous manor house (now an expensive hotel) in Storrington, West Sussex. How could we resist a glimpse of a miniature Castle Drogo?

Like Lord Walpole, Mr. Leonard Stocks answered my inquiry promptly and graciously. I had explained we would be traveling from Cornwall on a particular Thursday and could not guarantee a specific time of arrival. That was fine, he assured us. He would be at home all afternoon. He would be delighted to see us. Since I am rather reclusive myself, such politeness to a stranger always surprises and impresses me.

Everything about our visit to castle Tor was a surprise. On the scheduled Thursday afternoon, we arrived in Torquay for lunch and a quick walk around its inner harbor. Aware that Torquay had been an enormously popular summer resort since the mid-1800s, I had always avoided it. On the map it looked far too big, part of Torbay, an urban conglomeration of three adjacent towns with more than 125,000 people. I had somehow expected that its center might be crowded and tatty, defaced by postcard-and-popcorn kiosks, redolent of too many fish-and-chips shops.

But happily, like many seaside small cities in England, Torquay still retained some Victorian charm: pier; pavilion; long, curving seaside promenade; and well-tended public gardens. Its white stucco buildings and palm trees gave the town a vaguely Mediterranean air. Nor were we overwhelmed by people. In early April, Torquay was just busy enough to seem festive. Two young boys, ignoring posted warnings on the pier of NO FISHING ALLOWED, were intently watching their lines. One young couple, holding hands, stood in front of a seaside restaurant, studying its menu. Several older women, their careful curls tied down with bright challis scarves, accompanied by men in tightly buttoned jackets and tweed caps, walked slowly along the promenade. Other retirees or holiday-makers sat on benches in the gardens and basked in the afternoon sun. Several shop windows held posters advertising outings to tourist attractions within a day's bus ride: Dartmoor, Exmoor, Sidmouth, Lyme Regis. Torquay was clearly a favored spot for a genteel late-winter vacation.

When we left the harbor, I discovered that the residential suburb where Castle Tor was located was not what I'd expected, either. With its streets winding upward among the hills, Torquay's terraces reminded me of a gentler San Francisco. Plunging drives led down to many of the hillside houses, sometimes invisible behind high walls. Driving slowly along the designated road, we almost missed Castle Tor entirely. All that told us a house lay somewhere below was an open gate guarded by two unobtrusive eagles on pillars.

Walking down the drive, we found ourselves at the side door of a large white rectangular house, set very close to its neighbors. The garden, I thought, must be somewhere behind it. But where, exactly? A few minutes later, Leonard Stocks, a white-haired, vigorous, and cheerful man in his early eighties, came to the door, greeted us very cordially, and inquired when we wanted tea. Tea? I shook my head politely. Oh, no, we couldn't, really. But Mr. Stocks waved aside my protestations, suggested tea in an hour, and motioned us to follow him down a steep flight of stone stairs and around the corner of the house.

There, suddenly, was the garden. Both James and I gasped. After the elbowing, conventional houses on the street above, I could hardly take in what lay before us. We had emerged near the crest of a very high hill. Directly before us, opening out in a half-circle far below, was the brilliant blue water of the ocean. The houses behind us simply faded away in the vast sweep of that amazing blue. Few gardens could have competed with such a view, but Castle Tor magnificently rose to the occasion.

Stepping below us in several broad terraces, the serene garden was a measured composition of green lawns backed by ivy-draped limestone walls, stone-edged pools, shaped trees, clipped hedges, and sculptured topiary. A rectangular pool reflected the graceful trees in its mirrorlike water. Classical stone statues, with a patina of age and weather, dotted the green lawn. Dignified but enticing, it was a garden out of a medieval Italian fantasy.

Everywhere I kept noticing felicitous details: ornamental recesses and apertures lightening the severe high walls, white roses trained against the gray stone, stepping-stones across the large pool, three smaller descending pools like oversize saucers of water. But I always turned my eyes back to the dazzling view.

After we had surveyed the entire garden, including its Gothic gatehouse tower, complete with a working portcullis, whose architectural plans had come from Castle Drogo, Mr. Stocks led us into his house for tea. He served us cake on china plates and tea from his grandmother's lacily etched silver teapot, and as we sat in his sunny enclosed porch, talking easily about travel, London, the difficulties of keeping up a house even with daily help—he had been widowed for many years—I thought again how people who love and live with gardens often seem to have a special sweetness of spirit.

After tea, Mr. Stocks almost apologetically produced a small tin for our token one-pound contribution to the National Gardens Scheme. Several years before, he explained, he had tried opening the garden to the general public for two days under the usual NGS auspices. He had expected perhaps a hundred guests. But, drawn by the private garden's fame, more than seven hundred arrived the first day, five hundred the second. Unable to deal with such crowds, he now opens for the NGS by appointment; we were only his second visitors so far that spring.

Impulsive and intense, I worry a little in England about sometimes seeming too brazenly American. But Mr. Stocks had been so warm—calling me, in the nicest possible way, "dear" and "dearie"—that when we left, I ventured to give him a kiss on the cheek. I thought of his life alone in this large house, and I hoped that sometimes at night when the moon was out, he walked contentedly along the long reflecting pool in his garden.

Discovering Your Own Secret Garden

With so many guidebooks, listings, and open days, England's great gardens are not undiscovered. At Sissinghurst in Kent, the National Trust issues timed tickets during the high season. (Arrive, if you can, just before the noon opening hour, when many tour groups are still eating lunch, or come late in the afternoon.) One spring Sunday at popular Hidcote in Gloucestershire, we found ourselves politely edging our way in single file between the hedges. Great Dixter in Sussex, Tintinhull in Somerset, Mottisfont Abbey in Hampshire, Hever in Kent, Bodnant in north Wales, Powis Castle near Welshpool: in none of these, especially on a summer weekend, are you apt to feel lonely.

But because England has so many wonderful gardens, you will soon find your own favorites, perhaps small enough so that tour buses don't stop there, or large enough so that they absorb crowds, or distant enough from main roads so that only those in the know (like you) venture there. Especially if you are lucky enough to visit these enchanted places in late spring, early summer, or early fall, you may be able to wander down a grassy path all by yourself and feel that you are in your own secret garden.

On the April morning James and I arrived at Great Comp, near Sevenoaks, Kent, just before it opened at eleven A.M., we weren't even sure we'd come to the right place. No other cars were parked in the open space outside the gates, and I did not immediately see a sign telling us where we were. (English gardens do not exactly put up neon lights.) Behind a high fence I could glimpse some trees and lawn but not much else. Then I saw a rather ramshackle shed with an elderly man inside, near the gate, and I realized he must be selling tickets. So we had arrived.

Once inside Great Comp, I kept calling to James, "Here! Here! Come look over here!" Great Comp was wonderfully unpredictable, with an intricate system of criss-crossing and parallel grassy paths, so that I was never sure where I wanted to go next. Toward the terraces? Into the woodland? Past the daffodils? But what I remember most were the high-spirited "ruins," including fragmentary stone walls and turretlike oddments, ingeniously constructed from ironstone dug up during the construction of the garden. With no one else around, we did not need to act our age. So we scooted around corners, scrambled up a ruin with a kind of lookout, and waved at each other from behind stone mock-fortifications. Later we sat and munched our picnic sandwiches on a bench in an out-of-the-way corner, shaking off occasional leftover raindrops that spilled from an overhanging magnolia.

I find it impossible to choose a favorite garden. As soon as I think of one—Standen, in Sussex, with its hidden fernery in an old rock quarry and its bluebell woods—I immediately think of another. Perhaps Hever? I admired its Pompeian wall, with bays in which classical statues were framed by clematis and wisteria, and I sipped tea like a privileged friend of the Astors on the lakeside steps of the flamboyant Italian loggia. But surely Sissinghurst, especially when the Lime Walk is overflowing in spring with orange and pink tulips, white anemones, yellow daffodils, and purple grape hyacinth? What about Mapperton, whose crumbling Italianate walls are wedged into a remote Dorset valley? Leonardslee in West Sussex in late spring, with its billowing acres of rare rhododendrons and azaleas? I cherish small gardens and large ones. I enjoy opulent formal gardens, like Manderston, with its gilded gates, in the Scottish Borders, and romantic gardens, like Trebah in Cornwall, whose steep ravine, filled with flowering shrubs, plummets down to a secluded beach. Sezincote's Indian Bridge, decorated with Brahmin sacred bulls, part of a Moghul-inspired garden in Gloucestershire; Caerhays Castle's steep hillsides overhung with magnolias next to the sea in Cornwall; the large walled kitchen garden and towering brick dovecote at Felbrigg in Norfolk; the stone-edged rivulet trickling through Coleton Fishacre in Devon—once I begin to recall English gardens I have loved, I find it hard to stop.

So, inundated with roses and awash in daffodils, I will put aside my lengthening mental list. Instead I prefer to look ahead. Although I recently counted just over one hundred two-star gardens in my current *Good Gardens Guide*, I have only visited perhaps about a third of them. Sixty gardens to go! And what about the one-stars? If I should live to be a very, very old lady, might I have a chance at all of them?

A FEW FLOATING FACTS

Any bookstore in even a small English town will usually stock at least one garden guide. The Good Gardens Guide, updated every year, is sometimes available in well-stocked American bookstores, too. Gardens of England & Wales, known as "the Yellow Book," an inexpensive paperback that lists private gardens open in aid of the National Gardens Scheme, is also issued annually.

Once in England, check local Tourist Information Centres; almost every town of note has one. Many of these offices will give you a free brochure about gardens open locally.

3

Hitching a Ride on the Sweet Trolley

A muffled snort broke the almost complete silence of the dining room. At dinner in most country-house hotels, the English guests virtually whisper to one another, their voices discreetly sinking into the heavy damask linen and eventually disappearing into the patterned carpet. Only Americans seem to talk in normal tones. So when I said, quietly but distinctly, to the waiter at the sweet trolley, "I think I'll have a very small spoonful of the summer pudding, the tiniest slice of apricot gâteau with a dab of cream, and just one—well, perhaps two—of those little chocolate truffles," I found I had announced my carefully considered selection to the entire room. The snort came from the next table, where a gray-haired lady in a dark silk print, whose husband was frowning at her, tried unsuccessfully not to meet my eye. I smiled and instantly forgave her. I knew she was envious.

When I first learned that in England a two- or three-tier pushcart laden with desserts is called a "sweet trolley," I took to the term instantly. It suggested an old-fashioned genteel streetcar, the kind a young laughing Judy Garland might have clung to as she sang about finding love. Only this impeccably English streetcar was filled with strawberry Pavlova, Bakewell tarts, chocolate profiteroles, jam-filled cakes, quivery puddings, and a bottomless bowl of thick clotted cream.

Although until fairly recently the English were routinely attacked for bland or unimaginative cuisine, even those critics often had to come to a reluctantly admiring halt in front of the sweet trolley. If the English do not necessarily excel at, say, millefeuille pastry, they certainly know their way around anything put together with fruit, eggs, butter, a slosh of sherry or whiskey and/or heavy cream. Some scoffers, pointing to a preponderance of gooey, sticky, or creamy puddings, sniffily dismiss English desserts as "nursery fare" or "comfort food." Admittedly, *pudding* is often used in England synonymously with *dessert*, as in, "And will you have any pudding?" But, I wonder as I relish a cloudlike floating island redolent with the faintest hint of vanilla, what is wrong with comfort food? Would I be happier with a pear-ginger sorbet served with rosemary biscotti? I think not.

Nor do the English stint on choice. Not long ago, at a fairly ordinary Devon pub where James and I had stopped for lunch, I had no trouble deciding on my main course (my unexciting options were chicken salad, lasagna, or a ploughman's plate), but I was immobilized by the dessert menu. Scrawled on a blackboard whose painted heading read PUDDINGS were these possibilities: spotted dick and custard, hot apricot crumble flan and custard, rum raisin ice cream, orange Cointreau mousse sponge, strawberry daiquiri torte, pecan and treacle tart and custard, gâteau St. Honoré and rum raisin, apricot brandy and almond roulade, sherry trifle.

For anyone who has traveled much in England, this is an evocative list. It begins and ends with traditional English favorites, one a fruit-studded semisolid pudding whose unabashedly jovial name indicates something of its robust texture and the other a famously soggy concoction whose varying ingredients seem to depend on whatever may be lurking that day in the back of the refrigerator. In between are several French desserts, or, rather, English versions of them. Although the English have historically despised the French, they have never hesitated to reach across the Channel when it suits them, as tacitly acknowledged by the infinite variations of *mousse*, *torte*, *gâteau*, and *roulade* on English menus.

And, of course, there is custard. A thick yellowy sauce that tastes of sugar, cornstarch, and something that might be lemon or vanilla, English custard is only a distant country cousin of those delicate French emulsions of eggs, sugar, and cream. An English custard is meant to be poured with reckless abandon on cakes, puddings, pies, and anything else that will not collapse under the custard's viscous weight. Its reassuringly familiar taste slathers easily over any alarmingly foreign flavor—indeed, over any other flavor at all.

If anyone doubts that an English dessert is meant to subsume all the pleasures of the table, ponder the allurements of rum, Cointreau, daiquiris, brandy, and sherry. Some English recipes for trifle go even further, calling it *tipsy* trifle, a descriptive adjective that is also applied to certain puddings and cakes. I have yet to become even faintly dazed by the alcohol content of an English dessert—even by the misleadingly named Madeira cake, a fairly innocent treat that was originally served with a glass of Madeira—but perhaps that is because I become satiated with sugar long before the liquor has a chance to take effect.

Confronted with a panorama of English desserts, an American traveler needs to be prepared, or, after several nights, the sight of a sweet trolley might soon begin to evoke intimations of a hospital gurney. For a long time I did not discover how to take full advantage of the sweet trolley. Slogging earnestly through the rest of my meal, I tucked without a murmur into my meat, roasted potatoes, sprouts or peas or carrots, and waited stolidly for my reward to be rolled around to our table. Later that night, at midnight or two or three o'clock, I often bitterly regretted my indulgence—not really in the lemon sponge, whose fluffy tartness I still recalled with fondness, but in the preceding leaden courses. They were what had sunk me, I was convinced.

In the last few years, however, I have become a wiser woman. Now I begin by studying the *starters*, that plain blunt English term for a first course. (How much less tempting it is than *sweet trolley*. The English are straightforward about their priorities.) Often I can be quite satisfied in a competent restaurant by a fairly light starter, perhaps a warm mushroom tart or a plate of asparagus spears, which, supplemented by crusty rolls, can lead without embarrassment straight to a chocolate soufflé or rhubarb syllabub. Forget the meat, potatoes, and two veg; remember the waiting strawberry fool. Your waitperson may not approve of this abbreviated repast, but he or she will have to oblige. In less fancy places, without starters, go for salads but hold the mayo. Most pubs serve soup-and-a-roll as a main course; that, too, provides an honest pretense of a balanced meal.

Other precautions are also useful. On a potential dessert day— one when I suspect I will be unable to resist temptation—I try to reduce my heartening English breakfast to juice, cereal, and tea. Then I make sure I walk a lot, along footpaths, country roads, beaches, city sidewalks, even hotel stairs. Many miles, more mousse. I promise myself that as soon as I return home, I will focus relentlessly on grapefruit. Many promises, more pudding.

Then, of course, when the sweet trolley finally rolls around, I exercise restraint. Rather than indulging in an unseemly whole piece of lemon meringue pie, I ask for a slice so narrow that the server can barely cut it acutely. I request the smallest possible bowlful of banana pudding with a merest half-spoonful of cream. If the orange mousse only comes in an individual dish, I try to persuade my husband to share it with me. Even with such modest requests, I usually limit myself to three.

And if anyone at a surrounding table happens to notice this disciplined but undeniably catholic approach, I have learned not to pay undue attention. I am not troubled by overheard remarks, nudging elbows, or sidelong glances. Remember the lady with the stifled snort? When her turn came for the sweet trolley, she looked at me, smiled shyly, and promptly ordered the waitress to dish her out three desserts.

4

Looking for Literary Landscapes

For more on a book lover's obsessions in England, see the next chapter,
"A Suitcase Full of Books."

Because of books, I grew up believing that England was a magical country, inhabited by such fascinating characters as Dick Whittington's cat, Toad of Toad Hall, Sara Crewe, King Arthur, Sherlock Holmes, Oliver Twist, and Maggie Tulliver. For years I didn't bother to sort out its real geography. Instead, on a vague mental map, I brushed in patchy fields with wandering hedgerows, windswept moors, rocky pastures on misty hills, lonely miles of jagged seacoast, and a labyrinth of gas-lit London streets. Starting with nursery-rhyme places, I soon added Ratty's great River, Christopher Robin's Forest, Bilbo's peaceful Shire, Doctor Doolittle's Puddleby-on-the-Marsh, and the mysterious London park where Mary Poppins once descended from the sky with an open umbrella.

Only as an adult did I eventually learn that the River was actually the Thames, the Forest was still a wild tract outside London called Ashdown Forest, the Shire recalled J. R. R. Tolkien's Worcestershire countryside, and anyone longing to see Mary Poppins could walk through Hyde Park, look wistfully up at the sky, and hope.

As I grew older, I expanded my imaginary map. Riding sedately in a barouche landau (a vehicle I longed to climb into when I later encountered one in an English country-house museum), I visited Jane Austen's quiet villages and country estates. I rambled over the Brontës' wild moors, hastened through the foggy London streets of

Dickens's novels, and wandered over Hardy's Wessex heathland. Standing with Lancelot, I watched Elaine, the lily maid of Astolat, float on her funeral barge through Camelot. With Evelyn Waugh, I fell under the spell of aristocratic Oxford, and, paying respectful attention to Matthew Arnold, I heard the melancholy withdrawing roar of Dover Beach. When E. M. Forster took me to Howards End, I watched with dismay the approaching pall of suburbia as I stood under the ancient wych elm.

When, over the years, I delved into murder mysteries, I tracked the Hound of the Baskervilles across Dartmoor, roamed through the brooding fen country with Dorothy Sayers, ventured to the wind-swept north Norfolk coast with P. D. James, and pottered happily in quaint, cozy, but corpse-strewn villages with writers like Agatha Christie, Margery Allingham, and Ngaio Marsh.

Not every literary journey I took to England was a romantic one. When I travel for pleasure, I do not usually seek out the bleakest, most depressed or despoiled landscapes. But when I read, I sometimes go there. No wide-ranging reader should avoid D. H. Lawrence's ravaged Midlands, George Orwell's grimy London, or Beryl Bainbridge's depressed Liverpool.

Anyone wanting a kaleidoscopic literary tour through unidealized postwar England can seek the wildly diverse company of Peter Ackroyd, Martin Amis, Alan Ayckbourn, Anita Brookner, Anthony Burgess, Caryl Churchill, Margaret Drabble, Nell Dunn, John Fowles, William Golding, Graham Greene, Ted Hughes, Philip Larkin, Doris Lessing, Iris Murdoch, Joe Orton, John Osborne, Tim Pears, Anthony Powell, Barbara Pym, Bernice Rubens, Fay Weldon, David Lodge, Julian Barnes, and Joanna Trollope—among many others. No one writer's England is quite like anyone else's

So when someone asks me, "How would I go about planning a literary tour of England?" I cannot give a short fast answer. I first need to know which literary England they mean: the one remembered from their favorite children's stories, or from classic novels, or from Shakespeare's plays, or from the eighteenth-century essays and poems of Johnson, Dryden, and Pope? Are they more interested in the Lake District of the Romantic poets, Thomas Hardy's Wessex, or the age of King Arthur, as envisioned by Malory or Tennyson or T. H. White? Do they prefer a stroll through Lodge's Birmingham or Drabble's Hampstead?

I usually start by reassuring the tentative planner that anyone going to London can hardly *escape* a literary tour. Throughout London, round blue plaques attached to buildings clearly announce their illustrious former residents (see Chapter 6, "Lolloping Around London"). Glancing upward, a casual pedestrian might note, for example, that A. A. Milne spent twenty years at 11 (now 13) Mallord Street, where he wrote much of *Winnie-the-Pooh*; that Oscar Wilde lived at No. 34 Tite Street from 1884 until 1895, when he went to jail; that our own American writers, Nathaniel Hawthorne and Mark Twain, once occupied, respectively, 4 Pond Road, Blackheath, and 23 Tedworth Square, Chelsea.

Studying these blue plaques is a kind of literary education in itself. American writers in England, for example: Who were they and why did they come here? How did English culture and society affect their work? I have no trouble imagining Mark Twain on the Mississippi or in Virginia City, Nevada, but in London? Nathaniel Hawthorne in Piccadilly?

Minor names often tease at my mind: What exactly do I recall of Thomas Hood, who once lived at 2 Robert Street, south of the Strand? Why have I never heard of Joanna Baillie, a Scottish dramatist and poet who evidently spent most of her life in Bolton House, Hampstead? Here at 65 St. Paul's Churchyard, a plaque tells me that John Newbery established his bookselling and publishing business in 1744. I've heard of the Newbery Award for children's books; why don't I know anything about John Newbery?

Bookish travelers who don't want to depend on the simple serendipity of blue plaques can easily locate several authors' houses preserved as museums in London. Among the best known are Thomas and Jane Carlyle's former home at 24 Cheyne Row in Chelsea; the Dickens House Museum at 48 Doughty Street; Keats

House, Wentworth Place, Keats Grove, in Hampstead; and Dr. Johnson's House, 17 Gough Square.

Outside London, a book lover could hopscotch across the country by planning stops at famous writers' houses now open to the public, from T. E. Lawrence's Clouds Hill, a modest bungalow near Wareham, Dorset, to Rudyard Kipling's impressively magisterial manor, Bateman's, in the Burwash valley of East Sussex; from John Milton's cottage at Chalfont St. Giles, Buckinghamshire, to Byron's family estate, Newstead Abbey, near Linby, Nottinghamshire.

These literary shrines vary in their accessibility. For example, Pope's Grotto at Twickenham, in private ownership, is currently only open on Saturday afternoons, and then strictly by prior appointment, while Beatrix Potter's Hill Top, a little seventeenth-century house at Near Sawrey, Ambleside, Cumbria, owned by the National Trust, is open five days a week from spring to fall, with a special audiovisual show on Beatrix Potter's Lake District available at the nearby National Trust Visitor Centre in Keswick.

Some of these sites are so well known that in high season they are apt to be mobbed. Arrive early or, even better, just before closing hour, at the Brontë Parsonage Museum in Haworth, Keighley, West Yorkshire, if you want to try to recapture the former isolation of its bleak moorland setting. And no matter when you arrive at Shakespeare's fabled Birthplace or Anne Hathaway's Cottage in Stratford-upon-Avon, you'll likely have plenty of company.

Although, like most book-loving tourists, I have dutifully paid my respects at some of these literary meccas, I do not always find an author's-house-as-museum particularly interesting. To me, a house without a living occupant seems empty and lifeless, no matter how much carefully preserved memorabilia fills its rooms. Even when I stare hard at, say, Dickens's desk—as well as his scuffed favorite chair, well-worn books, personal pen and inkstand—I feel only a faint tremor. I find it very hard to conjure up the shade of Dickens sitting in front of me, writing his books. And what does this mute desk really have to do with the rich, vivid, and utterly engrossing world of *Bleak House*?

In *Writers at Home*, a compendium of engaging essays on British writers' houses, Jonathan Keates eloquently describes such preserved rooms as inspiring "a species of haunted, tomb-like sadness comparable to no other: the lovingly-amassed rows of first editions, the display case devoted to the publications of the Society—dismal little altar of the cult—the caricatures and signed photographs, the lifeless array of manuscripts and letters, the terrible collection of personal objects like things tossed aside in a headlong flight from death, none of these can bring back what we have come to find."

Yet sometimes a chance glimmer of insight does bring me closer to a person behind the authorial mask. At Chawton, Hampshire, Jane Austen's home during the last eight years of her life, I was lucky to find myself alone by a small chair in the parlor, facing a window looking on to the village road. It was not a busy day in Chawton; a few people passed by, perhaps on their way to a footpath that led across an adjoining meadow. Maybe the path ended at the village church or parsonage or a grand country house like Netherfield.

Suddenly I felt what it might have been like to be Jane Austen, sitting there calmly but observantly watching the passing world. I could also picture her a few feet away at the family table, where she wrote, ready to slip her pages under a book if an unwelcome visitor intruded. Outside, in the afternoon sunshine, I could sense the peace in her cottage garden, blooming that summer day with the old-fashioned flowers—larkspur, geraniums, daisies—she might have tended. During my brief stay at Chawton, I could almost catch the quiet music of the tenor of Jane Austen's life.

If I know enough about a writer, I can sometimes blow away the unseen dust from fossilized rooms. At Virginia and Leonard Woolf's home, Monk's House, in Rodmell, Sussex, and at nearby Charleston, where Virginia's sister Vanessa Bell and Duncan Grant lived, I wandered through the houses with great excitement because I could mentally fill them with actual people, including guests like Ottoline Morrell, John Maynard Keynes, E. M. Forster, Clive Bell, and others, a cast of vivid characters whose parties, conversations, and domestic dramas I had shared through hundreds of pages of diary, memoir, autobiography, and even photographs.

I felt, in fact, a little abashed at my intrusion into these once-private spaces—especially Virginia's small, sparely furnished bedroom. Reached only by an outside entrance, it must have been a detached retreat that felt peculiarly her own. Standing in that room, next to her plain, narrow bed, I thought of a haunting passage from *Mrs. Dalloway*: "Like a nun withdrawing, she went upstairs. . . . There was an emptiness about the heart of life; an attic room. . . . The sheets were clean, tight stretched in a broad white band from side to side. Narrower and narrower would her bed be."

When I came to Virginia Woolf's "hut," an unpretentious, almost ramshackle unheated studio at the back of the garden, I was enormously moved to think of the fiercely protected hours, the intensity of effort, that she spent there. I could easily evoke her elegantly thin, bent figure, secure and absorbed in this sequestered room.

Even when I do not pursue authors' houses, I find I am often swept into a literary ambience in England. Sometimes I am startled by an unanticipated name or place I know. A few years ago, as James and I were nearing the border of West Dorset and Somerset, I noted in my driving atlas that we would soon pass by the village of East Coker. "East Coker! It's got to be the same one!" I said triumphantly to James, who looked puzzled until I told him that "East Coker" was both the title and the setting of one of T. S. Eliot's magnificent *Four Quartets*.

Detouring into the village, we stopped at the church, where, it turned out, Eliot is buried. It was a still summer afternoon, and the small hushed town, with its tidy houses of warm golden Hamstone, nestled among gentle green hills. Beyond, the fields were dotted with ancient farmhouses, grazing cows, and scattered sheep. I thought of Eliot's tortured visions of early twentieth-century urban life and then of this sheltered, seemingly timeless countryside. I could better understand something about the tide of growing conservatism that eventually swept Eliot back to this church.

Not long afterward, we were turning down a country lane toward our rented cottage in Cornwall when I saw on the map that we were not far from the town of Helford. That name, too, caught my attention. "Isn't that where Mary Yellan was from?" I asked James. Mary is the courageous heroine of Daphne Du Maurier's novel of intrigue and adventure, *Jamaica Inn*, which we had recently listened to on tape. The next day we drove to Helford, tucked along the wooded estuary of the Helford River, and its seductive charm soon led me to a bookstore and several more of Du Maurier's best-sellers.

Without exploring Cornwall, I might have thought the landscapes of her novels exaggerated, overly lush and theatrical. But that was what her Cornwall was really like: the jagged, sea-beaten coast whose cliffs are mostly wild and unspoiled; the stark, undulating expanse of Bodmin Moor, broken by strange rock formations; a dampish green tangle along the banks of hidden Frenchman's Creek, where Du Maurier's pirates could lurk unseen, waiting for a moonlit night and a rising tide.

We did not see Menabilly, the estate where Du Maurier lived for many years and her inspiration for Manderley, the eerie centerpiece of *Rebecca* ("Last night I dreamt I went to Manderley again."). Although Cornwall's countryside does not disappoint, I was afraid Menabilly might. Menabilly is not open to the public. But this past April James and I did take a steep public path along the edge of the Menabilly estate, down toward the small bay—still tranquil and secluded—where Rebecca's body was found. I could almost glimpse the great house through the trees, high above the bay. I think I preferred imagining the rest.

Any book lover traveling in England eventually looks around and realizes that he or she has stepped into the pages of a half-forgotten book. During a stay in Exmoor, on the North Devon coast, I discovered we were in the heart of Doone country. We had come to Exmoor not because of R. D. Blackmore's novel, *Lorna Doone*, which I read and loved when I was perhaps thirteen, but because I am irresistibly drawn to places where tumbling, sky-swept moorland meets the sea. Once there, however, I bought a new copy of the leisurely, old-fashioned romance, and when, one misty morning, we crossed heather and bracken to little Oare Church, where Lorna was married and shot, I felt as if I were walking through a tantalizing half-remembered dream.

I think of Thomas Hardy almost everywhere in his beloved "Wessex," a surprisingly vast countryside, still mostly rural, that extends from Hampshire through Dorset to Cornwall. But I seldom seek out the specific sites he fictionalized, partly because I do not love his novels, which I find masterful, profound, but irredeemably gloomy. Instead, because I love this part of England—its rolling green hills, bits of heath, thatched cottages, stone manor houses, prehistoric monuments—I let the land work its own magic. Looking down into the deep, remote valley of Batcombe ("Owlscombe"), for example, whose fields and pastures are outlined by centuries-old hedgerows, I can easily recover the slowly paced, traditional rural England whose seasons, customs, and beliefs Hardy has kept alive in his stories and poems.

Wherever I go in England, books are waiting for me. Passing recently through the popular seaside resort of Torquay in Devon, I noted a hotel sign that proudly reminded travelers that Agatha Christie had once sought anonymous refuge here. In London, we often stay in the former home of Sir John Betjeman, once poet laureate, a flat now maintained and rented by the Landmark Trust. The flat itself is in Cloth Fair, a street just outside St. Bartholomew's Hospital, setting of Ben Jonson's play *Bartholomew Fair* (see Chapter 21, "At Home in Cloth Fair").

Not only in England, but also in Wales and Scotland, I find at unexpected times that I am in the company of a writer I have loved. One misty September afternoon on Scotland's Isle of Skye, as James and I were driving north from Armadale along a coastal road, I asked him to turn off and swoop down into the hamlet of Ornsay. Something about it sounded familiar. As we took a brief walk around the rocky inlet that shelters an inn and a few houses, I kept turning to gaze at the whitewashed lighthouse just offshore. It looked lonely yet inviting, a shelter from the wet fierce winds that often whip through the Hebrides. What would it be like to live there, listening to the ocean beat against the rocks, with the hills of Skye rising behind?

Then I remembered. Isle Ornsay! Of course! The lighthouse cottage on that island—connected at low tide to the mainland—was once the refuge of Gavin Maxwell. His *Ring of Bright Water*, a dramatic and moving story of his sojourn among wild otters, had so enchanted me that I eventually read his other haunting memoirs (see Chapter 5, "A Suitcase Full of Books"). A recent biography had revealed much about Maxwell's troubled life; that is where I came upon Isle Ornsay. From here, across the water, if I knew exactly where to look, I would also be able to see the site of Camusfearna, Maxwell's isolated Highlands cottage. I had not been searching for Maxwell, but he was here.

For someone who is a meticulous planner, such an unforeseen encounter has a special piquant pleasure. I could, of course, consult the innumerable books on literary sites, like *The Oxford Illustrated Literary Guide to Great Britain and Ireland*, whose maps are almost covered with pointillistic dots, suggesting possible stops. But although I love to read about literary landscapes—the settings of novels, memoirs, poems, or plays, as well as the actual places where writers lived—I seldom need to arrange a special journey to find them. As long as I travel in England, I am sure *they* will continue to find me.

A Few Floating Facts

Guides to Literary England

So many books have been written on literary England that they cover several shelves in a good used bookstore (many are now out of print) or in a large library. Browsing in either place, as well as consulting new books in any well-stocked bookstore, will yield rewarding finds. Here is a sampling of very different possibilities:

The Oxford Illustrated Literary Guide to Great Britain and Ireland (1992) lists and briefly describes actual (not fictional) places with literary associations. An index of writers gives cross-references to these places. Some citations in my 1981 edition are wonderfully obscure: Middleton Stoney, it seems, is the former home of John Gay's patrons, who financed his play, The Beggar's Opera (1728). But if I were driving through Rolvenden, Kent, I might like to know that Frances Hodgson Burnett based The Secret Garden on a high-walled garden at Great Maytham Hall.

A Writer's Britain: Landscape in Literature, by Margaret Drabble (1979), is an intelligent, compact essay on the changing attitudes of British writers toward their landscape. This essay shows off Drabble's critical acumen, scholarship, and verve: "It is no accident that Tennyson is so fond of words such as glimmer, wan, dim, ghastly, misty, dusk, chill, dreary, drooping, sodden, drenched and dewy . . . for they describe the half-tones, the melancholy, the dim wetness of a Northern world."

Literary Britain: Landmarks, Landscapes and Houses of the Great Writers and Poets, with photographs by Bill Brandt (1986), has facing pages of literary text and Brandt's illustrative black-and-white photographs. A similar book, but in color, is Michael J. Stead's Literary Landscapes (1989). I have a special fondness for a faded copy, sent to me by a thoughtful reader, of Literary England: Photographs of Places Made Memorable in English Literature, by David Scherman and Richard Wilcox (1943), which I read as a child and which introduced me to England.

Writers and Their Houses, edited by Kate Marsh (1993), collects fifty essays by prominent current authors on literary masters of the past in Great Britain and Ireland, with a gazetteer to writers' houses. It is great fun to read P. D. James being authoritative on the life and houses of Jane Austen, Michael Holroyd on George Bernard Shaw, Malcolm Bradbury on Laurence Sterne, and more.

Writers at Home, a book organized by the National Trust in 1985, *also offers essays by well-known contemporary writers-biographers on ten authors' houses owned and open to the public by the National Trust. Quentin Bell surveys the Bloomsbury homes in East Sussex, for example, including Charleston Farm House; Ronald Blythe describes Coleridge at Nether Stowey.*

London has its own copious annotators. Literary London: A Readers' Walking Tour, *by Andrew Davies (1989), is packed with information. Many other general guidebooks also include literary walking tours.*

Books abound on specific writers and their landscapes. The Landscape of Thomas Hardy, *by Denys Kay-Robinson (1984);* Thomas Hardy's England, *by John Fowles and Jo Draper (1984);* Shakespeare Country, *by Susan Hill (1987);* James Herriot's Yorkshire, *with photographs by Derry Brabbs (1979);* Daphne Du Maurier's Enchanted Cornwall *(1989);* Nigel Nicolson's *The World of Jane Austen (1991); and* Brontë Country, *edited by Glenda Leeming (reissued 1994), are only a few examples.*

The British Tourist Authority, 551 Fifth Avenue, Suite 701, New York, NY 10176, may be helpful with specific requests about literary tours. The B.T.A. can also provide addresses for local tourist information centers, located virtually everywhere in England. These centers often stock books or pamphlets on local writers and literary heritages. On our last trip to Cornwall, for example, I purchased a forty-eight-page pamphlet, "Cornwall's Literary Heritage," describing all kinds of enticing literary associations with sites throughout Cornwall, from Arthurian legends to minor memoirs.

Tourist information centers also cater to special interests. Shropshire Tourism, The Music Hall, The Square, Shrewsbury, Shropshire, SY1 1LH, for example, provides "Brother Cadfael Car Trails," a driving itinerary for fans of Ellis Peters's Brother Cadfael mysteries.

With an atlas of Great Britain, a little research, time, and determination, any reader can construct his or her own tour. My stepfather, an English professor who had written his dissertation on the visionary poet-artist William Blake, once planned a very successful trip to London around Blake, from the poet's lodgings in Lambeth and print shop in Soho to his art (mostly at the Tate Gallery) and, finally, his grave at Bunhill Fields.

If you are curious about the sites associated with Shakespeare, Dickens, or several other major writers, consider one of the organized walking tours available every day in London. Many of these tours have literary themes (see Chapter 6, "Lolloping Around London").

5

⚔⚔

A Suitcase Full of Books

Forget cashmere sweaters, skirt lengths of Harris tweed, Wedgwood teacups, and satiny black umbrellas. A book lover carries home souvenirs that look plainer, weigh more, but last a lot longer.

Only in England would I pounce with delight upon a second-hand copy of *Down Among the Donkeys*. Browsing through the hodgepodge bookstalls outside London's National Theatre, I certainly wasn't looking for anything on donkeys. But attracted by its odd title, I leafed through Elisabeth Svendsen's 1981 memoir, a lively and well-written account of how she came to found a donkey sanctuary in Devon. Then, paying the hovering bookseller two pounds, I wedged the book into my crowded shoulderbag and managed to ignore my husband's muttered query: "*More* books?"

When I'm in Great Britain, I always buy more books. Some travelers worry about what reading material to carry with them; I obsess about what I can take home. Together with crumpets and three-fruit marmalade, a certain kind of book—quiet, circumscribed, intensely local—has become my favorite British souvenir.

Many years ago, I bought books in Britain mainly because they were cheap. During my graduate school days of the 1960s, I could acquire certain texts—the definitive *Piers Plowman*, for example, or Yeats's collected poems—more easily and inexpensively from a Blackwell's mail-order catalogue, based in Oxford, than from any Berkeley bookstore. And, taking my word as sole credit reference, Blackwell's graciously permitted me to charge and only billed me months later.

In those years, literary paperbacks also seemed more plentiful in

Britain than in America. *Paperback* at home originally meant pot-boilers with lurid covers; I remember once in the 1950s being surprised to find a paperback copy of Faulkner's *Sanctuary* on my mother's shelf, since I knew that he represented Literature, which then only came in hardcover. Until well into the early 1980s, I would avidly search Foyle's racks of Penguins, hoping to find classy titles unavailable in America. I came to think of that perky black bird, stamped like a discreet seal of approval on an orange book jacket, as a symbol of British superiority.

But after book prices in Britain eventually soared, finally to levels even higher than at home, I began to buy books there for different reasons. Over the years, I had become fascinated with the particular—and sometimes peculiar—passions that individuals in Britain nurtured, whether restoring a vintage Victorian yacht, or training falcons, or operating antique locomotives, or assembling vast collections of butterflies or bone china or bamboo. When I found a book that articulately explored one of these passions—like Ms. Svendsen's love for donkeys—I felt as if I had been given the privilege to examine the wellspring of someone's life.

Such books, usually in the form of memoir, also provided details about daily life that, as a tourist, I was seldom able to experience. I learned to comb National Trust gift shops for local titles, head for bookstore displays marked REGIONAL or OF LOCAL INTEREST, and watch for out-of-print memoirs in sidewalk stalls. I knew what I was looking for: something that took me off the well-traveled road.

During a recent trip to the Highlands, for instance, I picked up Alison Johnson's *A House by the Shore: Twelve Years in the Hebrides* (1986), which described with gusto how she and her husband converted a derelict old house on the remote island of Harris into a flourishing small hotel. Although I did not have time that trip to stop at Harris, I felt as if I had been there, for Ms. Johnson's anecdotal book led me on a long, idiosyncratic personal tour, from hidden sand beaches to a fairy hill, and cheerily chatted at length about her neighbors.

Not every such guide has to be nonfiction. After Ms. Johnson's memoir, I discovered Alice Thomas Ellis's witty, haunting novel, *The Inn at the Edge of the World* (1990), in which five lonely people seek refuge one Christmas in an inn (not, as far as I could tell, Ms. Johnson's) on a Scottish island. Because of Ms. Ellis, I was able to dwell for a time among the magical selkies or "seal people," next to the fierce Hebridean winter sea, an ever-present and unpredictable force in the novel. Now I am eagerly looking forward to Finlay J. MacDonald's *Crowdie and Cream: Memoirs of a Hebridean Childhood* (1982). Since none of these books are currently available in the United States, I know that without my stash of souvenirs, I'd have missed an intriguing sojourn in the Hebrides.

Most of my best local-color book buys suddenly appear without warning, calling to me seductively, if in a distinctly minor key. My considered and more obvious choices of better-known works are often less successful. Sometimes when I travel to a literary site, I feel impelled to buy the relevant classic, which I intend to read or reread practically on the spot: *Lorna Doone* in Exmoor, *The Mayor of Casterbridge* in Dorchester, *Sons and Lovers* in the Midlands. But at the end of a long touring day, I can rarely give good literature its due. So I usually portage these unread books home, where they take their place on shelves already heaped with high intentions.

I have better luck with what I think of as casual biography, books that do not pretend to magisterial status. I read them with the glee of a visiting tourist who has an unexpected, prolonged, intimate glimpse of a celebrity or even a semicelebrity. On a recent trip to England, I grabbed from a secondhand bookstall Michael Coveney's *Maggie Smith: A Bright Particular Star* (1992), Lyle Dorsett's *Joy and C. S. Lewis: The Story of an Extraordinary Marriage* (1988), and *Olivier at Work: The National Years* (1989), an informal collection of reminiscences by Olivier's co-workers, including Michael Gambon, Anthony Hopkins, and Jonathan Miller. Even after spending much time in England, it is not always easy to feel like an insider, but admiring, gently gossipy books like these can temporarily do the trick.

Sometimes I discover a biography of a less well-known British subject with whom, over decades, I have cultivated an ardent if one-sided relationship. Douglas Botting's 1993 biography of Gavin Maxwell, best known as author of *Ring of Bright Water* (1960), was a prize find. When I saw *Gavin Maxwell: A Life* on a shelf of new arrivals in a London bookshop, I startled the gray-haired lady next to me with a little cry of excitement. During a difficult time in my own life, I had once delved with an uneasy sense of kinship into Maxwell's bleak, torturous but often lyrical memoirs, *The Rocks Remain* (1963), *The House of Elrig* (1965), and *Raven Seek Thy Brother* (1968).

I had wondered what Maxwell was really like; after his death in 1969, I assumed I would never know. But through Botting's intelligent, sympathetic, yet balanced narrative, I learned a great deal about this gifted, charismatic, but deeply troubled man—as well as about the Highlands, Marsh Arabs, shark fisheries, and some of the fascinating people, places, and animals in his world. I had the grateful awareness of unlooked-for illumination that sometimes happens when an acquaintance deepens into friendship.

Not all the books I look for in Britain are about people. I find it hard not to pick up enticingly illustrated guides to flora and fauna, imagining that I am carefully preparing myself for close encounters. I now own several authoritative books about British trees, which, unfortunately, I am still seldom able to identify correctly, because my authorities are never in hand when I am under a tree. Although I always promise myself to study those books later, they tend to end up next to *The Mayor of Casterbridge*.

I find animals more fun to read about than trees. Flipping through *Nature Lover's Library: Field Guide to the Animals of Britain* (1984), I stopped at a remarkably engrossing entry on "Helping Hedgehogs to Survive." Its several pages on hedgehogs were filled with drawings of these small, spiny, and quintessentially British mammals, and the entry included such enlightening information as: "If a hedgehog is seen to froth at the mouth and twist itself about, it is not sick but is spreading the frothy saliva on its fur and spines with its tongue. The purpose of this behaviour is unknown, but it is quite normal." Now that I know how to react if I see a frothing hedgehog, I compla-cently think of myself as a tourist with a difference.

So I happily contemplate my newest stack of souvenirs, just unpacked, as yet unopened: Katy Cropper's *A Dog's Life in the Dales* (1992), the story of a young shepherdess in Yorkshire; P. Y. Betts's *People Who Say Goodbye* (1989), childhood memories of a woman, born in 1909, who now lives in seclusion in Wales; Sylvia Haymon's *The Quivering Tree: An East Anglian Childhood* (1990); and Elisabeth Svendsen's recent sequel *For the Love of Donkeys* (1993).

Reading these books will probably have consequences. After fin-ishing Ms. Svendsen's first book, I rearranged my travel plans to include visits to her sanctuary (now sheltering six thousand donkeys on nine farms), as well as to an otter sanctuary, a seal sanctuary, and an owl sanctuary (see Chapter 19, "Touring England's Ark"). Next summer I want to take a ferry to Harris. Private passions, exposed in just the right kind of book, can be catching.

6

Lolloping Around London

A Note on Lolloping

I only lollop when I am in England. At home, I sometimes "loll," "lounge," and "move forward with a bounding or leaping motion," as my several dictionaries define *lollop*, with a cautionary note: "Brit. dial." But I do not lollop. Since no one in Minneapolis would understand me if I spoke in British dialect, I also cannot *swan about* (prance around in public, showing off), wear anything absolutely *flash* (gaudily loud), or haughtily dismiss a fancy fake-Tudor birdhouse as impossibly *twee* (unbearably cutesy).

As soon as I arrive in England, my vocabulary acquires an English patina. Enamored of words, I absorb them almost without thought. So I immediately begin referring to *lorries*, not trucks; *lifts*, not elevators; a *flat*, not an apartment; a *tin* of tuna, not a can. I know enough to *book* a seat at a restaurant or a theatre, not just to make a reservation or buy a ticket. I can discern that an *aubergine* is really an eggplant, *courgettes* are zucchini, and English lettuce is what I call Boston. If I order a mixed salad, I understand it will be filled with cut-up hard tomatoes, cucumbers, and raw onions, not a variety of greens.

With rather embarrassed bemusement, I find myself asking James to *hoover* the front room rather than vacuum it. I tell a grocery-store clerk to put my purchases in my *shopper* rather than in my shopping bag. I'm apt to explain to an inquiring salesperson that an expensive item is far too *pricey*.

When someone has proffered a nice but unspectacular idea, perhaps for lunching at a particular restaurant, I might well exlaim, "Brilliant!" ("Brilliant?" I then ask myself incredulously. "Did I just say that? About *lunch?*") *Brilliant*, in Britain, is merely a slightly upper-class way of commending something. Or maybe it is not upper-class at all. Trying to decide what British locution is "U" (upper-class) or "non-U" (alas, not) is very tricky, as Nancy Mitford pointed out forty years ago, in a witty essay reprinted in *Noblesse Oblige*.

As soon as I pass through customs at Gatwick, *lovely* begins to pop unbidden out of my mouth. An Anglophile I know calls this "an attack of the lovelies." "That would be lovely," I say to the taxi driver who asks if he should stop right here. "Lovely," I tell the waiter who points to our table. "Oh, how lovely," I say politely to the friend who has brought out a tea tray with scones on it. As soon as the taxi driver, waiter, or friend has turned his or her back, James looks at me wickedly, grins, screws up his face, and purses his lips. Prissily, he says in a phony mock-whisper, "Oh, yes, how *lovely*! Perfectly *lovely!'* But even James cannot entirely suppress my lovelies.

I do have my limits. Despite tweaks of temptation, I have yet to promise anyone that instead of phoning, I'll give a tinkle on the tellie. If I refer to the ladies' room as the loo, I never suggest that I'm going there to spend a penny. (As a veteran traveler to England, I confess I do remember when pay toilets required one or more of those long-vanished huge copper coins.) Although, caught up in the British spirit, I may sometimes call out to James, who has just negotiated a tortuous road, "Well done!" or "Good show!," I never, ever tell him that everything now is going to be tickety-boo.

Dismayed to hear myself sounding too affectedly British, I am also startled when I sound too American. Talking to British friends, I occasionally have to stop in the middle of a sentence and explain what I've just said. Sometimes a well-worn bit of slang appears quite peculiar: *pigging out*, for example, or *give it a shot*, or *a real blowout*. Once, when a British couple mentioned they'd soon be staying in an Italian village where we wanted to take a future holiday, I said, "Great! Then you can scout out the territory for us!" As I instantly pictured myself in buckskins and a coonskin cap, they smiled politely.

But no matter how I try to prune my speech of twining Anglicisms or knotty American slang, I hope, at least in London, I can continue to lollop. *Lollop* has an easy, carefree sound, with a swinging kind of rhythm that suggests someone sauntering down the street. On my happiest days in London, that is exactly what I do.

*   *   *

Perhaps London's secret is an oddly haunting aroma—a faint, blended scent I can't ever quite analyze. It may suddenly waft out from a quiet tree-lined Kensington square before the morning traffic has reached full pitch on nearby Cromwell Road. Or I may notice it when I first arrive, emerging from Victoria Station onto the confusing bustle of Buckingham Palace Road. Once I paused, arrested by its evanescent sharpness, just as I turned onto a rather ordinary shop-lined street near the Barbican.

I remember standing on the sidewalk, a few yards from the hidden entrance to a Safeway, trying to dissect that elusive aroma. It was, I thought, definitely gray and damp, perhaps something that emanated from wet wrought-iron railings, cement pavements, and rain-soaked old buildings, pitted and pockmarked stone that had slowly absorbed drizzle for a hundred years or more. It was a little acrid, too, with that whiff of wet iron, and perhaps also an overlay of endless cups of dark, grayish tea, steeped to the bitter taste of metal, drunk in long-vanished Lyons Corner Houses and faded tearooms.

Somewhere in that mixture I could catch just the suggestion of something fresher, reassuringly moist and green—grass, bits of lawn, the stems of daffodils or pansies or wallflowers, sprigs of daphne or cistus, in a concealed garden square around the next corner or maybe the corner after that. Could I also conjure up a slight dank odor of turbid moving water, a distant breeze from the blackish Thames as it slowly surges through the city on its way to the sea?

Part had to be the odor of urban decay, an almost universally familiar brew of garbage on the curb—I'd seen it sometimes, during England's labor disputes, heaped in huge, stinking piles—added to lingering gas and oil fumes, faintly burned rubber, and stale urine in alleys, tunnels, and dark corners never washed clean by the heaviest of rains.

Of course I didn't linger long, wrinkling my nose and staring at the almost empty street. I never like to feel conspicuous, especially in London, and in my purse I had a daunting grocery list. But the sharp, damp odor reminded me that I had returned once more to an ostensibly plain, straightforward, commercial city—a city that, however handsome, asserts itself with a certain pomposity, granitic dullness, and even deliberate blankness, with none of the soft, alluring airs of Paris or Venice. I stood for a few moments and savored the indefinable smell. I'm back, I thought happily. This is it. London. How I've missed it!

I easily lose count of how often I've been to London. Since that first summer in 1960, when I was a college student studying in a special program at the University of London, I suppose I could chalk up about twenty visits, some for only a few days, others for a week or two, one for seven months. The sum of my time isn't so astonishing—perhaps two years, added all together. I'd never claim to know London as a native does.

But I love London. At unpredictable times, I get lonesome for it. I climb into a steamy, dirt-streaked American taxi, with broken seat belts and sprung seats, and I wish I could be magically whisked into a stately black London cab, careening around the tightest corner with a certain sedateness. Dutifully admiring a prized Minneapolis garden, with its unrelenting rows of timid roses in rectangular beds, I think longingly of the tumultuous blooms spilling over circuitous paths in English gardens. On a blistering July afternoon in Minnesota, I have a momentary vision of myself walking along the

Thames, a wet mist dampening my face, with my turtleneck pulled up almost around my ears.

Preparing for an occasional business trip to New York, I glance over a rather thin listing of Broadway's current plays, looking for just the right combination of intelligence and entertainment. I wish I could see instead what's on right now at the Almeida or the Royal Court or the National Theatre. In London, I remember wistfully, plays often start by seven-thirty P.M., so I can get to bed at a reasonable hour, and besides, I can make my way home safely and easily, by foot or in one of those nifty cabs.

Sometimes, as lunchtime approaches, I want to walk into one of London's infinite street-front delis and buy a fresh-cut sandwich—egg and cress or smoked salmon on whole wheat. I'd eat it on a sunny bench near the Serpentine in Hyde Park. I want to pour myself a glass of sweet cider and finish my picnic with a raspberry jam tart or a small carton of hazelnut yogurt. Then at one-fifteen P.M., just after lunch, I wish I could slip into a nearby church and sit for an hour while listening to a free organ concert of Bach and Handel or perhaps to a young soprano singing Grieg and Mendelssohn.

On a rainy afternoon I'd like to browse through a deserted upper room at the Victoria and Albert Museum, examining intricately enameled china vases or gracefully curving eighteenth-century silver teapots or multicolored Venetian glass swans. Then I'd warm up with tea and scones in the crowded cafeteria downstairs and afterward dash in and out of a few boutiques, whose prices leave me a little breathless, on nearby Beauchamp Place.

Sometimes I can shut my eyes and open them in memory on Regent Street or Birdcage Walk or the Victoria Embankment. I get flashes of red double-decker buses jammed together in traffic along Knightsbridge, pigeons fluttering in Trafalgar Square, emerald lawns in Regent's Park, crackling-new books—not available yet, if ever, in the U.S.—stacked near the cashier's desk at Hatchard's. At such moments, London seems very close, and I think I can almost imagine that wonderful, rainy, acrid smell.

Not long ago, Isobel, a friend of mine who has visited London many times, said resignedly, "Well, I guess I'll probably go back to London for my vacation. I'd thought about a few other places, but after all, I do speak the language and I know how to get around in London. The trouble is, I've been there so many times that the city no longer holds any mystery for me."

I did not bother to remind Isobel of Samuel Johnson's famous dictum: "When a man is tired of London, he is tired of life." If she had fallen out of love, I certainly could not argue her back in again—either with London or with life. Cities are like people; who can ever satisfactorily explain why he or she loves one and not another? Venice, not Rome? Amsterdam, not Brussels? San Francisco, not New York? Above all, London, not someplace else? Crowded, chilly, increasingly expensive, grimy, touristy, demoralized London? Yes, above all, London!

I waited for my friend Isobel to continue, to challenge me a little defensively, to ask, as a few friends and acquaintances do, "Since *you* seem to go so often, what do you and James *do* there? I suppose you go to the theatre, but what else? Museums? And then what?"

But Isobel changed the subject. So I was left pondering her plaintive remarks and her unasked questions. Off and on, as I thought about her again, I gradually began to answer her in my mind. Okay, I said, here is what I do in London. I go back to London for pleasure—not to work, not to visit relatives or friends, not to buy or sell or collect, not for any of the reasons that might make London a different city for me, but for the sheer fun of it. And although my fun might not be yours, I'd like to share a few secrets with you.

First, I'd tell her, right after collecting your bags and before heading into London, stop at the airport newsstand. Buy a copy of the daily London *Times* and the current *Time Out* magazine. You need to tune in to the tempo of the city. On the Gatwick Express to Victoria, sleepy as I am, I always take samplings from the *Times*. I remind myself what really matters here: overfishing by Spanish trawlers, new threats from Brussels to British sovereignty, a cabinet minister's extramarital adventures, a marquess's drug addiction, an

out-of-sync Anglican bishop's mildly radical views about abortion or
divorce, a rescued dog or stalled trains or a bungled operation by a
National Health doctor with an ominously foreign-sounding name.

On the back page, I glance at the weather map, remembering that
even the staidly officious *Times* cannot safely predict what the
London weather will be like tomorrow. Their helpless forecasts turn
ambiguity into a complex art form: "Dull but dry, with bright intervals" or "Sunny patches with showery spells, then clearing, with rain
later."

I quickly skim through a few columnists who somehow seem to be
more acidly personal, defiantly biased, and slyly entertaining than
the earnestly balanced writers who compose their careful views for
the newspapers I read at home. I delight in the caustic report of
goings-on in a Parliament whose members are often still, amazingly,
recklessly quotable. (I still treasure Denis Healey's remark, many
years ago, that criticism from Geoffrey Howe was "like being sav-
aged by a dead sheep.") I look for the usual columnists' comments,
suffused these days with scorn, pity, or tolerant bemusement, about
the beleaguered royal family. I need to catch up on them, too.

Then I finish off with the page of "Letters to the *Times*," a vintage
tea chest of British manners and mores. Dignified politicians write
solemn exposulatory epistles about trade, diplomacy, and Brussels.
After indignant protests about French lambs or local lager-louts or
female Anglican priests, country gentlemen conclude with a
flourish, "I remain, sir, yours most sincerely . . ." and then attach the
evocative names of their houses: The Feathers, Tiverton; Rose Cottage, Lulworth; The Old Rectory, Bexhill-by-the-Sea. Elderly ladies,
retired military officers, and others evidently oppressed by too much
time write to correct spellings, annotate historic dates, announce
bird sightings, and warn of disappearing hedgerows.

Now that I'm feeling firmly back on English ground, I excitedly
turn to *Time Out*, a weekly compendium of everything going on in
London, published each Wednesday. I regard it as such an essential
guide that upon arrival in London on Tuesday I will unhesitatingly
buy an almost outdated issue rather than wait a day for the new

edition. I want to start planning immediately and try to figure, impossibly, how to fit everything into my precious time, whether it is two days or two weeks.

A Night—Many Nights!—at the Theatre

First I run down the theatre listings, rapidly absorbing *Time Out*'s capsule reviews, ferociously opinionated, which I'll later supplement with milder critical comments in the daily and Sunday *Times*. Not only do I note what's on at the National Theatre or Royal Shakespeare Company, both of whom have enviable records, but I look for more offbeat recommendations as well.

London offers lunchtime theatre, for instance: fairly short plays, usually minimally staged, beginning anywhere from eleven A.M. to one P.M. Tickets are cheap. During one summer week, an adventurous but penurious theatregoer could have attended lunchtime performances of Tennessee Williams's *The Chalky White Substance*, seats at £5 ($9), at the Jermyn Street Theatre, near Green Park, and John Steinbeck's *Of Mice and Men*, £4 ($6.40), at the King's Head in Islington. Just a short train ride into southeast London, St. Dunstan's College was offering Euripides' *Cyclops*, the only complete surviving Greek satyr play, for only £3 ($4.80), a mere 50p (90 cents) to seniors. Doc Watson's *Riotous Acts* ("a musical chronicle of a theatrical plot") was free at the Theatre Museum in Russell Street, as was Full Tilt Theatre's outdoor performance at Victoria Embankment Gardens of *Immortal*, described, rather archly, as "a stilt-walking tale of vampires, Tibet and ageing-reverse cream." From Williams, Steinbeck, and Euripides to vampires on stilts in a London garden, how could any theatre lover resist?

Travelers who only think of London theatre in the West End—the cluster of theaters around Piccadilly, in the Haymarket, or along Shaftesbury Avenue—should pay special attention to the listings under "Off-West End" (London's equivalent of Off-Broadway) and "Fringe Shows" (Off-Off-Broadway). Some of the best productions open at the Almeida (Islington), the Royal Court (Sloane Square), the Hampstead Theatre, the Richmond Theatre, the Greenwich Theatre, Riverside Studios in Hammersmith, and other, lesser-known venues, all short jaunts on the Underground.

What about Stratford, for instance? No, not Stratford-upon-Avon. The other Stratford is a working-class London suburb no tourist ever sees. At least, until recently, I had never thought of going there. But then James and I read about a highly praised musical version of *Zorro!* at Stratford's Theatre Royal. Off we went, almost an hour's ride on a number 24 bus from St. Paul's, to a once-grand old theatre, full of gilded swirls and former royal boxes, that now sits, marooned by traffic, in the midst of a grimy, overcrowded shopping center and not far from a busy outdoor bus terminal.

But for the two hours we spent inside Stratford's faded, rather shabby theatre, we forgot our immediate surroundings. *Zorro!*, which played with zest to an audience largely of enthusiastic children and their parents, was great fun. The small touring troupe, doubling and redoubling in roles, sang, danced, and mimed with the kind of professional razzle-dazzle we have come to expect from the best British theatre.

Even the inventive staging, clearly operated on a budget, was impressive, demanding—and winning—an imaginative complicity from the rapt audience. When dashing Zorro galloped away—on a kind of broomstick hobbyhorse whose bobbing head was just visible above a waist-high curtain rapidly unfurled across the stage—we cheered and stamped with the rest. As Zorro dueled with his evil brother, both leaping and clashing swords with panache, the row of restless, whispering children in front of us froze into an admiring silence. (British actors sail through swordfighting as gracefully as they do Shakespeare's verse.)

Not only does *Time Out* help me decide what plays to see but also how best to afford them. It reminds me not to forget London's Half-Price Ticket Booth, where mainstream theatres with less than full houses will often sell discounted tickets—a third or a half off, with a small added fee—through a special booth in Leicester Square, usually open Monday through Saturday from noon to six-thirty P.M. The buyer must pay in pounds, not with a credit card—so have cash ready—and must take, for better or worse, whatever seats slide under the ticket window. Long lines form early outside this booth, but don't turn the corner into Leicester Square, look at all the people waiting ahead of you, and give up and go home. The line moves fast.

Best bets at the booth are long-running plays (except smash musicals), new and unreviewed plays, and occasional plays that are too thoughtful, serious, or experimental to win much popularity. (Unless they are securely slotted in repertory, the latter plays probably won't last too long after they reach the Leicester Square booth.)

Other cost-saving possibilities exist. The National and Royal Shakespeare companies offer a limited number of cheap seats ("day-seats") on the day of performance; on an uncrowded day, we can easily move to a better seat. Some theatres offer half-price tickets (including the best seats) to senior citizens (known in the U.K. as OAPs—Old Age Pensioners) or students who appear at the box office half an hour before the curtain goes up.

Anyone who likes gambling can try hanging around outside a theatre just before show time and hope for some respectable-looking private party to offer one or two tickets he or she can't use. Bargaining is possible. (I've bought an occasional ticket this way and never had a problem. But beware, I've been told, of unscrupulous touts, who may be selling bogus tickets.)

I don't always try to cut costs. Sometimes I'm willing to pay top prices for the best seats, figuring that we've already spent enough on airfare and lodging to make those seats a sensible investment. Similarly, although many people who visit London swear that they can always get tickets at the last minute, I care so passionately about what we see that I usually take as few chances as possible.

So several weeks before we leave for London, I procure a more-or-less current *Time Out* and *Sunday Times*. (Any moderately large city, like Minneapolis, probably supports a newsstand or bookstore that stocks current British magazines and newspapers. A fairly big library may carry the *Sunday Times*.) If I discover a play I cannot bear to miss, I call the theatre I want (both publications give phone numbers), cite my credit card number, and ask to have our tickets held at the window. The cost for the phone call is unalarming, perhaps five to eight dollars—I talk fast and don't dither—and the resulting seats have always been superb. Although I could use a toll-free number to one or two American ticket agencies, they do not handle every theatre and their prices are much higher.

Even if a play is sold out, I do not give up. On one trip to London, I longed to see *Riverdance*, a dazzling fusion of Irish dance and music. Although the limited engagement had been sold out for months, on the morning we wanted to go I called the box office three times to inquire about possible returns. The first agent said nothing was available. The second time a different agent offered us two tickets in the last row, which we turned down. On my third call, a third agent said, "This is very unusual, but in fact we've just had a return of two excellent seats in the middle of the dress circle." I was delighted but not astonished. In London, I expect the unusual.

Checking performance times, I am pleased to remember that matinees can occur on several days of the week, mainly (but not always) Wednesdays and Saturdays, and a few theatres schedule a late (four or five P.M.) weekend matinee, followed immediately by the regular evening curtain at seven-thirty or eight P.M. A truly avid and efficiently focused theatregoer, hustling from one play to another, could cram in ten plays or more in six days (although this wouldn't leave much time for anything else).

Although obviously no one, however eager, can attend two plays in a single evening, we sometimes manage to double our pleasure at the National Theatre. Besides its plays in repertory, the National offers periodic Platform Events. (These are unadvertised but announced in the theatre and in its monthly brochure.) For a few pounds—usually less than seven dollars—theatre lovers can buy reserved seats for an hour's onstage presentation by noted actors, playwrights, critics, and other theatrical figures. *Platforms* usually run from six to seven P.M., ending just in time for the audience to dash for an evening curtain. Programs are varied. On one visit, we had the chance to hear actor and writer Simon Callow give a mesmerizing monologue (without notes) on his biography of Orson Welles. Days later, noted critic Mel Gussow interviewed playwright Tom Stoppard in an onstage discussion of Stoppard's work. If we could have stayed a few weeks longer, we might have listened to actress Diana Rigg reminisce about her life in the theatre.

I love going to the theatre in London. Once in my seat, perhaps in a theatre with a flamboyant historic past and jewel-box architecture, I relax, putting myself in the hands of actors who are trained to speak the English language with care and precision. I hear Shakespeare that isn't muddled, mangled, or mealymouthed. I see Shakespeare—or Marlowe, Jonson, Wycherley, Congreve, and others—that is lively, furiously entertaining, mesmerizingly fierce. I can also seek out new English-speaking plays, American, Irish, South African, as well as British—Edward Albee, Arthur Miller, Tony Kushner, David Hare, Athol Fugard, Brian Friel—long before they hazard a run, if they ever do, on increasingly perilous Broadway.

And of course, at intermission, I can indulge in the kind of reasonable civilized tradition that often makes London seem like a pleasantly small town. I walk down the aisle to a nearby usher, buy a little carton of chocolate ice cream, and take it back to my seat.

Music and More Music

Although London's theatre is justly famous, the city has a vibrant musical life, too. Here I am forced to admit to areas of massive ignorance, of which *Time Out* reminds me by devoting huge sections to "Rock, Reggae & Soul," "Roots, Folk & Country," and "Jazz & Latin," while shoving "Classical" (a relatively short category) to the end. Since I am hopelessly retrograde in my musical tastes, skimming those first listings is, for me, rather like reading snatches of a foreign language—or, perhaps more accurately, a language whose words I recognize but whose grammar remains obscure.

What do I know of the Pet Lemmings ("currently touting a somewhat charming ska version of Kraftwerk's 'The Model' ")? Or of Ry Cooder, Vanessa-Mae, Rigid, Forget the Down, Sea of Rains, Poor Folk, Red House, Riotous Assembly, Counterfeit Stones, Daddy Longlegs, Shaking Vicars, Who Killed Bambi?, Spatter the Dew, Smashing Dishes, Smokin' Dogs, Kissing Pigs, Dear John, Ravers, Automatic Slim, Wild Swans, Lost T-Shirts of Atlantis?

I also like the venues where these musicians evidently hang out: Filthy MacNastys & The Whiskey Cafe, Fiddlers Elbow, Slug & Lettuce, Red Back Tavern, Polar Bear, Pint Pot, Harvey Floorbangers, The Fridge, Trolley Stop, Break for the Border, Frog & Bucket, Family Tree, Gossips.

As I whiz past these tantalizing references on my way to "Classical," I do sometimes pause and wish I could hear, for example, Zimbabwe's Chiweshe ("considered the greatest living female exponent of the mbira [thumb-piano]"), or the Peter King Quartet ("brilliant British bebop alto master,") or a "traditional Irish session, musicians welcome to join in."

But I never have enough time for classical concerts, whose listings call to me like a seductive violin. London has brilliant symphonic groups, including the London Symphony Orchestra (referred to, in shorthand, as the LSO), the Royal Philharmonic, the Royal Philharmonia, the BBC Symphony Orchestra, and the English Chamber Orchestra. The city is also home to the London Sinfonia, the Fires of London, the Academy of St. Martin-in-the-Fields, the English Baroque Soloists, and the Academy of Ancient Music. Chamber music, choral music, vocal recitals, instrumental duos and soloists, every kind of possible combination—a music lover has difficult choices from any week's calendar.

Concerts, like the theatre, often seem more civilized in London. On one recent visit, James and I walked to the South Bank on our first morning after arrival, a week before Easter. There I noticed a poster for a next day's performance—all day—of Bach's *St. Matthew*

Passion. We quickly bought tickets, glad that the concert would begin early on Sunday, so we would not be drooping with jet lag. (Last-minute tickets always seem to be available at the Royal Festival Hall box office.)

What I remember most from that concert was the absolute riveted silence with which the audience listened. The atmosphere in the hall was solemn, though not stuffy, with more evident feeling than I usually sense in church. At lunchtime intermission—a necessary break in tension—we easily bought sandwiches and picnicked on benches overlooking the Thames. Inside the hall, the first part of the music had been forebodingly dark; outside, the sun warmed our toes and sparkled on the water. Refreshed, we returned to the hall, where we both felt we had, for once, truly celebrated Easter.

On another Sunday morning, we suddenly decided to dash to Wigmore Hall, where a special "coffee concert" would take place at eleven. Wigmore itself is a pleasure, a restrained yet elegant turn-of-the-century hall with an Art Nouveau frieze and a glass ceiling. Sitting in one of its rows is rather like taking one's place in the large salon of a munificent music-loving friend. After listening to a young Parisian quartet playing Ravel and Beethoven, James and I politely lined up with the rest of the audience to receive a small glass of sherry—dry, medium, or sweet—or a cup of coffee. Sherry, we discovered, was included in the £7 ($11.20) ticket price.

Another civilized habit is attending lunchtime concerts, most of which are free. Like lunchtime theatre, these can take place from eleven A.M. until almost midafternoon, but most begin about one o'clock. Often they are held in churches, like St. James's in Piccadilly, or St. Martin-in-the-Fields in central London near Piccadilly, as well as several churches in and around the City (the now largely commercial sector of Old London) like St. Anne and St. Agnes, St. Martin's within Ludgate, and St. James, Clerkenwell. Watch for posted handbills and pamphlets listing current events at information centers. The City of London has its own information kiosk outside St. Paul's Cathedral, and it usually carries an assortment of handouts from City churches.

At the major concert halls in London—Royal Festival Hall, Queen Elizabeth Hall, the Purcell Room (all part of the South Bank Arts Complex); Royal Albert Hall; Barbican Arts Centre; the Royal Opera House; Wigmore Hall; St. John's, Smith Square; St. Martin-in-the-Fields—something is usually happening every day. At the National Theatre on the South Bank and the Barbican, free short concerts of all kinds, from accordionists to jazz trombones to sopranos singing Schubert, often resound in the lobbies, usually at lunchtime, late in the afternoon, or just before performances in the main halls. Sip a drink or munch a sandwich from the refreshment bar a few yards away, sit back, and enjoy yourself.

Because I don't want to miss some of these unadvertised events, I make sure we have the current monthly multipage brochures for the South Bank Arts Complex and for the Barbican. (If I can't pick them up at the Tourist Information Centre at Victoria, I try the British Tourist Authority headquarters on Lower Regent Street, just a few steps from Piccadilly Circus.) These brochures, listing all the goings-on, are as dense and tempting as an English plum pudding.

When walking around London, watch for signboards posted outside historic buildings and churches. One recent December in London, as we strolled by Westminster Abbey, I stopped to study a small poster on the wrought-iron fence. It advertised a six-thirty P.M. carol service in the Abbey a few nights later. (Since this was a service, not a concert, it was free.) When we slipped into a pew that night, looking in awe at the shadowy roof above us and glancing around at the decorated stone walls, filled with carved memorials that dimly glowed in soft scattered lighting, we instantly left the noisy, crowded street behind us.

An ecclesiastical pageant of splendidly robed prelates, with flashes of crimson and white, followed by the resonant choir, solemnly paraded down and around the aisles. At first singing close to us, the choir than processed by stages farther into the nave and chancel so that the carols seemed to fade slowly into the distance. At the end of the service, as we all held candles carefully lit from hand to hand, the ancient church shone with hundreds of flickering flames. The choir slowly surged by us again, raising their voices in a clear, soaring antiphony that seemed as ancient as the church.

London's great churches, and the musical traditions they pre-serve, come alive during such services. This is, after all, the function for which they were built. After walking through St. Paul's, for example, and studying its architecture and monuments, a traveler can best enter the spirit of the church by returning for matins, even-song, or a Sunday morning service. You don't have to belong to the Church of England; visitors are welcome. (See Chapter 21, "At Home in Cloth Fair," for the pleasures of Saturday morning choral matins at St. Paul's.)

Besides sacred and secular music, many other arts flourish in London. Opera fans can spend a small fortune on tickets at the Royal Opera House in Covent Garden (where a top seat for one recent performance was close to $250) or, much less expensively, attend operas sung in English at the English National Opera. En-gland's own famous Royal Ballet performs at Covent Garden, and dancers from all over the world appear in many London venues. One spring week I could have watched the Royal Swedish Ballet, a youth company from the Netherlands, several Indian dance groups, fiesta flamenco, Scottish country dancers, Irish folk dancers, and international tango groups. (In fact, I didn't watch them. Any of them. London, as most short-term visitors soon discover, forces constant and difficult choices.)

If my friend Isobel hadn't run out of space in her planning note-book, she could still consider *Time Out*'s other categories of enter-tainment: *Sport*, from football, boxing, cricket, cycling, greyhound racing, horseracing, tennis, rowing, to polo; *Film*, including, of course, repertory and art houses; *Comedy: Stand-up & Variety*; and *Clubs*, subdivided into groups like "House & Garage," "Hard House," "Soul, Funk, Jazz & Rap," and "Other Moves & Grooves." An example of "Other Moves": "*Naive* at Maximus: A new night for gender benders, cross dressers, and original party people." I can give no guidance here.

A Sampling of Museums

After we've slotted a certain number of plays and concerts into our alloted days and nights, I turn to the section in *Time Out* that describes the current shows at London's museums and art galleries. By now, I know myself well enough to realize that we're not going to see all those shows. We're not even going to be able to sample all the major ones. And if we tried to cover the entire British Museum, pore over every glass case in the Victoria and Albert Museum, and carefully study each Old Master in the National Gallery, we'd have to give up on doing anything else for weeks or months. Besides, I think I'd have a terrible headache. (See Section II, "Meandering Through Museums," for my views on enjoying museums.)

But *Time Out* does alert me to special, temporary exhibitions that I could see nowhere else—like the high-spirited, frequently zany entries in a contest for the design of contemporary playing cards (at the V & A, the usual nickname of the Victoria and Albert Museum), or coldly luscious Spanish still-life paintings (at the National Gallery), or African art (at the Royal Academy of Art), or Hans Holbein's astonishingly detailed Elizabethan portraits, all acutely contemporary in feeling (at the National Portrait Gallery). All these shows are, of course, now gone, but others, equally entrancing, always take their place. I try to make a reasonably short list of some of these possible stops.

If the mere idea of trying to surge with a crowd through the doors of the British Museum is alarming, I suggest exploring a lesser-known museum or gallery. London's specialty museums are one of the city's pleasures. On each visit, I try to see one or two that are new to me. On one cold but sunny spring afternoon, not quite warm enough for a long stroll in one of London's parks, I paced instead the tiny, historically accurate Elizabethan knot garden at the Museum of Garden History, charmingly housed in a former church on the south bank of the Thames in Lambeth.

In a grand tour of Britain's history, I've been introduced to kings and queens, prime ministers and soldiers, athletes and scientists at the National Portrait Gallery (see Chapter 12). From David Garrick to the *Phantom of the Opera,* I've met a galaxy of actors and actresses—through film, photos, paintings, and memorabilia—in Covent Garden's Theatre Museum (see Chapter 10).

Pretending to be a curious child at the London Transport Museum in Covent Garden, I've fiddled with the controls of an Underground train and scrambled into the driver's seat of a cutaway front of a red double-decker London bus (see Chapter 8). I've craned my neck to see the dangling toylike airplanes at the Imperial War Museum (see Chapter 9).

At the Museum of London, massive and labyrinthine, fittingly placed next to the old Roman London Wall in the City, I've flinched from the realistic flames in a multimedia show illustrating the terrible Great Fire of London in 1666. Not far away, in the small Museum of the Order of St. John, near Clerkenwell, I followed the history of the Knights Templar, medieval Crusaders to the Holy Land whose exploits and wealth made them both feared and revered, but who are now best known for St. John's ambulance brigades.

At the Design Museum, a gleaming contemporary structure on the south bank of the Thames (not to be confused with the Design Centre in the Haymarket, Soho), I have found myself, improbably, studying the evolution of the British vacuum cleaner. Touring the unassuming Geffrye Museum, I surveyed several centuries of the British "front room." In each of these museums, and in others, I've learned about aspects of British life and history I'd never have known or been able to imagine so fully otherwise.

Since I also like to revisit old favorites, I may never manage to get to all the intriguing-sounding museums I've yet to explore: the Guildhall, with its London maps and prints, as well as one of the most notable collections of clocks in the world; the Florence Nightingale Museum at St. Thomas's Hospital; the Shakespeare Globe Museum, near a full-size replica of the famous theatre; the Bethnal Green Museum of Childhood, with the national collection of toys, dolls, dollhouses, games, puppets, and children's costumes;

and the Horniman, an anthropological museum, with everything from musical instruments to an underwater conservation center.

London has so many museums that no one source can include them all. Try checking several all-purpose London guidebooks if you want to compile a fairly complete list. (I can't quite believe that a *complete* list would ever be possible.) Everyone has different passions. An old friend of mine who is an expert on pirates in English literature is devoted to the National Maritime Museum in Greenwich. Another friend, a movie buff, always heads immediately to the Museum of the Moving Image on the South Bank. A traveling grandmother of my acquaintance says emphatically that she and her charges absolutely never miss the dinosaurs at the Natural History Museum.

When I try to remember all of London's major art galleries and museums, I tend to get a little blurry—which is what happens if I also try to see too many paintings in one day. *Time Out* lists pages of galleries, from the permanent and passing collections at grand venues like the National Gallery, Tate, Victoria and Albert, Royal Academy, Courtauld Institute, Dulwich Picture Gallery, and Barbican, to fairly obscure "alternative spaces" that showcase work of young, contemporary, and/or unknown artists. Any standard guidebook will alert a London visitor how to find which art treasures.

After Museums, Then What?

If my friend Isobel was still wondering what to do in London, she might ask skeptically, "But after museums, then what?" I'd hand her an issue of *Time Out* with a page turned down at "Around Town: Family Events & Visitors' London." London has been entertaining visitors for centuries, and the city is full of inventive entrepreneurs who keep doing just that.

From one summer week's calendar, for example, I find vibrant evidence of Britain's continuing global interests. A Latin American festival, Gran Gran Fiesta, has moved into the outdoor spaces of the

South Bank for two weeks; a Cyprus Wine Festival—"a celebration of all things Cypriot," including, oddly, not only books and flowers but shoes—bubbles up at Alexandra Palace in Wood Green; a Pakistani Music Village features Qawaah singers and Bhangra drummers.

From Zippo's Circus, with acrobats and tumblers; a public meeting of the venerable Globetrotters Club, with a slide lecture on Madagascar; a traditional Country Fair Family Afternoon, complete with donkey rides and puppet shows, at a ten-acre model farm a short tube ride away at Finchley; to a tour of Kensal Green Cemetery, London's oldest public graveyard ("including the otherwise closed catacombs for which a torch [flashlight] is recommended"), London is full of possibilities, haunting and otherwise.

Where else would I ever have a chance to experience "Dialogue in the Dark"? In this installation presented by the Royal National Institute for the Blind in 1995, visitors were led into a vacuum of darkness beneath the Queen Elizabeth Hall and then directed through unspecified sensory experiences by a visually impaired guide.

If I wanted to sightsee in unusual ways, I could have signed up that same week for a three-hour cycling tour of Bankside, Docklands, East End, and the City. The London Waterbus Company organized day trips along London's canals, the Royal Institute of British Architects (RIBA) sponsored an hour-and-a-half tour of the Georgian architecture near its headquarters in Portland Place, and the Ramblers Association, marking its sixtieth anniversary, offered a free River Crane Walk and London Loop.

Walking is big business in London. Each week, professional guides lead dozens of short walking tours, usually two or three hours long, to all corners of London. For a few pounds, a guide will take you to Literary Bloomsbury, Oscar Wilde's London, Dickens's London, Lord Byron's London, Sweeney Todd's Fleet Street, Hampstead's Country Village, the Old East End, Kew Green and Gardens, Gastro-Soho Tour, Barbican and the City, Historic Islington, Borough to Belfast, Medieval London, Burlington Bertie's Strand,

Cornhill Alleys and Byways, Christopher Wren's London, Apples, Actors and Arias in Covent Garden, and the list goes on and on. Art and architecture, not surprisingly, attract fewer tourists than gore and scandal. So the most popular walking tours focus on themes like Murders, Music Halls and Millionaires; London by Gaslight; Haunts of Jack the Ripper; Apparitions, Graveyards and Alleyways; Ghosts of the Old City; Brothels, Bishops and the Bard; and Haunted Covent Garden.

Guides often enter enthusiastically into the calculated spirit of these tours. Returning one evening from the theatre, James and I were walking down a dark and fairly deserted street near St. Bartholomew's in the City area of London. It was a rainy, cold night, with wet mists swirling over the pavement.

Suddenly a man whisked around the corner, his black cape sweeping the ground, a black silk top hat on his head. He looked as if he might be dashing to catch a hackney cab to consult Sherlock Holmes at Baker Street. As he hurried past us, we looked at each other uneasily. Who could he have been? Where was he going in such a hurry?

A short while later, glancing out the rain-streaked window of our flat, I was startled to see him again. In St. Bart's churchyard across the street, a small group of rather bedraggled people—only a few carried umbrellas—huddled around the man in the flowing cape. He was talking loudly and gesturing toward the gravestones. His audience listened intently, following his gestures. After a few minutes, he beckoned peremptorily to them, turned, and strode through the churchyard and out of sight. The group scurried after him and disappeared into the rainy night. They were embarked, we realized, on a walking tour of Ghosts of the Old City.

Hotfooting It Through London

I have not yet followed a guide into the rainy night—or, in fact, into Dickens's London or Bohemian Chelsea or the Hidden Byways

of Clerkenwell. Fascinating as these walking tours often sound—
"Oh, James," I'll say, reading an intinerary aloud, "do you think we
should perhaps go tomorrow on the two o'clock walking tour of
Legal London and really experience the Old Bailey the way few
tourists can?"—tomorrow at two o'clock I somehow always find
something better to do.

I get restless on tours. I want to speed up or slow down. I wish the
guide would talk less or more. I have to laugh politely at jokes I
don't find very funny. I learn things I don't much care about, and I
never seem to get answers to questions I consider important. I look
at my watch a lot. I don't like fumbling for a tip at the end.

But I do like walking. In fact, walking in London, alone or with
James, is still one of my greatest pleasures. It is enthralling, free, and
easy. All I need is a raincoat, an umbrella, a warm scarf or pull-down
hat, and a pair of sturdy walking shoes. (I leave glamour behind at
Gatwick.) My only piece of essential equipment is a map. Even after
years of exploring London, I still carry a detailed folding "London
A–Z" in my pocket, and I openly consult it from time to time. I long
ago stopped worrying about whether I look like a tourist. I *am* a
tourist.

If I want my own personal guide, I need one who is quiet, unobtrusive, and lets me proceed at my own pace. Such an ideal companion is best found in a book. In recent years, many excellent
walking guides to London have begun to appear in American bookstores. *Londonwalks*, one of a sophisticated series for travelers on
foot, is a laudable example. I also look for the small, idiosyncratic
handbooks, highly personal and often published by little-known
firms, that sometimes pop up on a bookstore's travel shelves. *On
Foot in the East End*, by Robert Philpotts, for example, deftly escorts
its readers through such decidedly untouristy haunts as the
Whitechapel Bell Foundry, the Blind Beggar (a pub), and St.
George in the East, a notable church by Nicholas Hawksmoor, an
eighteenth-century pupil of Sir Christopher Wren.

But most of the time I merely open my map, plot a route, and set
out. I need my map because somehow, no matter how I concentrate,

London mysteriously (and more than occasionally) disrupts my sense of direction. As soon as I emerge from the Piccadilly Circus Underground, for example, my inner compass begins to spin crazily. I try to figure out where is up and where is down. After many months away, I have forgotten. Upper Regent Street? Lower Regent? Now which way is Jermyn Street? How do I get to Leicester Square? I check my map (but I'm still not always sure). Blundering on, I soon find myself in Chinatown, or Pall Mall, or in the back lane of the National Gallery. I have been in all these places many times before.

London Streets often lead me astray. As anyone who studies a map can see, the city is not laid out on a simple grid. Streets curve, turn sharply, open into garden squares, end abruptly. They even change their names. Once I lived for seven months at No. 7, Gledhow Gardens; it was actually on the Old Brompton Road (which, in turn, is different from the nearby Brompton Road, a street that eventually turns into the Fulham Road). Not far away, Gilston Road suddenly splits into two crescents, encircles a church inside an oval garden, and instantly becomes, elegantly and impressively, the fashionable address of The Boltons.

Intersections, like Piccadilly, can send me into a tizzy. (Although the British word *circus* actually refers to a point where several streets meet, Piccadilly Circus does have a certain air of three-ring confusion.) London authorities have tried to minimize chaos at many junctions with pedestrian subway crossings, but I can also get disoriented underground.

One late December afternoon, James, two friends, and I were ambling from Kensington Gardens to Knightsbridge. Heading toward a six-thirty service at Westminster Abbey (see above, under "Music and More Music"), we were in no particular hurry. When we felt tired, we'd take a taxi. Meanwhile we walked, chatted, and kept on walking. When we finally admitted to increasing cold and fatigue, we had reached Hyde Park Corner. Black taxis were whirling all around us, but we couldn't hail one. They whizzed by, FOR HIRE lights doused, shadowy figures tucked smugly in backseats.

Marooned on the south side of Knightsbridge, we were facing in the wrong direction. So, after surveying the endless flow of traffic, we dove into a warren of underground passages. Various connecting tunnels led to numbered exits, which in turn theoretically led to signposted destinations like Apsley House or Buckingham Palace. All this was supposedly explained on wall-side maps. (None of these maps told us how to get to Westminster Abbey.)

At first, I was confident. Couldn't we take this tunnel and end up on Park Lane, where we'd surely find a taxi? Emerging on Park Lane, we found ourselves behind an unbreachable wrought-iron fence. Down into the tunnel again. Another turning, still another, and up we were on Grosvenor Place. No available taxis here, either. Back to our burrow; another examination of a wall-side map.

Now we were all beginning to feel harried. Our watches agreed that it was ten after six. Twenty more minutes to make the abbey service. We had better walk—no, perhaps we had better jog. But where? Should we aim for the front of Buckingham Palace or behind it? Which would be faster? And then what?

Huddled in the wavering artificial light of the tunnel, everyone craned to look at my map. This was not so easy. Our current position, Hyde Park Corner, lay on a well-used crease, and the surrounding cluster of streets was half erased. Elbows jostled, voices rose, opinions clashed. Where exactly were we at this moment? Which tunnel exit now? My friend Felicity dashed in one direction. Reluctantly following, I called out a dissenting opinion. We were both wrong.

For ten minutes, like a scouting party of slightly demented rabbits, we tore up and down the tunnel, emerging to sniff the night air at different exits. Twice we found ourselves on a deserted little island, the fenced-off ground around the Triumphal Arch. Finally we bolted across its lawn, straddled the fence, and, risking our lives, crossed a murderous lane of traffic to Constitution Hill. Walking, half jogging, and muttering not entirely to myself, I am still not quite sure how we arrived at the door of Westminster Abbey a mere minute before the service started.

Unless I have a deadline, however, I don't usually care about getting lost in London. I saunter very happily here and there. An unplanned walk always brings new pleasures. One misty winter morning, soon after we had arrived for a week's stay in a Chelsea flat, James and I decided to take a brief walk to the Thames, just a few blocks away. We did not know the neighborhood at all. As the early morning mist dissolved into light rain, we walked down Beaufort Street to the river. There on our right, moored together, was a small village of houseboats, some long, luxurious, and fancily painted, others modest and cozy, a few decidedly mildewed and dingy. They rocked very gently on the wake of a barge that was slowly moving past. As we glanced into a few of the uncurtained windows, I tried to imagine what it might be like to sleep with the slap of waves against my wall or to drink my morning tea on a white-painted deck glinting with reflected light from the Thames.

Walking a little farther, we suddenly came upon a patch of bright green. Appearing around unexpected corners, London's gardens and squares are always a welcome surprise, but Cremorne Gardens, as the sign informed us, was quite special. I knew it had once been a famous, spacious pleasure ground, where crowds in the mid-nineteenth century thronged at night to enjoy music, theatre, dancing, fireworks, balloon ascents, and other amusements—jugglers, acrobats, gamesters—under hanging lantern lights. Years ago I'd read about this gaiety in Thackeray's *Vanity Fair*, and I vaguely remembered other nostalgic references to Cremorne Gardens in nineteenth-century writings. Now all that was left was this small, deserted park with a rain-soaked lawn and a few stone benches.

We walked onto a quay at the edge of the park and looked out over the river, where a wispy white fog floated and coalesced into a distant cloud. Half hidden by mist, the nearby Chelsea Bridge seemed to hang in the watery air. Seagulls clung to a buoy just off-shore, and a police boat slipped past into the fog. The Thames lapped softly against the seawall. It was hard to realize that just two bridges upriver, London's usual heavy traffic was hurrying past Westminster.

On our way back to our flat, I called James's attention to a starkly contemporary church front across the street. It looked oddly out of place among Beaufort Street's sedate classical facades. Since James, a modernist architect, always likes to investigate such anomalies, we walked over for a closer look. On an adjoining wall, I spotted a plaque.

Plaques—particularly round blue plaques—are part of an alert walker's pleasures. Blue plaques affixed to buildings or monuments in London reveal who once lived, worked, or died there; *who* might be anyone from Karl Marx to Winston Churchill, Byron or Nelson, the Duke of Wellington or George Eliot. To qualify, according to *The London Encyclopedia*, a candidate must have been dead for at least twenty years and have been born more than one hundred years ago. He or she should have made "some important positive contribution to human welfare or happiness" and be known to the "well-informed passer-by."

Reading these plaques thus becomes a mini–history lesson, especially when I puzzle over an unrecognized name, perhaps a long-ago prime minister, philanthropist, or obscure poet. (I've seen a guidebook, available in some London bookstores, that locates and identifies all of the blue plaques, now numbering close to four hundred. But it was too heavy for me to tote around.)

Who in this particular case was Sir Thomas More. Here, more than four hundred years ago, the great humanist scholar, Lord Chancellor to Henry VIII and a Catholic saint, lived for the eleven years preceding his death in 1535. Although the Tudor house had obviously disappeared, I could now see a narrow garden, hedged by a wall and entered by an archway at the side of the church. The entrance was open. Somewhat tentatively, we edged toward it.

As a traveler, I tend to be a little nosy. Although I never ignore a NO TRESPASSING or PRIVATE sign, I am often apt to explore—carefully, slowly, even gingerly—until I encounter an obvious barrier. James is even bolder. So we walked through the entrance, down the narrow garden, and to a door at the back of the church. The door stood ajar. Through an adjacent window I could see a room with a man at a blackboard, writing and talking to a few adults seated at tables. Just inside the door was an entry hall. James and I stepped inside.

In a few moments, the man noticed us and left his blackboard. Apologizing for disturbing him, I asked whether we might be able to view the church. Graciously, the priest—for he was part of the Catholic seminary that occupied the premises—offered to open the locked sanctuary for us. He stayed long enough to tell us about the history of the seminary, its students, and its work. Before returning to his classroom, he ushered us back to the garden and pointed to an ancient gnarled tree standing just past the door. "Some say that this mulberry has survived since More's day," he told us, "and that it once grew outside his door, here in what was then the country. I don't know, but it is certainly very old."

As we walked the few remaining blocks home, I thought of how much we'd seen in our hour's walk: mist on the Thames, a village of houseboats, a remnant of Cremorne Gardens, Sir Thomas More's mulberry tree. I thought, too, of More, his country garden, his martyr's death, the fluctuating power of the Catholic Church in England, today's dwindling number of priests, the obvious dedication of the priest who had been so hospitable. Then we stopped at the corner newsagent-deli to buy a *Times*, two croissants, and milk for our coffee. Our day in London had really only just begun.

That is the kind of walking I love most in London: wandering for an hour or two, turning down certain streets on a whim. I want to prowl into every mews we pass, discreetly surveying those quiet cobbled lanes lined with expensive cottages converted from former stableyards. (Which house would we buy if we had a million dollars? The dollhouse-size one with lacy white curtains at its leaded windows or the larger gabled one with a bright blue Dutch door and red geraniums in its flowerpot?)

Plotting a course from one point to another, I often try to maneuver through a maze of back streets. My detailed street map is full of possibilities. On such zigzag routes, I've suddenly found myself at the eighteenth-century Blewcoat School in Caxton Street, now the National Trust's London information center and shop. I've come upon pocket-size green spaces, like St. Mary Aldermanbury or Cleary Gardens, in the dauntingly commercial streets east of St. Paul's. Walking from the Albert Bridge along the river to the Tate Gallery, I've discovered old wharves and a secluded waterfront passage behind a new high-rise housing block. These unexpected pleasures don't appear in guidebooks.

Whenever possible, I head to the Thames. Crossing the river on one of London's many bridges, I stop in the middle for a long, contented look. My favorite perspective is perhaps from Waterloo Bridge at night, as James and I are returning from a musical or theatrical performance on the South Bank. Cars whiz by, but the city, starry with innumerable lights, rises on the far bank like a stage set. I try to identify the buildings—Charing Cross Station, the Savoy, Somerset House. In the near distance I can see St. Paul's dome, illumined at night, no longer hidden, as it is by day, among ugly encroaching skyscrapers. Now it floats serenely over London.

Fun as it is to explore London, I also like to walk through familiar places, noticing how they change in different seasons, times, and weather. On a hot summer afternoon, for example, Trafalgar Square feels as if the whole slightly crazy world—miniskirts, Levi's, saris, caftans, djellabas, lederhosen, strollers, wheelchairs, bicycles—has suddenly converged onto one chaotic spot just to feed a flock of fluttering pigeons. On a rainy winter morning, however, Trafalgar Square is gray and solemn. A dark forest of umbrellas moves slowly past the dripping stone lions. The pigeons, dispirited, huddle together. They seem to have dwindled; so have the tourists. But the square, almost deserted, now looks monumental.

When I walk in London, I notice all sorts of things. Although I cannot always attach dates to architecture, I admire the weighty presence, imaginative splendor, and ornamental intricacy of many of London's buildings. Most of all, I love their variety. Between a grand neoclassical marble portico and a curlicued terra-cotta facade, I might glimpse a sliver of a half-timbered, restored-Tudor pub. Pediments, arches, scrolls, bay windows, mansard roofs, gables, intricate brickwork, wrought-iron fences, leaded glass, all kinds of architectural embellishment: London's streets are an extravaganza of periods and styles. Most of these buildings have lived side by side long enough to seem quite companionable.

Many of London's streets are crammed with shops. As I quickly pass store windows, I marvel at the infinite variety of plaid cashmere scarves, tweed skirt lengths, and discreet silk ties on Regent Street. Turning into Oxford Street, I note, with bemusement, the skimpy rayon dresses and wedgy heels that seem to be young London's current uniform. On my next visit, I might see lace-edged petticoats, bustiers, and thongy sandals. Reassuringly, London fashions still seem slightly foreign.

I learn a little about everyday life in London from looking in windows. When I briefly stop to read a few white cards in the window of an employment agency, I try to imagine how an executive secretary could possibly survive here on £200 a week. I study the special offers in a discount travel agency. Amsterdam, Vienna, or Athens for only £75? If I lived permanently in London, would I be tempted to take an occasional weekend trip to Europe? Passing fruit-and-vegetable stands with meticulously arranged rows of squash, tomatoes, carrots, and lettuce, I check the current state of London's inflationary spiral.

On Oxford Street and its tributaries, I swerve past sidewalk racks of Indian-print skirts and cheap leather vests, flower carts spilling with roses and alstromeria, and the shrieking tabloid signboards that announce a tiny newsagent's shop. SLASHER'S MOM—HER STORY! FERGIE SHUT OUT! FLU: LONDON IN PERIL! I catch a pungent aroma of cheap curry in a darkened restaurant, smoky wisps of grease and long-simmered coffee from neon-lit takeaways, damp whiffs of the Underground at its entrances.

Nipping for a bargain-hunting moment into the temporary storefront of a Notting Hill Housing Trust branch, I note how many of these charity shops, selling secondhand and donated goods to aid the homeless, I've seen throughout London on this visit. Then I think of the raucous, disheveled young people, sharing paper bags of food and a bottle, huddled in their sleeping bags in a wide doorway on the Strand last night. It used to be only the old and ragged who camped out on the streets. Like American cities, London forces pedestrians to look at a few of the faces of disillusionment and despair.

But London has many other faces on its streets. As a curious traveler, I study as many of them as possible. Almost everyone in London walks quickly along, staring blankly into an indefinite space, and I can easily sneak a quick look without a returning stare. Although I see many foreign tourists, I catch glimpses of natives as well, from crisply helmeted bobbies to an occasional furled-up Londoner in a discreet dark suit, wearing a bowler and carrying a black umbrella.

Once I turn onto quieter, more residential streets, I encounter unlikely juxtapositions, signs of how the city has adapted to changing times. I admire a row of Georgian town houses, each with a strikingly elegant black numeral—and an occasional neon-lit BED AND BREAKFAST sign. Or a square of massive Victorian homes, with filigreed wrought-iron railings and window boxes, whose brass plates now advertise doctors' offices. Or white stone domestic palaces, with porticoes, pillars, and heavily curtained windows, that now fly the cryptic flags of the world's embassies.

I cherish London's distinctive neighborhoods: the academic fustiness of Bloomsbury squares, the posh smugness of Belgravia, the expensive exclusivity of back streets in Knightsbridge, the endless cheap hotels around Paddington, and the crowded Indian restaurants near Earl's Court. Some parts of London seem happily resistant to change. A small garden square, billowing with primroses and tulips, appears around a corner. Its black wrought-iron gate is securely locked, but I peer over the top into the garden, where I see an elderly resident on a bench, his Labrador at his feet, both snoozing in the sunshine.

Riding on the Top of the World

When I'm tired of walking, I take a bus. As soon as I see a red double-decker careening toward the bus stop, I hope it will be an old-fashioned Routemaster, whose rear platform, like a San Francisco cable car, is so temptingly easy to hop on and off. (I should probably mention that it is illegal to do this between official stops. However . . .) Leaping aboard, I head for the upper level, gripping the handrail fiercely as my purse and bags flap on my hips. Then, as the bus surges forward, I determinedly lurch toward the front. If I'm lucky, I land with a heavy plop on the first bench.

Settling in with a contented sigh, I look around. A panoramic window before me, a window at my side, perhaps even a clear view through a window on the other side. Rain-streaked, maybe, or blurred with dust, but windows all around. Below me, the crowded streets. At eye level, balconies, windows, facades, and architectural ornaments I'd never see from the ground. Ahead of me, the city unrolling on either side. My own howdah on top of a slow but genial elephant, lumbering across London.

I did not always love London's buses. Since they crisscross the city, penetrate far into the suburbs, and serve final destinations as remote as Hackney Wick, Golders Green, South Croydon, and Tooting, their routes are complex and circuitous. For years I seldom rode buses because I wasn't quite sure how or where they were going—and, since few conductors call out stops, I wasn't quite sure how or where I would be going, either.

But a few years ago, when I began to feel claustrophobic on the Underground, I decided to become a bus lady. It turned out to be surprisingly easy. On arrival from Gatwick at Victoria, I stop first at London Transport's information center for a current bus map and a week's Travelcard. (A Travelcard is an all-purpose pass for London's buses, tube, and trains. For further information, see "A Few Floating Facts" at the end of this chapter.) With a pass, I don't have to rummage in my purse or fumble for change as I board a bus. I also find I tend to take buses rather than expensive taxis if I've already paid for a pass. The bus somehow seems free.

With a bus map, I can see exactly where I'm going. I can change from one route to another. (London buses don't issue transfers; passengers pay according to length of journey. Just state your destination to the conductor.) Besides my bus map, I also use my trusty "London A–Z" to follow our route so that I know when to get off. Since buses do not stop at every corner—and, indeed, sometimes they careen along for several blocks between stops—I need to begin slowly sashaying down the aisle, while trying not to slide into someone's lap, well in advance.

I quickly learned the few necessary bits of bus lore. Look at a bus-stop sign to see if your bus stops there. This sounds elementary, but in a fatigued flurry, I sometimes rush to the reassuring symbol of a bus stop—hooray! at last! a bus stop!—and forget to check its numbers. Sometimes four or five buses might be listed, but my stop is down the street a few yards at the next sign. If the sign has an added notice, REQUEST, then the bus doesn't stop automatically. As it approaches, you hail it as if it were a taxi. Not noticing a request sign may mean watching your long-awaited bus sail by in front of you.

A word about waiting. Given London's tangled web of streets and snarled traffic, it is probably a miracle that buses run at all. They certainly do not always run on time. Attached to each bus-stop post, a schedule indicates, say, that the number 11 runs every eight to ten minutes during regular daylight hours. But this schedule is less accurate than reassuring. Don't worry, it intimates, and be patient. A bus will come.

I mention the number 11 because, on a trip to London not long ago, the number 11 was the main artery between our Chelsea flat and almost anywhere else we wanted to go. Sometimes the 11 appeared promptly. Sometimes it didn't. One evening, after a matinee at the Mermaid Theatre near St. Paul's, we waited on Ludgate Hill, stamping our feet and shivering in the damp cold breeze, for an 11 to appear. For forty minutes we watched other buses, with luckier numbers like 4, 15, and 172, zoom by. Our number never came up. Finally we took a taxi home. "Don't look back," James advised me in the taxi. As an old London hand, he knew that I might see an 11 just behind us. Or, worse, *two* of them. Frequently a long wait is followed by a stately procession of near-empty buses, which seem to have been loitering, out of sight, at some prearranged rendezvous. In fact, as we continued on several occasions to wait interminably for the 11, I concocted a scenario—which seemed, at the time, quite reasonable—in which, at a certain early-evening hour, all the number 11s gathered upon prearrangement on a deserted back street at the end of their run in the City.

I pictured the drivers, a convivial group, standing outside their buses, sharing a few lagers and crisps, telling jokes, exchanging news, until someone finally said, "Well, lads, off we go." Then they reluctantly climbed into their buses, started the engines, and headed out, all in a row. I revised this scenario, adding elaborate bits of stage business, every time we waited for an 11 for more than twenty minutes.

But most of the time a bus eventually came. And as soon as I'd clambered upstairs and dashed for my front-row seat, my irritation would disappear. The view was too entrancing to stay angry for long. On a number 11, a bus rider rockets and rolls through more of London than some sight-seeing tours: the inner sanctums of the City, beginning at the Liverpool Street Station; St. Paul's churchyard and cathedral; Fleet Street, with its literary and journalistic echoes; Aldwych, and a glimpse of theatreland; the Strand, the discreetly grand Savoy and bustling Charing Cross station; Trafalgar Square; Whitehall, the Horse Guards Parade, and Downing Street; Westminster Bridge and the abbey; New Scotland Yard; Victoria Station, where crowds spill out from the far reaches of England, not to mention Gatwick; Belgravia, Pimlico, and Sloane Square; and all the way through Chelsea on the King's Road to Fulham.

Other buses offer equally fascinating scenery. Climb aboard the number 19, for example, if you want to rumble past Sadler's Wells in

Islington, the famous legal complex of Gray's Inn, Bloomsbury, Oxford Street, Piccadilly Circus, Green Park, Hyde Park Corner, Knightsbridge, Harrods, Sloane Square, the King's Road, and across Battersea Bridge. Try the number 9 for Kensington Gardens, Knightsbridge, Piccadilly, Trafalgar Square, the Strand, and Aldwych. Or hop the number 15 for a giddy whirl from Paddington to the Tower of London. Let your fancy, and the bus map, be your guide.

When, out of your front-seat window, you see something—a museum, a palace, a monument, a shop, a pub—that you can't bear to miss, move quickly. Hurry to the head of the stairs, punch the buzzer, clutch the handrail, bump carefully downstairs, and leap off as soon as the bus stops. Sneak a glimpse at your map, take your bearings, and perhaps shake out your umbrella. Then just start walking. Another London adventure is about to begin.

A Few Floating Facts

If you do not already own a street-by-street folding map of London, pick one up at the airport when you arrive. You may even want two: a small one of London's central section, the size you can tuck into a pocket, and a larger one, covering outlying suburbs, for further excursions. If you really want to explore London, don't depend on the free maps handed out by airlines, tour leaders, or tourist information centers.

To purchase a weekly Travelcard, covering both London buses and the Underground, you will need a passport-size photograph. You can use one from a cheap snapshot booth. But if you bring a photograph with you, you can head right for the London Transport office at Victoria Station, or try the designated London Transport window at the Piccadilly Underground station. You can also purchase a similar pass before leaving the United States; check with the British Tourist Authority at 551 Fifth Avenue, New York, NY 10176 (toll-free phone 800-462-2748).

II

Meandering Through Museums

7

A Short, Eccentric Guide to British Museums

I am wary of museums. When traveling in England, Scotland, or Wales, I usually prefer to be outside whenever possible—wandering city streets, watching people, and peering into shop windows, or in the country, walking through sun-dappled woods or pacing a meandering footpath along a seaside cliff. Most museums, alas, are not outside.

Once inside a museum, I tend to become sleepy. I try not to blame myself too much: Travel is, after all, quite exhausting. Jet lag, late nights, unexpectedly early mornings, rich full days of exploring and investigating, constant change, and new sights—no wonder the sudden calm of a museum, its hushed atmosphere, muffled footfalls, lowered voices, stilled air, and dimmed special lighting all make me suddenly feel as if I want to lie down on the nearest bench and take a nap.

Museums induce guilt. I never closely examine everything even in most smaller museums, and I know I will never, ever take in half—perhaps not even a quarter—of the exhibits in the V & A. For years I avoided the British Museum because I felt so overwhelmed when I first walked into its vast labyrinthine halls. After tortuously finding my way to the famed Elgin Marbles, the great classical sculptures from the Parthenon in Athens, and studying them for an hour, I realized I'd only just begun to see them properly. And then my hour in the museum was up.

For an hour, I eventually had to admit, is about all I can handle in one museum visit, especially if I'm looking at art. Art requires attention. If I want to let color, line, texture, shape, movement (and more) work their magic, I need to stand or sit awhile and consider. I can't just look, nod, and move on. By the end of an intense hour, I'm blinking, colors blur, and paintings in the rooms ahead begin to multiply.

After I've left an art museum, the blurring continues. Too soon I forget much of what I've seen. I try to picture some of the paintings I recently examined so carefully, as if I were hanging them in a facsimile gallery in my head. But the walls have gaping white spaces, and many paintings I do recall now seem rather out of focus and lacking in detail. Other kinds of museums also become elusive, their cases of informative exhibits somehow vanishing after I've walked three blocks or read two letters in the *Times* or drunk one very small glass of sherry.

Yet on my trips to Britain, I continue to search out museums. I am drawn to art, which often delights, troubles, or enriches me, even if later I cannot always explain why. And, like most compulsive travelers, I am incurably curious. I like to learn new things—especially as I grow older, when I can feel, with some relief, my brain clicking and whirring, rackety but still functioning. Unchanging horizons grow constricting, and learning, as well as traveling, pushes them outward.

Museums have other attractions. On cold rainy days, they are travelers' havens. (In fact, avoid the most popular museums on those days, if you can. Remember how Frank Sinatra, singing about a foggy day in London town, warned that the British Museum had lost its charm? That happens. Too many dripping umbrellas. Too much wet wool. Too many people in front of the Rosetta Stone.)

In most cases, compared to many other forms of high-class entertainment, museums are inexpensive. Some great London museums, like the National Gallery and the Tate, are still free. Almost every museum anywhere in the U.K. offers a tearoom, cafeteria, or occasionally an excellent restaurant. (Try the small posh one at the Tate.) They have enticing shops. And they all provide "public conveniences" for ladies and gents. Hungry? Ready for a spot of tea? Want a restroom? Looking for artful souvenirs? Try a museum.

So I find myself detouring to a museum of plasterwork in Peebles, Scotland (where else could I learn about those elaborate friezes and coffered ceilings?), tracking down the Museum of the Order of St. John in a corner of the City (haven't I read somewhere about the Knights Templar of St. John?), and studying fragments of medieval glass in the stained glass museum in Ely Cathedral (how *did* they make those windows?).

I've walked past pens of old-fashioned, now rare, breeds of sheep and cows at the Cotswold Farm Park near Stow-on-the-Wold; listened to tapes of Northumbrian small pipes at the Bagpipe Museum in Morpeth; and studied the development of the postage stamp in London's National Postal Museum. I've toured a lawn-mower museum at Trerice, in Cornwall; a museum ship, a restored vintage yacht, at Inverness; and a butterfly museum and silk farm in Somerset.

But I've regretfully missed—so far—the National Waterways Museum at Gloucester with its historic canal boats; the Ironbridge Gorge Museum in Shropshire, where the first iron rails, wheels, and boat were made; Lincoln's National Cycle Museum, with more than 130 cycles on display; the National Tramway Museum in Derbyshire, where I could ride a vintage double-decker tram; the Wimbledon Lawn Tennis Museum; the Wedgewood Museum at Barlaston, Stoke-on-Trent; and many, many more. Will I ever get to the Historic Dockyard at Chatham, Kent ("the most complete Georgian dockyard in the world, now a living museum")? Or the Leicestershire Museum and Art Gallery, whose recent show on the English Civil War included Oliver Cromwell's shaving mirror?

Indeed, it its almost impossible to visit England, or any part of the United Kingdom, and not spot an intriguing museum across the street, around the corner, or a mile ahead. The British love museums. They have a strong sense of history (at least, their *own* colorful history), and they like to celebrate even its gloomier parts. (With or without a shaving mirror, Oliver Cromwell was not a lot of laughs.)

Most large towns, and many small ones, have local or regional museums. Some of these are sophisticated installations, with up-to-date facilities and carefully annotated exhibits. Others, often more fun, are jumbles of miscellany, with a kind of garage-sale view of history. At Morpeth's County Museum, a disarmingly casual collection called "Bygones" includes the labeled inventory from someone's 1941 kitchen, complete with turnip masher, mint chopper, and toffee hammer. ("A *toffee* hammer?" asked James incredulously. Invoking distinctly different childhood memories of candymaking, we argued for several minutes about its precise use.)

The British have always been great collectors. The traditional grand tour, once an essential part of any young gentleman's education, was also an expected shopping spree for European art, furniture, and knickknacks. Naturally, people needed to show off their collections. So the British eventually created hundreds, probably thousands, of museums—museums of children's toys (Bethnal Green Museum of Childhood in London), oast houses (the Whitbread Hop Farm in Kent), Roman antiquities (Circencester's Corinium Museum), enormous museums (the British Museum), and very little ones (the Thimble Museum in Biggar, Scotland).

Anyone who wants to understand the passion of British collecting would do well to visit the Thimble Museum. Located on the High Street in the small town of Biggar, the Thimble Museum occupies the front half of a little teashop. Biggar is the home of the international Thimble Guild (collectors and historians of thimbles), and the guild owner opened this museum in order to share his collection of 4,500 thimbles.

On walls lined with row after row of very narrow shelves, only inches apart, were thimbles made of every imaginable material (and some I hadn't imagined). I noted thimbles of wood, metal, china, and silver. Others were of agate, Murano glass, Caithness glass, cloisonné, Spode, and brass. Some thimbles were crocheted and ornamented with tiny flower ornaments and seed pearls.

Thimbles were grouped according to theme, period, and provenance. I saw a group from Istanbul and one from Kashmir, thimbles like dogs, Toby jugs, African tribeswomen, and Santa Claus. One had an infinitesimal village balanced on top ("Thimbly Village," 1992); an entire set illustrated *The Wind in the Willows*. In glass cases the guild showed off its rarest thimbles, including one dating back to the thirteenth century, with enlarged engravings to show details.

Think of the Thimble Museum when you next walk through one of the many historic country houses and castles open to public view. The collectors of these houses share the same spirit, only on a grander scale. These mansions hold centuries of furniture, carpets, paintings, sculptures, tapestries, china, silver, glassware, books, maps, clocks, and more, as well as unclassifiable oddments, like the Egyptian mummified cat at St. Michael's Mount, or the coaching box (a trunk like a giant round hatbox) at Traquair House, or the roomful of shelved stuffed birds at Powys Castle in Wales, or the lock of Napoleon's hair, carefully protected in a glass case at Sir Walter Scott's baronial Abbotsford.

Some critics of contemporary England claim, in fact, that the country has become one vast, increasingly musty museum, a theme park of Jolly Olde England, full of manicured ruins, ostentatiously thatched roofs, and unbearable cozy tearooms. (I understand their concern, but I think they exaggerate. I often wonder if these critics spend enough time outside. The English countryside is not under glass.) So if you're touring England, you might consider yourself already a museum visitor.

Since going to museums ought to be fun—remember, you are traveling in England for pleasure—you might ponder a few suggestions. First, of course, you do not *need* to go to museums at all. England is much more than its grand collections. If you leave London without ever entering the National Gallery—but one sunny day you took the morning train to Cambridge, mingled with black-gowned academics at Christ's College, ordered Lancashire hot pot at an old

Victorian pub with etched-glass windows, and arrived back in London in time for a last-minute ticket at the Royal Shakespeare Company—does it matter?

Even if you enjoy museums, you don't need to visit all of them. Ignore the advice of standard guidebooks. They always proffer recommended lists, especially in London: "The Top Ten" or "The Best of London," or "Three Days (One Day, A Week) in London." Most of these "must" lists include the British Museum, the Tate Gallery, the National Gallery, the Victoria and Albert Museum— and maybe the National Portrait Gallery, the Courtauld Institute, the Wallace Collection, the Museum of London, and more.

Such lists could easily make me feel that unless I rushed through the corridors of all these museums—the V & A alone has miles of them—I'd dismally fail to "see" London. But if I had three days in London and I tried to cram in most of these museums, when would I have time to walk along the Victoria Embankment? Take a boat trip on the Thames? Stroll through Covent Garden? Wait in line at the Leicester Square ticket booth? Ride on the top of a bus? Shop for a picnic lunch in Harrods's Food Halls? Sit in St. James's Park and watch the ducks?

So my third word of advice is: limit. Not only limit the number of museums you plan to visit, but also limit your time at each one. Of course, you may be able to maintain enthusiasm for far longer than I do. If you have energy and endurance, by all means go in the morning, eat lunch there, and only leave at closing. (Indeed, fewer tour groups will crowd you either at opening or closing times.) But depart, without guilt, as soon as your eyes droop or your feet hurt or your heavy shoulder bag sinks to the floor. When you begin wondering if it is too early for lunch, head for the door.

Once inside a museum, limit what you try to see. Tackling a huge museum becomes much less daunting if you mentally close off most of it and focus on just a small part. If you think you could never confess to having skipped the Raphael cartoons in the V & A, or the Elgin Marbles in the British Museum, or Leonardo's *St. Anne of the Rocks* in the National Gallery, you might check the museum shop for a miniguide, directing in-and-out visitors to the celebrated jewels of a collection.

Otherwise, resolutely divide a museum into all the exhibits you *won't* see and concentrate on the remaining few others. Divide and conquer. Before I plunge into a big museum, I usually decide in advance how I'll spend my allotted hour. When I go to the V & A, for example, I consider its overwhelmingly varied displays—from Islamic carpets to English embroidery to medieval stained glass to Indian Buddhas to Constable's landscapes—and usually avoid the most popular ones. (Wherever I am, when a tour group surges forward, I turn back.)

By now I've developed favorite nooks, an odd word to use for most visitors, who often find the V & A as drafty and cavernous as Grand Central Station. Years ago, on a wintry, rain-soaked day, I took the wrong turn on a stairway and eventually ended up in the department of English Ceramics. Tucked away in a high corner of the museum, it is always virtually deserted. On that day, half listening to the fierce rain beating on roof and windows, I warmed to the delicate flowers on tea cups, the exotic birds decorating soup tureens, the splashes of English color—the yellow of daffodils, the azure of bluebells, the pink of wild roses—on all imaginable varieties of translucent white china.

From these cases, I could imagine centuries of English life: eighteenth-century coffee drinkers, relishing their new addictive drink in gracefully curving pots; ostentatiously wealthy Regency landowners, indulging in intricately hand painted place settings for which each plate was decorated differently; an aging Victorian spinster on a genteel income who treasured her small commemorative bowl from Queen Victoria's Diamond Jubilee.

On my last visit to English Ceramics, I discovered the nearby renovated Glass Gallery. On the gloomiest day, it is impossible not to feel more buoyant in this luminous, light-reflecting room. Everything sparkles, from its ingeniously constructed green-glass stairs, leading to a mezzanine level, to its close-packed shelves. The shelves reveal a world of glass: vases, paperweights, tea caddies, miniature animals, salt and pepper shakers, Christmas ornaments, sculptures, and more.

In this ultramodern (and still relatively undiscovered) gallery, distracting labels have disappeared. Instead, each item, shelf, and case is numbered. At scattered computer terminals, a visitor need only type in those numbers and instantly learn, for example, that on Bay 23, Shelf 3, Label 9185 is an enameled opaque white glass vase, from Sunderland or Newcastle-on-Tyne, c. 1765, one of a pair. I felt rather as if I had a well-informed museum guide by my side who, quite politely, only spoke if spoken to. (The vase itself, adorned with rose, primrose, martagon lily, tulip, and bluebell, all in English spring colors, was enchanting.)

On the same afternoon I basked in the bright lights of the Glass Gallery at the V & A, I spent the other half of my allotted hour in the dark corridor of the Wrought-Iron Gallery. (No crowds here, either, only a few lost tourists hurrying toward Constable.) I learned a little about wrought iron: what it was, how it was made, when it was most used. But I also learned something about past ways of English life simply by admiring handsome wrought-iron artifacts: stove plates, fire baskets, trivets, toasting forks, pot hooks, sword stands, grates, and weathervanes.

When I left the V & A that day, I noticed the individual wrought-iron railings—like black ornamental exclamation points in front of creamy stone facades—on a residential Knightsbridge street. If I hadn't just examined eighteen different styles of wrought-iron balusters in the V & A's corridor, I might not have remarked on the elegance of those railings. From then on, I have paid a little more attention to one of the distinctive architectural elements that make much of London so attractive. What I see in a museum often makes me see something more clearly outside it.

Since my trips to England are full of many different pleasures, I know I'll never visit the V & A often or long enough to turn each corner of it into my own private nook. Nor will I see all of the British Museum or the National Gallery. I may never travel to the

Colour Museum in Bradford, West Yorkshire, where I could explore color, light, dyeing, and textile painting. I sincerely doubt that I'll ever find my way to a restored windmill in Marsh Mill Village, Lancashire, where a Clog Museum is waiting. But I'm glad England is full of such places. On a day when I need to take my imagination for a walk, I know I'll never have to go far.

8

On the Road . . . and Below It . . .
In the London Transport Museum

Watching London's bus drivers torpedo their red double-
deckers along the Marylebone Road, snake through
Oxford Street shoppers, or career around Marble Arch, I
have often wondered what it might be like to sit in the driver's seat.
In the London Transport Museum at Covent Garden, refurbished a
few years ago with a four million pound investment, I found out.

Stepping through the door of the museum, James and I were
whisked instantly into the past. The museum occupies the former
Central Flower Market, a great cast-iron-frame hall with a glass roof,
built in 1870. This huge enclosed space, filtering light through
the roof in greenish tones, shelters an amazing array of historic
transport: trams, trolleys, buses, underground trains, and more.
Cleaned and polished, they are efficiently parked in groups, showing the progress (and increasing complexity) of London's public
transportation.

Although I have slight mechanical aptitude or interest, I found
myself immediately captured by the museum's displays. A gleaming
replica of the first horse-drawn bus, introduced by entrepreneur
George Shillibeer in 1829, evoked the London of *Oliver Twist* and
Pickwick Papers. Rather like a bright green gypsy's caravan, ornamented with gaily colored rosettes and the gold letters of OMNIBUS,
Shillibeer's invention was a proud ancestor of today's grand red
double-deckers.

I followed the horse-drawn bus through its various permutations: The "knife-board" model, introduced in 1847, with back-to-back seating on the roof; the "garden seat," whose rooftop benches all faced forward; and the horse-drawn tram, which ran on rails. Except for the Shillibeer replica, the museum has acquired or restored actual buses and sometimes even provided them with realistic, life-size model horses. (No exhibit, however, re-created one of the disadvantages of horse transport: By 1900, London's fifty thousand animals deposited one thousand tons of dung a day.)

Early in the twentieth century, electricity revolutionized London's public transport. Walking through the section "Trams and Trolleybuses," I admired some of the stately vehicles that quickly appeared: a double-decker tram with larger upper balconies, from 1910; a "Feltham"-type tram car, with an Art Deco sleekness, from 1931 (and used in London until 1951); and lumbering red trolley buses, which survived until 1962 and were immediate forerunners of the motor buses.

Until I arrived at Section Three, "The Motor Bus," I had not realized that the familiar red bus, now one of London's landmarks, had undergone so many adaptations. The B-Type, introduced in 1911, looked like a highfalutin' Tin Lizzie; the 1921 K-Type, with an open top, daringly positioned the driver next to the engine; a 1931 model of the LT-Type, with its covered upper deck and added length, was shown in its wartime condition, with antiblast netting in the windows and hooded headlamps.

By now in a nostalgic mood, I greeted the RT-Type—a classic introduced just after World War II—as an old friend. With its open platform on the back and a roving ticket-issuing conductor, it was the London bus I learned to love on my first trip to England. Although succeeded by a newer generation of driver-only, toll-box buses, the venerable Routemaster—a derivation of that RT—still rolls through London. Like many passengers, I have on occasion been deeply thankful for an opportune (though illegal) chance to jump on and off the back platform of a Routemaster. Londoners have been so insistent about their fondness for Routemasters that

London Transport plans to keep five hundred of them running into the next century.

My chance to sit in the driver's seat of a big red bus came on the upper level of the museum, two mezzanine floors linked by a curved bridge across the bus and tram sections. Climbing into a cutaway front half of a bus, I plunked myself down behind the wheel, masterfully whirled it around, flicked my turn signals, and unsuccessfully tried to ignore the small boy who, waiting with his mother as next in line to be driver, stared at me with a mixture of disbelief and impatience.

The museum has many other hands-on displays, interactive exhibits, and even live actors. When I entered the section devoted to the London Underground Railway, I stopped briefly at a reconstruction of an early tube tunnel, where, in dim light, several grimy, shirtless workers—realistic dummies—were digging out clay and rocks with their shovels.

Later James asked me with a suppressed smile if I'd enjoyed talking to the diggers in the tunnel. I didn't know what he meant. To my mild annoyance, he insisted I return to the exhibit. When I did, I glanced quickly inside the tunnel and turned to leave, not noticing a new figure among the diggers. So when the man stood up, put his shovel down, turned to me, and began to speak, I gave a startled yelp. It took a moment before I realized he was an actor. Impeccably keeping in character, the laborer then began to discuss his job, its rigors and routine, until I edged away. For the rest of my visit, I looked very warily at any human figures in the exhibits.

Although the museum offers several examples of Underground railway carriages and engines, I have never fancied tube trains as much as bright red buses. I focused instead on the development of escalators: from wood (1912), to aluminum (1963), and, finally, styrene (1971). As a child, I used to wonder exactly what happened to the steps of an escalator after it flattened and disappeared. (As an adult, I've never been entirely sure, either.) So I was delighted to find a cutaway side view of a model escalator, with its intricate revolving mechanisms, to solve the mystery.

Like any good educational institution, the London Transport Museum gave me answers to questions I didn't know I had. I learned, for instance, that the top speed of an escalator is fixed at forty-four meters (about one hundred forty-four feet) per minute. "Any faster," explained a brochure, "and fewer people are actually carried because they hesitate when getting on or off."

Besides vehicles and machinery, the museum is a treasure house of smaller transport memorabilia, like signal stations, control panels, tickets, ticket kiosks, ticket-issuing machines, signs, lamps, uniforms, and architectural accessories, such as bronze poster frames. Pausing in front of a handsome 1907 Underground ticket window with deep green and white glazed tiles, I realized I had moved into another area of the museum's interest: design.

Long identified with design excellence, London Transport is particularly famous for its streamlined logo, a bright red circle bisected with a horizontal bar. Although it looks strikingly contemporary, the basic logo, with minor changes, has been in use since about 1913. Even the Underground map is a triumph, a diagrammatic design once considered revolutionary. Harry Beck, its draftsman, ignored geographical accuracy, limiting his lines to vertical, horizontal, or forty-five-degree diagonals, and using strokes of bright color. When a limited edition of Beck's map was printed in 1933, it was an instant success. Since then, the map has been copied, so the museum notes, by transport systems all over the world.

In 1908, Frank Pick, who was first a publicity officer and then London Transport's chief executive, began the long tradition of commissioning contemporary artists to create posters for the Underground. Part of the museum is a gallery for these posters. I was especially taken with a 1931 Fawkes poster illustrating stylized bluebells at Kew Gardens, an Underground stop. Another Kew poster quoted Matthew Arnold: "Dark bluebells drench'd with dews of summer eves." London Transport, I realized, has never lacked for aspirations.

No longer in doubt about the depth of pride and passion involved with London Transport, I was still surprised by the range of offerings in the museum's gift shop. I had expected such items as T-shirts, other souvenirs (like Underground toothbrushes), and, of course, model buses (all kinds, from National Express to a Black Prince, at a 1:76 scale). But I had never imagined the marketing potential for a video called *Central: A Driver's Eye View*, filmed from the drivers' cab of the Underground Central Line, or for entire books devoted to other individual Underground lines.

What perhaps best captured for me the spirit of the London Transport Museum, however, was *London Buses in Exile*. With respect, affection, and patient attention to historical detail, this illustrated book lists the whereabouts of every possible traceable bus no longer in London's service. Lake District Sightseeing operates DMS 1304, for example; a former RT2594 still rides the roads but on the Channel Islands; a restaurant in Jacksonville, Florida, took over 3183n, KYY913. Some of the pride of London Transport may be in exile, but, as the London Transport Museum so vividly demonstrates, those buses have not been forgotten.

A FEW FLOATING FACTS

The London Transport Museum is located in Covent Garden. It is open from 10 A.M. to 6 P.M. daily, with last admission at 5:15. It is closed December 24, 25, and 26. Admission is about $6 for adults; children five to fifteen and senior citizens pay about $4. The Museum Library and Photographic Archive are open to the public by appointment. The Transport Cafe provides snacks and light refreshments.

A twenty-four-hour Museum Information Line is available at 0171-836-8557. The museum's main number is 0171-379-6344.

9

The Imperial War Museum

I am not used to wandering among tanks and armored cars while fighter planes hover overhead. But one London afternoon I looked up to see a vintage Spitfire, one of the renowned small planes that won the Battle of Britain, hanging just above me. The sky—for that is what the soaring glass roof of the Imperial War Museum resembled—was crowded with other planes. A silenced threat, they floated quietly.

Although London's Imperial War Museum is one of the city's largest museums, I had avoided it for years because it sounded dull, suggesting endless cases of guns and medals. I did not like the idea of supporting the glorification of war, and I was further put off by the pretentious sound of *imperial*.

But then the Imperial War Museum burst into the newspapers. Peter Howson, a painter commissioned by the museum and the London *Times* to travel to Bosnia as Britain's official war artist, had returned to produce a series of grimly realistic images. One, which the *Times* called "terrifying in its art and in its impact," depicted the brutal rape by two soldiers of a woman with her head jammed down a toilet bowl. When the museum's artistic record committee declined to purchase the painting for its collection, headlines erupted in outrage.

Defending the museum's decision, an editorial in the *Times* commented: "We can sympathise with the dilemma of a museum which exists to record the wars of this century in words and images, weapons and other memorabilia but which is also a stop on the tourist trail, heavily visited by children and an important educational establishment for teaching history." I pondered this convoluted mission statement. If the Imperial War Museum was wrestling with an identity crisis, I thought I might investigate.

Visiting the museum took James and me into a part of south London we seldom see, a dingy quasi-commercial neighborhood southeast of Waterloo Station. Surrounded by a rather stark open park, the Imperial War Museum occupies an impressive domed building, guarded by two enormous naval guns from about 1912. The museum's solemn aspect reflects its original use as the notorious Bethlem Royal Hospital, better known as "Bedlam," which specialized in the care of the insane.

When we walked up the imposing stairs and into the spacious central gallery, I felt for a moment as if we had entered a children's amusement arena. Gleaming tanks and armored vehicles filled the floor. Not far from a polished dark green World War II V2 rocket, a white and black Polaris missile looked poised to take off from the sparkling beige tiles underfoot. Small planes, including the Spitfire, were suspended from the ceiling, like oversized dangling toys.

As I wandered around the floor, several boys gently jostled me, trying to get as close as possible to the exhibits. Nothing was roped off. They clearly yearned to climb into the sleek, cheerily yellow M3 Grant tank, General Montgomery's own personal vehicle from World War II; a zippy-looking Daimler Mark 1 4X4 armored car, used for reconnaissance; an M4 Sherman tank; and a menacing Jagdpanther tank destroyer, freshly painted in camouflage colors of green and mustard.

Although, standing next to these massive vehicles, I shivered a little at their obvious power—their huge treads, swivel guns, and plated armor—I, too, was undeniably fascinated. I could envision one of the tanks rolling down the street of a terrorized town, its turret gun slowly turning, its driver barricaded (or trapped) inside. Perhaps like the small boys, I wondered, rather guiltily, what it might be like to control all that power. I tried to imagine peering from that tiny slit window. But both the boys and I heeded the warning signs, reinforced by periodic recorded announcements: "Please do not touch or climb on the exhibits."

As I walked past World War I artillery pieces—a German one-man Biber submarine—and vehicles of war so miscellaneous they included a red two-story omnibus (the B43, the actual first bus that George V, a sheltered monarch, ever boarded), I was always aware of the airplanes hovering overhead like giant birds. From the mezzanine, I could examine them more closely.

Like the tanks, the airplanes were intriguing, but more for their intricate and elegant design than for brute strength. An early two-man reconnaissance aircraft, the BE2c, whose bilevel curving light wings seemed startlingly delicate, looked as if it might have been built for the set of *The Magnificent Men in Their Flying Machines*. I also liked the gaudy, stubby North American P-51 Mustang, with a black-and-white checkerboard nose and a bold, swirling inscription of its name: BIG BEAUTIFUL DOLL.

Before we had gotten to the first floor, where more ominous implements of air warfare were displayed—anti-aircraft guns, cockpit sections of several World War II fighters, and a BAC Thunderbird 2 missile, among others—I was captured by the public-address system. Announcing that "Operation Jericho" would begin immediately, a voice urged anyone wishing to participate to proceed directly to a lower floor.

Operation Jericho, we'd learned at the front desk, was a simulated flight in a Mosquito aircraft, duplicating a daring bomber raid on February 18, 1944, over occupied Europe to Amiens Prison, to try to free captured members of the Resistance. Perhaps because I'd been lulled by the relative benignity of the museum so far, I thought the simulated flight sounded fun.

Tucked into a corner of the museum, a kind of large metal egg was anchored to a platform. Together with one other couple, James and I clambered through an open hatch into the shell of a cockpit, with three rows of seats and a movie screen in place of a windshield.

We sat down and fastened our seat belts. As the heavy door swung shut on our darkness, I suddenly remembered my occasional claustrophobia. Then the shaking began.

Although I have watched many film clips of World War II aircraft, I had never known how bumpy—how jarringly rocky, how continuously and nauseatingly rough—their flights must have been. For what seemed like forever, we dipped and bounced, guided (the audio told us) by Group Captain Pickard and his navigator, watching the streaming sky and unstable ground below. It was actually only minutes before we vicariously swooped and dropped our bombs over Amiens Prison, but when the door slid open again, I felt like cheering. Besides, the mission, our "pilot" had told us, had been a success.

After we got out, as I was testing my equilibrium on the flat, unmoving surface of the museum's floor, I took the time to read a serious of informative placards about the results of this raid. Although two hundred fifty of the seven hundred inmates at Amiens escaped, some were soon recaptured, and in the process, one hundred two inmates and civilians were killed. On the way home, Group Captain Pickard and his navigator, investigating the downing of another plane, were themselves killed. It was not quite the smashing victory I'd assumed.

For the rest of our time in the museum, I never really felt celebratory again. At the beginning of the main permanent exhibits on World Wars I and II, large photographic blowups with captions lined the walls. The museum did not intend to evoke a simple response. One picture showed a smiling soldier, giving a thumbs-up, next to a blurred battle picture with the caption: *The essence of war is violence and moderation in war is imbecility—Lord Macaulay, 1831.* Lying in a hospital bed, a big-eyed child with a bandaged head was accompanied by the comment: *War is a part of God's creation— Helmuth von Moltke, 1848–1916.*

Many of the exhibits in this section focused on the details of war as a complex operation. I had heard of the infamous Enigma cipher machine; there it was, a small box looking like a miniature telephone switchboard. There were also British semaphore training cards and flags, a parachute flare, a pigeon basket and pigeon message container, trench signs (PETTICOAT LANE, SUICIDE CORNER), respirators, gas masks, secret reports and maps, propaganda posters, a dummy tree used as an observation post, and countless other paraphernalia from the two wars.

The museum provides more than exhibits in glass cases to convey something of the feeling of war. We plunged through darkness into a mock-up of a frontline World War I trench on the Western Front, dimly lit at night by flashes of distant explosions and smelling of stale air. Dummy soldiers spoke with taped voices as they exchanged a watch or wearily climbed a fence to try to rescue two prisoners from enemy trenches. The last soldier was covered with bloody bandages.

Because hordes of visiting schoolchildren were crowding through the main World War II galleries, chattering and even shouting, we did not see all of its grim displays. But we did manage "The Blitz Experience," in which the museum painstakingly reconstructed an air-raid shelter and a blitzed London street in 1940 complete with heaps of rubble. A special temporary exhibition, "London at War," included a wartime cinema, sections of a prefab house, a fashion shop, and even a window of a Lyons Corner House, a restaurant chain older visitors to London can still easily remember. One room was inscribed with the names of the sixty thousand Londoners who died during the war.

By this time we wanted to leave war behind us. But I felt we ought to tour, however briefly, the art galleries on the second floor. The museum rather astonishingly owns some twelve thousand items, by artists as varied as John Singer Sargent (whose *Gassed*, one of the museum's most famous paintings, is a dramatic contrast to his better-known society portraits), Sir William Orpen, Augustus John, Sir Stanley Spencer, Graham Sutherland, and Edward Ardizzone. Only a relative few, obviously, can be displayed at any one time.

I did not concentrate very closely on many of the paintings in these galleries. The exhibits on the lower floors had affected my vision; too much of this carefully hung art seemed self-conscious. It was eclipsed by the detritus below—gas masks, rubble, and bloody bandages—as well as by unbearably clear photographs and lists of names.

Although I did not see everything the Imperial War Museum had to offer, I left in a shaken, sober, and thoughtful mood. In an introduction to the museum's souvenir guidebook, its past director, Alan Borg, states that the all-embracing nature of modern war makes the museum a comprehensive record of the twentieth century. He adds: "The collections range from tanks and guns to works of art and films, yet our real subject is human behavior."

A FEW FLOATING FACTS

The Imperial War Museum is located on Lambeth Road, SE1. Telephone 0171-407-6434. The nearest tube stations are Lambeth North and Elephant & Castle.

It is open daily from 10 A.M. to 6 P.M. Admission is about $7 for adults, $4 for children five to sixteen. Free admission from 4:30 to 6 daily, but check first to see if this offer is still available.

10

On and Off Stage at London's Theatre Museum

*E*merging from darkness, a strange but gorgeous creature hung in the air. His body was covered with red and blue scales, his green wings were tinged with red, his feet were clawed. Next to him floated a fantastic apparition with a green tail, green scaly legs, and red and blue butterfly wings. Flaming out from black walls and black ceiling, these fairies—costumed figures from a 1994 production of Purcell's semi-opera, *The Fairy Queen*, at the Royal Opera House—were a startling but appropriately dramatic introduction to London's Theatre Museum.

From Edmund Kean's 1833 death mask to a mocked-up modern dressing room, from David Garrick's 1760s waistcoat to John Lennon's stage suit, from Victorian music-hall bills to an early *pointe* ballet shoe, the Theatre Museum provides the grandest of backstage tours. Besides historical information and artifacts, it includes regular guided tours and brief workshops on costumes and makeup with the price of admission.

Although the museum, formally known as the National Museum of the Performing Arts, is centrally located in Covent Garden, the entry on Russell Street (in the old Flower Market building) is not always easy to find. Covent Garden now contains a labyrinth of shops, an open-air market, street performers, and crowds of sightseers. A few signs that point to the museum are misleading. On a recent visit, James and I circled the milling plaza twice before finding our way to the right door. Once inside, we had little company; tour groups have evidently not yet discovered the Theatre Museum. Yet anyone who comes to London at least partly for its theatre would find this museum irresistible.

Entering the museum is rather like entering a darkened theatre. A small elegant box office, now shuttered, stands just inside. This blue and white confection, with faux marble garlands and insets, was designed by Cecil Beaton in 1950 for the Duke of York's Theatre in nearby St. Martin's Lane. Beyond the box office, past a ticket and information counter and an unassuming gift shop, is a changing panorama of exhibits: on our visit, lavish costumes from several Purcell tercentenary productions and an ornate black miniature stage, complete with gold elephants' heads.

But this ground floor is only an opening act. A long ramp leads downward, lined first with handprints of current theatrical celebrities and then with black-and-white enlarged photographs from the past, including the fleshy, ruined face of Herbert Beerbohm Tree as Macbeth in 1911 and a young, ravishingly handsome John Gielgud in 1938.

In an underground hall on one side of the ramp, the Paintings Gallery, a showy room with large clustered columns of pink faux marble, mirrors, and banquettes, houses "Picturing the Players," a selection from Somerset Maugham's collection of eighty-two theatrical oils and watercolors. Executed before the invention of photography, these paintings offer quick if frozen glimpses of legendary performances: David Garrick as Richard III in 1760, Edmund Kean in the same role in the 1820s, William Davidge as Malvolio in 1846.

On the other side of the ramp, in a display called "Recording Performance," we were able to watch the famed Victorian actor and producer, Herbert Beerbohm Tree, silently swaggering and posturing as King John. This brief scene from an 1899 production was one of many film clips from the past. On another video screen, Ian McKellen and Diana Rigg narrated a documentary on how a contemporary performance is now recorded on film.

What happens backstage moved front and center in the next

gallery. To suggest the complexities of staging an intricate production, the museum has prepared an elaborate exhibition on the National Theatre's popular version of *The Wind in the Willows*, which we had seen only a few nights before. Multimedia and interactive displays illustrate the roles of the casting director, the voice coach, the movement and fight directors, stagehands, electricians, wigs and makeup, props, publicity, and more. For each professional associated with the show, a brief résumé indicates his or her special training and subsequent career.

The depth of detail was fascinating. I discovered, for example, that the squirrels' tails were made at first of bristle, until ostrich feathers proved more realistic. Pork pies, for an onstage picnic, were molded in clay, cast in plaster, made with latex, painted, and then filled with cotton wool. Weighing in my hand sample bricks, I saw why Toad's prison wall was made of airex bricks glued onto canvas backing; a plywood brick was clearly too heavy. I marveled at designs for the steam-engine and for Toad's 1910 Mercedes, both of which had chugged, hooted, and honked across the stage. All props were constructed in a mere seven weeks.

From computer-generated drawings for the aluminum structure of the framework that supported all the settings on the revolving stage, I understood why fourteen stagehands were required to operate the massive system and change its scenery. In a video of rehearsing actors, who were being instructed by a movement director to behave as foxes or moles or badgers, I watched hands curl into claws, feet tiptoe like soft paws, and pursed mouths spit out an occasional warning "Pfffft!"

Becoming the Phantom of the Opera didn't look like as much fun. In an adjacent gallery called "Slap!," illustrating the art of makeup, a video showed the step-by-step process of creating the Phantom's grotesque face. Beginning with a mold for the mask, formed on the actor's face with a plaster bandage, the whole process took two obviously excruciating hours—shortened on film, but still daunting.

After these tantalizing previews, the main gallery unfolds a full panorama of theatrical history. Glass cases contain models of theatres, set designs, paintings, engravings, costumes, props, and all kinds of memorabilia. Prominent figures merit cases of their own. Sometimes an object evoked a momentary sense of a performer's vital self: a dangerous-looking sword Edmund Kean used as Macbeth; a heavy jeweled costume worn by a phenomenally strong Feodor Chaliapin; a surprisingly small waistcoat belonging to David Garrick, who was only five feet four inches tall; Noël Coward's red silk dressing gown, complete with monogram.

Some of the artifacts have their own history. Admiring the hand-painted, dazzling costumes designed by Nicholas Roerich for *Le Sacre du Printemps* (*The Rite of Spring*), presented by Diaghilev's Ballets Russes, I was reminded that this startlingly innovative production had caused a riot when it opened in Paris in 1913. A few pastel drawings worked up from sketches made in performance offer rare clues to the now-vanished choreography.

Although it was tempting to linger in these corridors, moving from a model of a Restoration playhouse designed by Christopher Wren in 1674 to Julie Andrews's ballgown from *My Fair Lady* in 1958, I kept an eye on my watch so that we wouldn't miss the scheduled makeup and costume demonstrations. (They usually take place at least twice a day; times vary.) Conducted by professionals, these half-hour shows provide their own kind of beguiling theatre.

Crowded into a tiny alcove with an energetic group of English college students, all enrolled in a theatre course, we sat on stools for our makeup lesson. The makeup artist, a brisk young woman in her twenties, chose a student (from many eager volunteers) as her model. Working swiftly, the artist explained exactly what she was using—what kinds of base, shadows, and lines—to turn this pale teenage girl into a convincing old woman. When she had been properly wrinkled and withered, the girl was delighted. "I'll wear this on the streets all day," she announced.

Although the lively student audience called out many teasing comments and questions, they gave their loudest gasp when the artist answered an inquiry about her training. She had attended a three-month makeup course at a very well regarded London school of theatrical makeup, she explained, which virtually guaranteed good jobs to all its graduates. But the price of the course—she paused a moment for effect—was £7,000 ($11,000).

After the makeup lesson, we all trooped off to the Studio Theatre, a small auditorium, for the costume session. Another young woman, Maureen, who moved quickly and authoritatively around the stage, began by pulling extravagant hats from a large box and tossing them into the audience. Whoever caught a hat was supposed to put it on. Watching the students preen and clown in their plumed, feathered, and sometimes overpowering hats, Maureen pointed out how their costumes had already begun to turn them into actors. Then she began to organize a sort of playlet.

Helping one girl into a bejeweled brocade Tudor gown, Maureen declared her the heroine. A boy who already sported earrings and nose studs put on a Regency jacket; with his hands on the lapels he suddenly assumed a rakish stage presence. Another boy who donned a dramatic red vestment was instantly a priest. By the end of our half hour, Maureen had assembled a cast, provided an instant plot, directed elementary stage movements, and given the students the chance to perform a boisterously melodramatic scene inspired by their flamboyant costumes.

When we all trooped out of the auditorium, James and I reluctantly decided that we needed to draw the curtain on our afternoon at the Theatre Museum. Although we still had not seen everything the museum had to offer, we had tickets in a few hours for a play. Whatever the evening performance might offer in stagecraft and acting, we would now see much more of it.

A Few Floating Facts

The entrance to the Theatre Museum (the National Museum of the Performing Arts) is located on Russell Street in Covent Garden. The nearest tube station is Covent Garden. Telephone 0171-836-7891. The museum is open Tuesday through Sunday from 11 A.M. *to 7* P.M. *Admission is about $6 for adults, $4 for children five to sixteen, $15 for a family ticket of two adults and up to four children.*

11

The Pleasures of London House Calls

*P*oking about in other people's houses is part of the fun of traveling in Great Britain. Anyone with the price of a ticket can regularly call at hundreds of historic country houses and have a look around. But a visitor to London doesn't have to leave town for this pleasure. During a recent December stay, James and I explored three grand, yet very different, London houses: Apsley House, Spencer House, and Leighton House.

Although Apsley House stands at Hyde Park Corner, one of the busiest intersections in the city, not everyone who passes the house notices it. A massive and impersonal building with a dignified classical facade protected by a wrought-iron fence, Apsley House might well be a bank or a government office. Once known as "No. 1 London" because it lay just inside tollgates separating the city from countrified Knightsbridge, today the house is marooned on a spit of land among whirling buses and taxis. A pedestrian has to make a determined effort to reach it, searching for the proper exit in a confusing warren of subways linking Knightsbridge, Grosvenor Place, Constitution Hill, Piccadilly, and Park Lane.

Apsley House was not always so retiring. Designed by neoclassical architect Robert Adam and built between 1771 and 1778, it was eventually acquired by the First Duke of Wellington, whose triumph over Napoleon at Waterloo had made him a national hero. Using funds voted by a grateful Parliament, the duke enlarged and redecorated the house into a suitably palatial residence. He remained at Apsley House during his long public life, which included a brief period as prime minister. Although the Seventh Duke donated the house and its contents to the nation in 1947, the Wellesley family, the duke's descendants, continues to live there in private apartments.

On the bleak winter morning we visited Apsley House, it was hard to imagine the politicians, soldiers, diplomats, aristocrats, and all the necessary servants who must have paced, or hurried, through the rooms when the First Duke was in residence. Despite an expensive three-year restoration—it reopened in 1995—Apsley House seems rather dark and lonely. Our footsteps echoed on the mosaic floors of the cavernous front halls, which are lined with paintings and marble busts of the great man. Wherever he looked, Wellington would have been able to see flattering versions of himself, his austere, sharply angled face set into lines of irreproachable dignity.

As we then walked slowly through the public rooms, I realized that the entire house was a testament to Wellington's achievements. Aware that Wellington had, for the time, saved their thrones, European monarchs endowed him with costly treasures: paintings, sculpture, gold, silver, and china. Apsley House became a showcase for these splendid gifts. Now it remains a kind of imperial museum, reflecting an earlier era of power and wealth.

In the ground-floor Plate and China Room, radiant glitter and gleam temporarily dispel the house's gloom. In one glass showcase, the gilded-silver round Wellington Shield (1822), heroically sized and adorned with reliefs from the duke's career, shines like a miniature sun. It is set off by two magisterial silver-gilt candelabra (1816–1817), at least five feet high, decorated by figures of soldiers of several nationalities, reliefs, and motifs of war and victory. This ornate three-piece set was a gift from the merchants and bankers of the City of London, who knew, like the kings and emperors, how much they owed the duke.

I never thought I would feel something like awe in the presence of mere china until I saw the Sevres Egyptian Service. Ordered by

Napoleon as a divorce present for the Empress Josephine (who re-
fused it), the service, whose sixty-six plates depict Egyptian scenes,
eventually became a gift to Wellington from Louis XVIII of France.
The formal centerpiece is an authentically detailed Egyptian
temple, based on Karnak, Dendera, and Philae, and flanked by
seated godlike rulers. I tried in vain to imagine myself at the table,
talking across these sepulchral replicas.

The duke could obviously entertain in lavish style without ever
running out of dishes. Besides the Egyptian Service, the room displays selections from the Prussian Service, depicting the duke's life
and campaigns, a gift from the king of Prussia; the Saxon Service,
from the king of Saxony; and the Austrian Service, from Emperor
Francis I. Each set of china has its own impressive accoutrements:
one hand-painted and gilded ice cream bucket, for example, resembles a majestic funeral urn.

Should the duke have tired of contemplating his exemplary deeds
on china, he had many other opportunities for enhanced self-regard.
The room also holds parts of the Deccan Service, some one hundred
twenty-five pieces of silver parcel gilt, various silver commemorative
objects, and the duke's Campaign Plate, which the catalogue discreetly described as "an assemblage of relatively simple functional
silver."

Although I did not study closely the many bejeweled medals the
duke had accumulated from foreign rulers, their titles rang like a knell
for a vanished world: Order of the St. Esprit (France), Royal Military
Order of Maximilian Joseph (Bavaria), Order of the Elephant (Den-
mark), Imperial Military Order of Maria Theresa (Austria), Order of
the Lion (Baden), Order of the Golden Fleece (Spain), and many,
many more. Other cases contain mementos of Waterloo: ten of the
duke's batons, looking like royal scepters; ceremonial gold and silver
snuffboxes; daggers and swords, including Napoleon's court sword,
taken from his carriage after the battle of Waterloo.

Napoleon is almost as compelling a presence in Apsley House as
the First Duke. Commanding the curve of the formal main staircase
is a towering marble statue, almost twelve feet tall. At first glance it

appears to be an undraped Greek athlete. But the herculean figure is, in fact, sculptor Antonio Canova's 1806 portrait of Napoleon. Purchased from the Louvre after Napoleon's downfall, it was given by George IV to Wellington. Lit from a skylight above, the statue seems almost luridly naked (and cold) in this decorous hall.

Upstairs in Apsley House, we passed through a series of stately reception rooms, luxuriant variations of silk upholstery and hangings, intricately woven carpets, sparkling chandeliers, gilded mirrors, marble tables, great porcelain vases, and Adam chimneypieces. On the walls hang the First Duke's notable collection of paintings, many of which he received as gifts. The Waterloo Gallery, the grandest room of all, boasts works by such masters as Jan Breughel, Rubens, Velazquez, Ribera, van Dyck, Jan Steen, and Goya. Tall windows on one side of the Waterloo Gallery overlook the not-so-distant rush of traffic around Hyde Park. But the muffled uproar only makes the gallery seem even more remote from any kind of everyday life.

In the dining room, faint light through half-drawn curtains illuminates the mahogany table, set with part of the Portuguese Service, which originally consisted of a thousand silver and silver-gilt pieces. Created over four years, between 1812 and 1816, it is described as the single great monument of Portuguese neoclassical silver. Although I had been awed by the displays in the Plate and China Room, I was still unprepared for a twenty-six-foot silver-gilt centerpiece featuring symbolic figures of the four continents paying tribute to the allied armies of Britain, Portugal, and Spain, not to mention sphinxes, wreaths, garlands, spears, arrows, coats of arms, horses, and other ornaments. Dancing silver-gilt figures around the edges of the centerpiece were originally linked by ropes of silk flowers. The whole effect would have been one kings might have envied.

Since much of the rest of Apsley House is reserved for the First Duke's descendants, we did not see Wellington's private rooms. Several reproduced illustrations from an 1853 guide to the house, however, showed his suite as relatively plain and somber—possibly a welcome retreat from all that gilded silver. Just outside a basement gallery, devoted to changing exhibitions on the First Duke and Apsley House, a case displays Wellington's death mask, made three days after his death in 1852. It is a necessary reminder that even the duke was mortal.

As we left the regal pomp of Apsley House, I remembered how, in 1831, a London mob that deeply resented the duke's adamant opposition to the Reform Bill, which expanded representation in Parliament, had rioted one night and broken the windows of Apsley House. The indefatigable duke had then fitted iron shutters on the house. Although the shutters were removed long ago, when I looked back at Apsley House I thought I could almost still see them, closing off the duke's palace from the threatening hurly-burly of the modern world.

If Apsley House is a solemn monument to a soldier and statesman, Spencer House, London's only great eighteenth-century house to survive intact, is an exuberant shrine to lovers. John, First Earl Spencer, began the house in 1756 as a fashionable new home for his childhood sweetheart, Georgiana, whom he had secretly married the year before. The marriage was a love match, then a rarity in aristocratic society, and the earl intended the house to reflect their mutual devotion in its spirit and decoration.

Like Apsley House, Spencer House is on a very visible site in the heart of London. With one facade that borders on Green Park, its lofty windows look out on Londoners hurrying across the park toward Piccadilly, Buckingham Palace, or Victoria. But its actual entrance is not so easy to find. Even its existence is something of a secret. Because the house is only open to the public on Sundays, it does not appear in many tourists' guidebooks. Our taxi driver had never heard of it, though he knew St. James's Place, a quiet cul-de-sac that also shelters the exclusive Dukes and Stafford Hotels.

The exterior of the house is as noble as Apsley House's. On the west front, above a neoclassical arcade and attached portico, a handsome pediment is crowned by statues of Bacchus, Flora, and Ceres—symbolizing hospitality, beauty, and fertility. Since the young earl prided himself on his artistic antiquarian taste, he chose as an architect John Vardy, who specialized in adapting designs from imperial Rome. (Lord Spencer was a member of the Society of the Dilettanti, a group dedicated to "Roman Taste and Greek Gusto.") But when the house was well under construction, the earl decided to change architects. James "Athenian" Stuart, Vardy's successor, was an exponent of the newer and allegedly purer Greek style. So Spencer House became a blend of both.

Like most long-standing houses, Spencer House has been adapted and redecorated over the years. Damaged by a bomb blast in 1944, it was then occupied by such varied tenants as Christie's (the auctioneers), the British Oxygen Company, and the Economist Intelligence Unit. But in 1985, when Jacob Rothschild's investment firm acquired it, Lord Rothschild began an extensive and painstaking restoration. He decided to retain and embellish aspects of several periods of the house; even a modern work of art, a bronze Giacometti lantern, hangs over one grand staircase. Now, its rooms filled with newly acquired period furniture and loans of art from sources including the Tate Gallery, the National Trust, and the Queen, Spencer House not only serves as a suite of company offices (not open to the public) but also as a sumptuous setting that can be rented for social occasions.

Although I found it hard to imagine gala parties in Apsley House, I wish I could have attended one in Spencer House. Its meticulously re-created eighteenth-century interiors are light and airy, painted mainly in soft shades of white, gold, rose, green, or blue, and embellished with coffered ceilings, plaster friezes, polished marble, and freshly applied gold leaf. The effect is astonishingly rich but not overbearing. Along the western side, tall windows frame views of Green Park. On our winter afternoon visit, the bare trees formed delicate traceries through the glass.

Even today, if I were a guest in the dining room with its faux marble columns, I could sit beneath a glittering glass and gilt-metal chandelier from the Palace of Satara in India. I could admire two marble-topped side tables designed by the architect Vardy, sporting carved masks of Bacchus, winged panthers, and festoons of vines. Looking upward, I could study a gold-and-green gilded ceiling surrounded by a frieze based on an engraving of a Roman temple. Guests probably do not now take advantage of certain eighteenth-century comforts: one pillar cabinet held a hidden coal-basket for plate warming and another provided discreet space for two chamber pots.

Perhaps the most spectacular room in Spencer House is the white-green-and-gold Palm Room, where the gentlemen retired after dinner. With lavishly gilded columns simulating palm trees, whose cream-and-gold fronds whoosh upward to the ceiling cornice, the Palm Room looks rather like a deliciously artificial stage set. Even the gilded furniture and hanging light fixture are ornamented with palm fronds, for a neoclassical architect saw the palm tree as a symbol of marital fertility.

Throughout Spencer House, the decor incorporates symbols of love and marriage. "There is nothing too *serious* here," our guide assured us, pointing out a Bacchus head on a doorknob, a statue of Venus, and a plaster medallion of the Three Graces. Spencer House is especially known for its Painted Room, one of the most famous eighteenth-century interiors in England, in which the architect Stuart celebrated the classical theme of The Triumph of Love. A chimney-piece frieze copies the *Aldobrandini Wedding*, a Roman painting; a circular panel over a mirror shows a Greek wedding; an oval panel over the door reveals Venus being unveiled by Hymen, the god of marriage. In one painting, two turtledoves perch on a garland of roses; others show music, drinking, and dancing. The whole green-and-gold room, festooned with painted and gilded roses, evokes festivities and high spirits.

After such splendors, emerging onto a gray London pavement was something of a shock. But our last house tour quickly whisked us back into an exotic world. Set close to the sidewalk on a Kensington street, Leighton House unpretentiously fits into its prosperous residential neighborhood. Much smaller than either Apsley or Spencer Houses, it looks unexceptional with its restrained redbrick exterior. Built between 1864 and 1866, then added to over the years, Leighton House was the home for thirty years of Frederic, Lord Leighton (1830–1896), a resoundingly successful Victorian artist. Although Leighton's classical and idealized subjects, combined with his eventual peerage and presidency of the Royal Academy, have made him appear to later generations as a staid academician, his house is anything but dull.

Conceived as a studio and as a showcase for Leighton's art collections, the house is also a determinedly private home. Its original plan included only one bedroom and bathroom for the owner, besides servants' quarters, for Leighton did not want overnight guests who would interfere with his work. Although the windows of the dining room look out on a back garden, the rest of the house seems to turn inward, away from any view.

What Leighton House focuses on instead is its magical interior. When we passed through a small entryway into the staircase hall, Kensington suddenly disappeared. A shimmering blaze of blue-and-green tiles covers the walls of the hall and adjoining anteroom, including panels of solid dark blue tiles, designed by the skilled ceramicist William de Morgan to reflect colors from Leighton's collection of Syrio-Isnik sixteenth- and seventeenth-century ware. On the floor is a black and gray-green mosaic; Corinthian marbelized columns with gilded capitals lead into the next room. In such surroundings, perhaps it is not surprising that I did not immediately notice such accessories as a bronze cast of the Dancing Faun, a potted palm, and a stuffed peacock.

Walking through the anteroom, past a library and a dining room on either side, we entered the astonishing Arab Hall, a vision from the Arabian Nights. Light from a gilded dome suffused a small but soaring room filled with mosaics, tiles, friezes, and marble. A fountain splashed gently into a black marble pool in the center of the floor. Except for the sound of dripping water, the room seemed hushed, a feeling emphasized by the delicate latticework from Damascus screening the windows and gallery above.

Intricate blue-and-green decorative tiles, arranged in panels, seemed almost to writhe with birds, flowers, vines, and fanciful arabesques. Looking closely, I could see where a line chipped across the glaze "cut" the necks of the birds, thus making them acceptable to a strict Islamic culture that banned the representation of living creatures. But the designs remain vibrantly alive.

Although Leighton was devoted to art of the past, he was also a friend and patron of many contemporary artists. The dazzling effect of the Arab Hall is partly due to Walter Crane, who designed its encircling gilt mosaic frieze of birds, prancing deer, and mythological scenes, and to Randolph Caldecott and Edgar Boehm, who modeled and carved the extravagant capitals of the columns. Hanging over the black marble pool is a resplendent Victorian gasolier—an up-to-date version of a chandelier that burned candles—made of beaten copper and gilded wrought iron, a work of art designed by Leighton's architect, his friend and fellow Royal Academician, George Aitchison.

Much of Leighton House is, in fact, an art gallery. Although the artist's original furnishings and collections had to be sold at his death, a private trust of friends and admirers, determined to preserve something of his legacy, purchased some drawings and paintings at the sale. Acquisitions continued, and today Leighton House displays not only a selection of Leighton's own work, such as *The Death of Brunelleschi*, *Desdemona*, and *The Vestal*, but also many fine Pre-Raphaelite paintings, such as Burne-Jones's *The Uninterpreted Dream* and *Morgan Le Fay* and Waterhouse's *Mariana*. The first-floor Silk Room, named for its wall hangings, was Leighton's own top-lit picture gallery; his former winter studio now serves for rotating exhibitions.

Leighton's imposing main studio dominates the upper floor of the house. No mere utilitarian space, it is both spacious and ornamental, with gilded domes and an apse. Here Leighton surrounded himself with beautiful objects as well as art materials; photographs show it crammed with paintings, sculpture, carvings, and furniture. His musical evenings were legendary: Clara Schumann performed here, as did other famed musicians.

Although the vast studio, now denuded of much of its furniture, seems somewhat bare, the Leighton House official brochure advised us to imagine it "banked with hothouse flowers, draped with tapestry and oriental rugs and filled with a brilliant throng of artists, litterateurs and esthetes." Leaving the studio, we walked a few steps to the adjacent zenana, a tiled alcove brought by Leighton from Cairo and named after the traditional part of an Indian house where women and children were secluded. The plushly cushioned zenana extends as a balcony over the Arab Hall. Standing behind a rope that closed off the alcove, we could admire Walter Crane's pseudo-Persian frieze at eye level. Since the house was quite silent, we could also hear the faint dripping of water from the fountain below.

Every visitor to Leighton House receives a free informative brochure, with a cover picture of the Arab Hall and an accompanying legend: "Relentless Perfection." Although the word *relentless* is perhaps a harsh way to describe surroundings with such a sense of luxuriant ease, it does suggest the intensity of Leighton's desire to create and furnish a home that would itself be a work of art. It was just this passion that linked all three of these grand London houses.

A Few Floating Facts

Apsley House (The Wellington Museum) is located at Hyde Park Corner. Besides the adjacent Underground station, it can be reached by many buses that stop at the top of Knightsbridge. It is open from 11 A.M. to 5 P.M. Tuesday through Sunday. Admission is about $5 for adults, $3 for seniors and students. Children under twelve are admitted free. Telephone 0171-499-5676.

Spencer House is located at 27 St. James's Place, between Piccadilly and the Mall. Reservations for a guided tour can be made Tuesday through Friday from 10 A.M. to 1 P.M. at 0171-499-8620. The tours are given on Sundays only, between 10:30 A.M. and 5:30 P.M. Admission is about $10 for adults. No children under ten are admitted.

Leighton House (Leighton House Art Gallery and Museum), at 12 Holland Park Road, is a short walk from the Kensington High Street Underground station. Telephone 0171-602-3316. It is open Monday through Saturday from 11 A.M. to 5:30 P.M. Admission is free.

12

Listening in at the National Portrait Gallery

As though amused by all the fuss about his posthumously uncovered skullduggery, Robert Maxwell, half laughing, glances casually at me. Next to him, Lord Mountbatten, an overwhelming and stern presence, stares directly, almost challengingly, until I lower my eyes. The self-made publishing magnate, born Jan Ludwig Hoch in Eastern Europe, is an unexpected companion to the last viceroy of India, aristocratic friend of princes.

In a few steps, I find myself among a crowd of politicians. Anthony Eden, standing with square shoulders in front of a brocaded screen, looks vigorous and dapper. Harold Macmillan, however, is a disillusioned old man with wrinkled skin and thinning hair, lids almost closed over his eyes. Alec Douglas-Home, also old, seems much happier. Informally dressed for a day in the country, he has brought along a fishing pole and his favorite retriever. I notice others nearby whose names, if not always faces, I know: Winston Churchill, Edward Heath, Clement Attlee, Aneurin Bevan, Hugh Gaitskell, Harold Wilson. I wish I could hear what they are saying to one another.

But in England's National Portrait Gallery, founded in 1856 and now housing a collection of over nine thousand works, I am free to imagine some of those conversations—and others equally unlikely. Whenever I am in London, the gallery invites me to a free ongoing party, where I can eavesdrop among famous guests. When I first visited this museum as a college student many years ago, I discovered portraits of many people I'd come to know through literature and history courses: Queen Elizabeth I, Cromwell, Nelson, Wellington, Jane Austen, Samuel Johnson, Byron, the Brontës, Disraeli, among many others. Everyone I'd ever heard of seemed to be there.

As I walked through the gallery that day, I'd recognize a face and hurry over for an introduction: "So *this* is really Shakespeare!" As I stood in front of a much-reproduced picture of the Bard, which was the gallery's first acquisition, I pondered his dark, lustrous eyes. What meaning could I find there? I liked his little gold earring.

I studied every portrait closely, hoping for some illumination. How would Jane Austen appear in this sketch if she were laughing? William Blake looks so normal! Why hadn't I known about that extraordinary dimple in Byron's chin? Was Milton really once such a sweet-looking young man? Why was it so hard to think of Milton as *young*?

Sometimes a picture provided clues to more than a single person, as did *Queen Victoria Presenting a Bible*, a painting by T. Jones Barker. In this grandiose large painting, Prince Albert stands protectively behind Victoria. The queen, whose tiara, jewels, and off-the-shoulder ruffled gown do not effectively disguise her receding chin and dumpiness, is handing a Bible to a grateful subject. Dark-skinned and heavily muscled, he kneels before her, an animal skin thrown over his tunic, an improbably feathered turban on his head. If he stood, he would tower over her; but, of course, he does not stand. What better introduction could I have to Victorian imperialism?

Over many years, I have returned often to the meandering halls of the National Portrait Gallery, with its five levels and almost thirty rooms, to renew old acquaintances and make new ones. A few years ago it opened a new set of Later Twentieth Century Galleries, covering the period since 1945, and from the moment I walked into the first room, where Mountbatten and Maxwell dominate one wall from on high, I felt as if the party were in full swing.

Whoever thinks of England as dismal and faded need only spend an hour in these post-1945 galleries. The people one encounters here, through drawings, paintings, sculpture, caricatures, silhouettes, photographs, and ingeniously mixed media, are alike only in being famous. They come from many social and ethnic backgrounds, and, as their brief biographical placards reveal, they have devoted their lives to wildly different passions.

May Warnock, born in 1924, described as an "academic, philosopher, and public servant," served as mistress of Girton College, Cambridge, in the 1980s. Ian Bothan, born in 1955, is a revered cricketer. Elizabeth David (1913–1992), seen holding a glass of wine in her kitchen, was a cookbook author who dramatically influenced British cuisine. Arthur Michael Ramsey, Baron Ramsey of Canterbury (1904–1988), with a face carved rather like a Cézanne landscape, was the one hundredth archbishop of Canterbury. Miriam Rothschild, born in 1908, a zoologist and parisitologist, compiled six volumes of *Rothschild's Collection of Fleas* for the British Museum.

Juxtapositions can be both amusing and thought-provoking. In a 1985 photograph, Rudolf Nureyev, his expressive face already ravaged, reclines somberly in a gorgeous red patterned caftan against a black and gold couch. Next to him, in a cozy family group, Queen Elizabeth II and Prince Philip smile blandly at their grandchildren. Not far away are a bronze half-length sculpture of David Gascoyne, a surrealist poet born in 1916; a large, glossy portrait of singer Joan Sutherland, looking rather airbrushed; and a huge oil painting of Bobby Charlton, a footballer (soccer player) born in 1937.

Other stars of contemporary British society in this gallery include Graham Hill (1929–1975), a racing driver who won the Monaco Grand Prix five times; Chris Bonnington, born in 1934, a mountaineer who reached the summit of Annapurna II in 1960; and Dorothy Hodgkin, born in 1910, who was awarded the Nobel Prize for her work on the structure of Vitamin B_{12}. In a wonderful oil painting by Maggi Hambling, Hodgkin is seated at her littered desk, fiercely concentrating on her structural models, her loose white hair flying. Hambling has even given her four hands, all in motion.

That sense of energy pervades the gallery. Even when their subjects appear contemplative, artists provide their own intensity. The head of fashion designer Zandra Rhodes, done in resin and glass by Andrew Logan, accents her startling sparkly pink hair; the heavily modeled surface on Jacob Epstein's bronze of composer Ralph Vaughan Williams is nervously alive; David Hockney's acrylic painting of Sir David Webster, general administrator of the Royal Opera House, shimmers in cool green tones; Michael Ayrton's oil portrait of composer William Walton ripples into fractured planes. It would be very possible to come here only to study artistic technique.

But I just plain have fun at the National Portrait Gallery. Sometimes, as I walk its halls, I fantasize about creating my American version of this museum. How would I define famous? What categories would I exclude? Who, exactly, would get in? Who could I substitute as a smash opening duo for Maxwell and Mountbatten? Steven Spielberg and JFK? S. I. Newhouse and Brooke Astor? I mentally arrange a wall of, say, late-twentieth-century politicians and social activists: Eisenhower next to Malcolm X, Betty Friedan with Lyndon Johnson, Joseph McCarthy and Ronald Reagan. In the writers' room, could J. D. Salinger hang next to Sylvia Plath? E. B. White with Faulkner? Pearl Buck and Norman Mailer? The possibilities dazzle.

Unlike many museums, England's National Portrait Gallery quietly lets its visitors know that having fun is fine. One recent acquisition is a video portrait of Duncan Goodhew, an Olympic gold-medal swimmer born in 1957. Marty St. James and Anne Wilson, the artists, have arranged eleven video screens on a wall, with added amplifiers for occasional sound. First the screens flash different shots of a swimming pool; then Goodhew's feet on the edge of the pool; next his head, naked back, and hands; then last, strokes in the water. As he dives (on all the screens) into the pool, the sound of his splash suddenly fills the room.

Surfacing, he appears first just as unblinking eyes, then as a bold domed head, and at last with a grinning face. Another shot proudly highlights the medal on his dripping chest. In the final screens, his goggled face filmed underwater, Goodhew is swimming away, metamorphosed suddenly into a strange sea monster. In a museum that so teases the imagination, a sea monster seems quite at home.

A FEW FLOATING FACTS

The National Portrait Gallery is located next door to the National Gallery, with an entrance on St. Martin's Place, just off Trafalgar Square. It is open Monday to Friday, 10 A.M. to 5 P.M.; Saturday, 10 to 6; and Sunday, 2 to 6. It is closed on major holidays. Telephone 0171-306-0055.

13

The Barbara Hepworth Museum at St. Ives

Bronze abstract shapes nestle among palm trees, stands of bamboo, and glossy green shrubs. A few stone sculptures also lurk here and there among the foliage, like brooding monoliths from a lost modern age. Beyond one wall of the small garden, a seagull is nesting on someone's brick chimney, part of a crowded roofscape of chimney pots and gray slate shingles softened by green and gold lichen. Over another wall looms the pinnacled fifteenth-century stone tower of the parish church, and standing on the garden path, I can just glimpse in the distance a patch of shining sea.

Who would imagine that this enchanted place is actually a museum? But then consider where the Barbara Hepworth Museum and Sculpture Garden is located, in the surprising town of St. Ives. Once a fishing village and then a mining center, St. Ives, at the southwest tip of Cornwall, is now a popular seaside resort of some eleven thousand people, with wide sandy beaches, a windsurfing school, and harbor-front shops filled with seashells, fudge, and shiny jewelry.

Although many seaside resorts support art galleries, usually specializing in dramatic maritime landscapes, St. Ives is distinctive. Ever since the painter J. M. W. Turner discovered St. Ives's charms on a sketching tour in 1811, the town has attracted many artists, of whom the best known are James McNeill Whistler, Walter Sickert, Ben Nicholson, Peter Lanyon, Patrick Heron, potter Bernard

Leach—and, of course, sculptor Barbara Hepworth. (Writers have also loved St. Ives; Virginia Woolf spent holidays here as a child, and many of her memories reappear in *To The Lighthouse*.) To celebrate and house this proud artistic heritage, in 1993 the Tate Gallery opened a new branch, the Tate Gallery St. Ives, in a gleaming white modernist building set just above Porthmeor Beach.

So the pleasures of a visit to the Barbara Hepworth Museum and Sculpture Garden can easily expand to include sunbathing, swimming, surfing, shopping, coastal walks, and the Tate St. Ives—not to mention clambering around the winding, old cobbled streets above the harbor. Although St. Ives is not undiscovered, it is not yet flooded with Americans, who are perhaps daunted by the six-hour train ride, or even longer drive, from London. In spring and fall, St. Ives seldom seems crowded at all. A day in St. Ives, centered around the Barbara Hepworth Museum and Sculpture Garden, can be a thoughtful and leisurely delight.

When we arrived by car one morning last September, James and I looked for the bypass that would bring us around the top of the town to one of the well-marked public parking lots. (Our favorite is a miniscule one just above Porthmeor Beach, but it fills up very early.) Another possibility is to park at the rail station in nearby Lelant and catch the Park and Ride train, a short but stunningly scenic route past Carbis Bay. On our first trip, some years ago, we made the mistake of driving blithely into the center of St. Ives, where a confusing labyrinth of narrow, frequently one-way lanes usually slows traffic to a painful crawl.

Walking downhill into the old town—the newer suburbs of St. Ives, like most modern outer rings of historic towns, are not especially attractive—we headed right for Porthmeor Beach. One of five local beaches, Porthmeor is a festive, colorful sight on a sunny day, with multistriped sunscreens set up on the golden sand and bright red, yellow, and white sailboards skimming over the aquamarine water. On gray, misty days, unless the rain is too dispiriting, we like to walk across the vast, empty expanse of sand from one end to the other, seeking the firm sand at the edge of the surf. At the western end, we can climb up steps to join the Cornwall Coastal Path.

This section of the longer South West Coast Path runs from St. Ives southwest toward Zennor, encompassing part of what Barbara Hepworth called "the remarkable pagan landscape which lies between St. Ives, Penzance and Land's End," a landscape she felt had a deep effect on her art. Bracken, heather, sparse pastures, and arduously cultivated fields run right to the edge of rocky cliffs that hurl themselves into the sea. Behind the coastline, the barren moorland is dotted with prehistoric standing stones and stone circles, as well as ruins from the now defunct tin and copper mines. With only one day, we do not walk far, just long enough to savor the silence, the wind blowing across the moor, and the views back to dwindling St. Ives and then far out to sea.

Returning to Porthmeor Beach, we are always ready for lunch. St. Ives offers many possibilities. One warm, bright April day, we assembled a picnic from a sampling of the tiny shops that crowd among bed-and-breakfasts on the narrow, hilly streets near the harbor. Seated on a public bench just above the beach, we feasted on fresh crab and whole-wheat sandwiches, Jaffa oranges, strawberry tarts, and cider, while we watched two barefoot children trying to dare each other into dipping their toes into the cold water. On another, rainier visit, we took refuge in an inexpensive waterfront cafe for tea and scones and tracked a solitary walker, swathed in yellow raingear, tugging his dog along the deserted beach.

Our favorite lunchtime treat is the rooftop restaurant at the Tate St. Ives. (A ticket to the Tate includes a visit to the Barbara Hepworth Museum, now part of the Tate.) There, perched above St. Ives, in an informal all-white dining room, designed with the same modernist panache as the rest of the museum, we can look through the panoramic windows over the town and sea.

On our last visit, the food at the Tate was simple but delicious, with a short menu that included quiche, fresh John Dory whitefish with vegetables, crab salad, and a rich bread pudding topped with clotted cream that should have been a meal in itself. The views, however, are what make the dining room so spectacular. Walking slowly through the two rooms and terraces, we admired how each window framed a different picture: complex angular compositions of tiled roofs in muted colors, flying seagulls, clouds over the bay, the beach, rocks, and sea below.

Since we had not long before toured the museum's permanent collection and had to leave St. Ives by midafternoon, we descended quickly past four floors of coolly white, well-lit galleries. In the entrance foyer we paused to soak in the rich colors—reds, blues, yellow, white, and a splash of black—of a huge abstract stained-glass window by Patrick Heron. Surrounded by so much white, Heron's window has the effect of an exuberant shout.

It is only a short walk to Trewyn Studio and Garden, now the Barbara Hepworth Museum and Sculpture Garden, clearly signposted from the center of town. Dame Barbara lived here from 1949 until her death in a studio fire in 1975, when she was seventy-two. In her will she asked that her executors establish a permanent display of some of her works at Trewyn, as well as keeping her working studio "as closely as possible as it has been in my lifetime." (Since it was damaged in the fire, the interior of the studio has been reconstructed.) Hidden on Barnoon Hill behind high walls in a narrow street, Trewyn gives no clue on its exterior of what awaits within.

From the street, the entry leads directly into a downstairs room that was once Hepworth's kitchen, dining room, and bathroom. Now it holds a ticket desk, bookstall, showcases illustrating segments of the sculptor's career, and a wall of photographs. The photographs are mesmerizing, compressing her intense life into a rush of images: a sweet-faced Yorkshire girl of ten; a simply dressed art student at twenty-one in Italy, shyly half smiling, her eyes cast down, standing with her first husband, sculptor John Skeaping, whose arms are crossed as he stares straight at the camera; a svelte young woman of twenty-eight, dressed in black slacks and tank top, cigarette dangling from her mouth, next to painter Ben Nicholson, her second husband; the mature and celebrated artist at sixty-one, her weathered face etched with character, standing alone in a breeze blowing across the harbor of St. Ives.

Upstairs is the studio, also once used as a bedroom and sitting room. It is a spare and luminous room, with white walls and ceiling, a few pieces of white or ivory-colored furniture, and windows on all four sides. With its ivory curtains drawn back, light floods into the airy space, glinting off the polished dark wood floors and the white pedestals of many polished sculptures, including one with slate and nested marble stones (*Oval with Two Forms*, 1971), a rounded, pierced shape carved from a rich brown Nigerian wood (*Epidauros*, 1960), and several sheet-brass arcs threaded with strings (*Curlew*, 1956).

At one end of the studio, a door beckons into the garden. This is the green heart of the museum, a tangle of trees, shrubs, and flowers that in a very small circuit suggests something of Cornwall's wild beauty. Barbara Hepworth created the garden herself, and it still seems a very personal place. In one corner is a little white shed, with windows on three sides and a saggy bed, chair, mirror, and table visible inside. An outdoor table with chairs is shaded by a sun umbrella. Looking over my shoulder, I almost expected I might see the sculptor herself strolling out from the house.

This sense of immediacy—of a vibrant presence, departed moments ago—became even stronger when I crossed to the annex, where the artist did most of her plaster and stone carving. The workshops remain almost just as she left them, with stained jackets and smocks hanging on the wall, mallets, chisels, and other tools laid out ready for work, bottles of spirits on the shelf, and white stone dust thick on various surfaces. Half-carved stone and marble sculptures, just emerging from the rough blocks, seem to cry out for completion, but, according to Dame Barbara's explicit wishes, they remain unfinished.

If the abandoned workshop is somewhat chilling, the garden is very much alive. White daisies spill in profusion around the base of one sculpture, pink feathery astilbe hovers near another, and dense lilypads cluster on a tiny pond crossed by a rough stone slab. As the garden path dips and turns among trees and shrubs, sculptures appear unexpectedly, perhaps in a sheltered niche or in a grassy clearing. The art exists in harmony with palm trees, bamboo, and flowers, as if these abstract shapes contained some kind of organic essence.

Without any sense of crowding, the garden easily holds a surprising number of sculptures—on our last visit, three large stone carvings and eighteen bronzes, some small in scale and others imposing. *Four Square (Walk Through)* (1966), Hepworth's largest work, consists of four bronze squares balanced on two levels. The centers of the squares are cut out so that one's eye crisscrosses the spaces. Walking through this sculpture, which seems as natural as walking along the path, adds another sensuous element, both to the sculpture and to the garden.

Bronze with Strings (Spring) (1966) is a bronze oval, almost circular and pierced in the center, with its inner concave space threaded by strings. Its curving shape relates to the stone-walled circular pond in front, and its strings uncannily evoke something of the feeling of the tall, feathery bamboo behind. Hepworth changed and moved her sculptures around, and so periodically does the museum, but each seems to have been created just for the place it now occupies.

In the far corner of the garden stands *Conversation with Magic Stones* (1973), Dame Barbara Hepworth's last major work in bronze. Three tall bronzes, notched and indented rectangles, rise like sentinels from the grass; three boxlike shapes lie on the ground, as if tumbled by age, like many of Cornwall's prehistoric stones. Walking among these irregular haunting forms, I felt as if they might indeed be holding some kind of indefinable conversation.

It is hard to leave Barbara Hepworth's garden. But St. Ives does display more of her work elsewhere: a moving *Madonna and Child*, a memorial to her son Paul Skeaping, in the nearby church; sculptures near the railway and bus station, outside the guildhall, in the library, in two courtyards of apartment buildings, in the new Tate, and in Longstone Cemetery, where Dame Barbara is buried.

It is also hard to leave St. Ives. On a clear windy day, when surf foams into the bay, after hiking to the beach I buy an ice cream cone and explore the cobbled lanes among cottages whose window-boxes burst with pansies and geraniums. Glancing into a few uncurtained windows that face toward the sea, I wish I had a talent for painting. Then, I think, I could justifiably settle in for the summer. And every day, when I'd painted just long enough, I'd put down my brush, cross a few streets, and head for some silent conversation in the Barbara Hepworth Museum and Sculpture Garden.

A FEW FLOATING FACTS

The Barbara Hepworth Museum and Sculpture Garden, on Barnoon Hill in St. Ives, is open from April 1 through September, Monday to Saturday, 11 A.M. to 7 P.M., and Sunday 11 to 5. From October to March, it is open Tuesday through Saturday, 11 to 5, and Sunday, 1 to 5. Admission is charged.

III

At the Water's Edge

14

♕♕

New Views on
an Ancient River

After many trips to London, I thought I knew the Thames. I had seen the river from embankments, bridges, and boat trips upstream to Hampton Court and downstream to the Tower and Greenwich. But one recent spring in London, James and I acquired four fascinating new perspectives on the river: from a little-used pedestrian pathway, inside Tower Bridge, through an underwater tunnel, and at the Thames Barrier below Greenwich.

We discovered our first perspective by accident. Most visitors to the South Bank Arts Complex, which includes the National Theatre and Royal Festival Hall, come and go via Waterloo Bridge or the Hungerford Foot Bridge, which lead to the West End. Since we were staying in the City, the old commercial heart of London (see Chapter 21, "At Home in Cloth Fair"), our pedestrian route took us in the other direction along the Thames, across Blackfriars Bridge, and then onto Paul's Walk, a paved riverside path that runs between the river and St. Paul's Cathedral.

Few other walkers ever seemed to use this route. After passing Gabriel's Wharf, a small development of shops and restaurants just east of the National Theatre, we were always almost alone. On the busy Victoria Embankment, the Thames is closed off by stone walls and lined by ships converted to restaurants. But on our route along the South Bank, it was startlingly empty. (New developments, however, are planned for this area; it may not remain lonely long.

Further down the river, for example, the reconstructed Globe Theatre and its related museum have recently opened.)

Concrete landing steps, leading downward, unexpectedly appeared at intervals along the pathway. None have gates at the top.
At night, as we walked home, I peered at these beckoning staircases
until they suddenly disappeared into the dark, swirling water. As the
water lapped over the steps a few feet away, I sometimes glanced
nervously over my shoulder. Here the Thames seemed faintly Dick-
ensian, evoking the untamed and sinister river of *Our Mutual Friend*
or *Oliver Twist.*

After crossing Blackfriars Bridge, we descended again to a pedestrian path toward St. Paul's. In the daytime, several benches along
this path provide a private and protected picnic spot, far removed
from street traffic. We sometimes chose to eat our sandwiches on
one of these benches, so we could watch boats moving up and down
the river. Across the river, a monumental but faded power station,
now destined for a radically new design and eventual use by the
Tate Gallery, is shouldered by ostentatiously modern office buildings, providing a large-scale lesson in changing urban architecture.

After such a close view of the river, our next perspective on the
Thames zoomed upward. In 1994, Tower Bridge, one of London's
landmarks, celebrated the centenary of its opening. With its two
massive Gothic towers, dramatic drawbridge, and gracefully
swooping shore spans, Tower Bridge dominates the lower reaches of
London's Thames. One morning James and I decided to take a
guided tour of this famous bridge.

Our tour incorporated an elaborate multimedia show, over an
hour long, that described and explained the history, design, and
actual workings of the bridge. To my surprised pleasure, I found the
show not only informative but often amusing. It began in the darkness of the North Tower, where two animated dummies, one a
workman and the other a former Lord Mayor, loudly argued with
each other across the chambered space. I found myself turning from
one to the other, as if their taped voices were real. Following a short
film, with excellent and vaguely familiar actors, a ghostly image of

the architect—who did not live to see the bridge finished—sent the tour group on its way. (The way includes some walking and steep stairs.)

Although other segments of the tour vividly illustrated the actual construction of the bridge and its intricate hydraulic system, which operates the two giant bascules of the central drawbridge, I was most entranced by the sky-high walkway between the two towers. Dazzling views opened east toward the Docklands and west toward the Tower of London, St. Paul's, and the Houses of Parliament. Glassed-in girders and crosspieces keep the walkway enclosed enough to prevent undue vertigo, although photographers can open a few small sliding windows.

Below the South Tower, the Engine Rooms house much of the original giant machinery—boilers, accumulators, and engines—that operates the bridge. (Here, too, an animated dummy, Toby the Coal Stoker, can easily startle an unnoticing visitor with a sudden tape-recorded spiel.) Many hands-on displays are geared to children or to those who, like me, only dimly grasp the basic principles of physics. I studied cogs and wheels, experimented with a miniature wind machine, and finally made James sit on a large piston while I gleefully operated a hydraulic device that forced the piston (and James) to slowly ascend several inches.

In the well-stocked gift shop, whose scope extends beyond Tower Bridge to the Thames in general, I browsed through several souvenir booklets. In "London's Royal River," one picture in particular caught my attention. It showed a luminous night view of the Thames Barrier, a mammoth series of movable steel gates, built in a line across the river, that can be raised to protect London from flooding. The gates, a short distance from Greenwich, were only officially opened in 1984, and they are not yet on most tourist agendas. We decided to investigate.

Our trip to the Thames Barrier unexpectedly provided us with still another river experience. Instead of taking a boat from the Tower to Greenwich and then on to the Barrier, we decided it might be faster to try the Docklands Light Railway, with its quick overview of the most recent, and much-ballyhooed, redevelopment of the riverfront, and then walk through an underground tunnel from the Docklands to Greenwich.

The light, airy Docklands train, which whizzed speedily through a moldering section of London, not yet developed, and then past brand-new marinas, office blocks, and Docklands condominiums, was no preparation for the Greenwich Foot Tunnel. From a flower-bedecked station at Island Gardens, we walked in moments to an entrance to the tunnel. I hadn't considered how far underground it might be. Since we'd just missed the elevator, we hurried down a gloomy circular staircase. It was very long. At the bottom, we found ourselves in a kind of huge pipe.

Suddenly I remembered I am sometimes vulnerable to claustrophobia in extreme situations. This definitely seemed extreme. "What if the lights go out?" I tremulously asked James. I remembered London power outages. "Oh, well, at least we wouldn't get lost," he answered, ever cheerful. "We'd just feel our way along the wall." I looked at the curving pipe and sniffed the musty, clammy air. All the weight of the Thames lay above us. I figured we could make it across the river, underwater, in about twenty minutes if we walked fast. We walked fast.

When we emerged at Greenwich, I was glad to hop aboard the last boat to the Thames Barrier. Although the boat was packed with schoolchildren (according to a teacher, the Barrier and its museum are a favorite scientific day trip), the short voyage down the river was pleasant as well as educational. Most shipping has long since disappeared from this stretch of the Thames, but a few signs of industry still cling to the banks—piles of metal from scrapped cars waiting to go to Germany, huge mounds of sand from the North Sea, a sugar factory, ramshackle warehouses. Away from tourist London, the Thames is still a working river.

In half an hour, the Barrier loomed impressively before us. With its six colossal hoods, wood shells covered with narrow strips of curving stainless steel, the Barrier looked like a gleaming set of hulks from outer space. The hoods protect the actual operating machinery of the gates, enormous rocking beams moved by linkages to two hydraulic cylinders. Our captain announced we were unusually lucky that day, for two shieldlike gates were raised for inspection and cleaning. Ordinarily, the gates, which form a wall against the water, lie like lurking steel traps just below the surface. If necessary, they can be raised in minutes.

Although visitors cannot dock at the actual gates, they can tour the Thames Barrier Visitors Centre. Besides a buffet restaurant and a riverside park, the center provides a museum with working models, displays, a video film, and a multimedia audiovisual show. The multimedia show illustrates the history of London and graphically shows how the city is gradually sinking, while the video film gives a detailed presentation of the Barrier's design, engineering, and construction. Watching cranes lower impossibly huge pieces of metal into place, measured for correct position within millimeters of an inch, I could understand why some call the Barrier "the Eighth Wonder of the World."

Since we had missed the boat back to Greenwich, we left the shiny, high-tech world of the Thames Barrier for a slow, crowded bus back to the city in rush hour. We rode past the dwindling dregs of river industry, grim-looking terrace housing, and, after Greenwich, miles of sprawling south London. For over an hour, we caught not a single glimpse of the river. But our excursions along, under, and on top of the Thames had made their impression. I knew that somewhere near, perhaps just hidden behind a few tall buildings, the Thames still ran through the heart of London to the sea.

A FEW FLOATING FACTS

The British Tourist Authority can supply maps of the Thames, with its attractions and new developments easily pinpointed. The telephone number for the B.T.A. in the U.S. is 1-800-462-2748.

Tower Bridge can be reached by the Tower Hill tube or London Bridge tube. It is open for tours daily from 10 A.M. to 4 P.M. Admission is charged. Telephone 0171-709-0081.

The Thames Barrier Visitors Centre is near Greenwich, at 1 Unity Way, Woolwich, on the south bank of the Thames between the Blackwall Tunnel and the Woolwich Ferry. It can be reached by car, via the A206 Woolwich Road; by buses 177 and 180; by train, after a fifteen-minute walk from Charlton Station, which is served by Charing Cross, Waterloo East, London Bridge, and Dartford. It is open daily, except Christmas, Boxing Day, and New Year's, 10 A.M. to 5 P.M. weekdays, 10:30 to 5:30 weekends. Telephone 0181-854-1373. Admission is charged.

River cruises to the Thames Barrier leave from Westminster Bridge embankment (lasting 75 minutes) and from Greenwich (25 minutes). For Westminster service, phone 0171-930-3373; for Greenwich service, 0181-305-0300.

15

A Beacon on the Cornish Coast: The Lieutenant's Quarter

Whenever I have the chance to stay near an ocean, I want to get as close as possible. I'm not easily sidetracked a few miles away to a nice little inn or over the hill into a sheltered inland village. I want to look out my bedroom window at all that water and, if the wind is right, listen at night to surf pounding against the shore. When James and I arrived for a week's stay at the Lieutenant's Quarter, one of several holiday cottages converted from a disused fortification on St. Anthony Head, the very tip of the Roseland Peninsula in Cornwall, I knew we had come to the right place.

Like many other cottages owned by the National Trust on unblemished parts of the English coast, the Lieutenant's Quarter was not easy to find. When I consulted my map before leaving our launching pad of St. Ives, the distance from St. Ives to St. Anthony Head, across from St. Mawes and Falmouth, seemed at first deceptively short—perhaps an hour, no more. But soon I discovered that we would have to dip and swerve across southern Cornwall on crowded two-lane A roads and then turn off on a minor B road to a ferry across the River Fal. That was the easy part. Once on the other side of the Fal, we would need to thread our way through a maze of even more minor roads. Finally, if we made all the right turns, we could edge our way down what turned out to be almost three miles of a narrow lane to our waiting cottage at the tip of St. Anthony Head.

It was at the King Harry Ferry that our week on the Roseland Peninsula really began, a week of ocean, wooded estuaries, medieval churches, peaceful gardens, and cliffside walks. The ferry road led past hilly farmland and secluded hamlets, with signposted names like Come-to-Good, Cowlands, and Goonpiper, and zigzagged down a steep hill to the banks of the Fal.

The Harry Ferry, as we soon began calling it with resigned affection, is a very slow diesel-powered barge pulled on underwater chains across the river. Its movement was so quiet and stately that sometimes, after we'd driven on board, I'd look up from my newspaper (acquired in the outside world to which the ferry connected us) and find that we had arrived at the other shore without my noticing we'd ever left. From morning to early evening, the Harry Ferry runs almost every half hour. But knowing its schedule wasn't much help. It was impossible to time our arrival exactly via the country roads, on one side, or the sometimes clogged main roads on the other. If we were early, we parked in line and waited. If the ferry had just left, we watched it as it ponderously clanked across and back. Sometimes, muttering, I took out my map and wondered about the much longer overland loop around Truro.

But the Harry Ferry reminded us that once we left the A39, we were entering a slower, more tranquil world, one where Cornwall still has not succumbed to the fever of raging tourism. Our road took us from the ferry across the upper neck of the Roseland Peninsula, named not for its roses—though they bloomed, gloriously, in many cottage gardens—but from the Cornish word *ros*, meaning promontory. Turning down the peninsula, we drove its full length, through more tiny villages, until we found ourselves on the long narrow road that ended at St. Anthony Head.

Although our small one-bedroom cottage was one of three adjoining conversions, the walls in the single-story stone building were so thick that we never heard our neighbors, and we seldom saw them come or go. We might have been alone on St. Anthony Head, a windswept, isolated cape with an almost complete circle of spec-tacular views. Stepping out our front door, we could gaze across the water to St. Mawes, a former fishing village whose harbor is now dotted with sailboats, and farther west toward the larger port of Fal-mouth. At night the lights of Falmouth glittered as if it were a metropolis.

But we did not think of cities and people when we stood on the tip of the headland. Then we looked far out to sea, often straining to make out a ship moving across the horizon. Smaller boats, their sails white against the dark water, hurried toward their sheltered anchorage in Carrick Roads, the long deep inlet between Falmouth and St. Mawes that is the third-largest natural harbor in the world. Just below the point, St. Anthony Head lighthouse, a handsome whitewashed stone tower built in 1834, still warns mariners of the lethal Manacles reef farther south.

Because the National Trust owns large swaths of land on this beautiful peninsula, we could explore much of it on foot. One sunny morning, sandwiches and thermos stashed in a shoulder bag, we set out on a leisurely six-mile circular walk from our cottage door. Rounding Zone Point, just past our headland, we soon left any sign of human habitation as we headed northeast on the coastal path. On the landward side, pastures and fields ran down almost to the cliff edge, but a hedge, just low enough so that we could see over it, protected us on the seaward side of the path from any sudden slide to oblivion. Ahead we could see our clearly defined route, winding along the cliffs, disappearing down a hill, and reappearing on the next upward slope.

A slight breeze blew in from the sea, cooling us from the warm sun overhead. The path was well trodden—we met several other walkers, all of whom stopped to chat for a few minutes—and we could safely keep our eyes on the miles of brilliant blue sea. Our pace was comfortable. In little more than an hour, we reached Porthbeor Beach, a rock-strewn stretch of sand far below. Descending a very narrow, almost entirely vertical set of stairs, we lazed awhile on the beach, wading in the lapping fringe of the fiercely cold water and then napping in the shade of the precipitous cliffs. Not much farther, we circled above Towan Beach, larger and almost as secluded, although, by using a side path that led in minutes to the main peninsular road and a parking area, several families had pitched their umbrellas on the sands.

Turning onto this path, we cut across the peninsula, past Porth Farm, whose refurbished stone buildings are now also National Trust cottages, and emerged on the banks of Porth Creek. From hot sun and bright spreading ocean, we had suddenly entered another characteristically Cornish landscape, the serene backwater of a slow-moving estuary. Our cool damp path led along the creek under the shadow of overhanging trees. As we walked below the trees, we could smell the rich moist rot of the tangled undergrowth. We walked almost in silence, not wanting to break the hushed quiet. A family of white swans floated by, five cygnets sedately sailing behind their mother.

Soon the creek emptied into the Percuil River, and our views widened. Coming upon a thoughtfully placed bench, we stopped for a picnic lunch. Before long we were joined by an English walker and his grown son; friendly and talkative, they stood on the path, watching us munch our sandwiches, long enough to tell us all about the father's ninety-three-year-old aunt in Vacaville, California, who had recently died. At least in Cornwall, a coastal path is seldom as lonely as it seems.

Once again on the path, we arrived in early afternoon at Place House, a startling sight after oceanside fields and tangled riverside. After the path curves inward around a small bay, Place House, built in 1840, rises like a French château among fervently mown green lawns. Guided by a National Trust leaflet, we walked as unobtrusively as possible down a silent overgrown lane that ran so close to the house, we could see into its walled garden. At the end of the lane, almost hidden in the trees, was the former parish church of St. Anthony.

Although St. Anthony is now disused—the dismal word *redundant*, implying a kind of failure, is the proper Anglican designation—it still freely offers a remarkable meditative atmosphere, the gift of many English medieval churches. (St. Anthony mostly dates from the twelfth and thirteenth centuries.) Although the small church was swept and tidy, the surrounding graveyard was not. Many gravestones were toppled, others half buried under noxious weeds and high grasses. The only monuments still kept reasonably tidy were those relating to the family whose descendants evidently still lived in Place House. In the mansion's walled garden, the perennial border was immaculate.

When we had circled the little bay, I had noticed a sign posted at a tiny quay: PLACE TO ST. MAWES FERRY. What kind of ferry could possibly run between this isolated spot and the lively port a mile across the estuary? I peered toward St. Mawes, but I could see no sign of a ferryboat. According to this schedule, however, one ran every half hour. Since much of the afternoon still lay ahead of us, James and I decided to return from the church to the quay and wait for the next (and almost unimaginable) ferry.

"The Ferryboat leaves from Place Quay at high water, and at low water from some steps 150 yards north east of the Quay," we read. We scrupulously examined the shoreline—exposed rocks, barnacles, a tethered rowboat—to try to discover whether the tide was out or not; we were a little embarrassed that we couldn't tell. But in a few minutes another couple emerged from the riverside woods. They were obviously serious ramblers, packs on backs and fearsome boots on their feet. They strode determinedly to a spot on the bank just above some seaweed-covered moldering stone steps that led into the water. James and I looked at each other. The tide must be out.

Just before the half-hour scheduled departure, we could see a black dot on the horizon moving closer. As it grew bigger, it assumed an odd shape—recognizably a boat, but unlike any I'd ever seen. The Place–St. Mawes ferry was a sort of open small scow, with an outboard motor, a makeshift one-person cabin perched on the front, and room for several people to sit on benches in the back. Its pilot was a raffish-looking young man with a leering grin and a cigarette dangling from his mouth. We clambered on, paid our pound fare, and put-putted across the water in ten minutes to St. Mawes.

Our ferry ride gave us just time enough for a brief exchange with
the other two passengers, who turned out to be pleasant and
friendly. Somehow—conversation in England often leads with mysterious speed to animals—we learned about their older unmarried
daughter, a veterinarian, whose passion was rescuing discarded
racing greyhounds, four at a time, and giving them a home. Like
the earlier tidbit about someone's aged aunt in Vacaville, I always
treasure such nuggets out of nowhere, perhaps because they give
me a tantalizing peek into the lives of people I would otherwise
never know.

St. Mawes is an enchanting little town, whose whitewashed stone
houses rising in terraces above the harbor give it a Mediterranean
air. Although tourists flock here in midsummer, in June only enough
of them walked along the narrow streets to make the town seem on
holiday. Since we wanted to take the ferry back to Place in an hour,
we decided to pause for refreshments at the Idle Rocks, a venerable
hotel overlooking the fleet of sailboats dipping and swaying at
anchor. For a little more than a pound, we were served tea and
coffee from a white ceramic service, brought to us on a tray as we
lounged on a stone-walled outdoor terrace in the sunshine like
yachting grandees.

After catching the three-thirty P.M. ferry back to Place, we
walked ever more slowly back to St. Anthony Head, still an hour
away. In the open now, next to the sparkling water and shaded by
an occasional windblown pine, the coastal path took us past fine distant views of the Falmouth docks, which lie on the inland side of a
promontory that ends at Pendennis Castle. Pendennis is one of a
chain of coastal forts built by Henry VIII as a defense against the
French; its twin, an austere, almost abstract idea of a castle, with low
circular buildings in the form of a cloverleaf, guards the other side of
the inlet at St. Mawes. When the path led us to St. Anthony Head
lighthouse, we huffed and puffed up, up, up to the public parking
area near the National Trust holiday cottages—and home.

As we strolled in front of the Lieutenant's Quarter that night,
drinking our decaf and looking toward the blinking lights of Fal-

mouth, I knew I wanted to see more of waterside Roseland. What lay on the upper reaches of the Fal, before it emptied into Carrick Roads and flowed past Falmouth into the sea? In St. Mawes we had seen a notice for a ferry to Falmouth. That ferry would be our next destination.

This time we approached St. Mawes by road, driving up one branch of the peninsula and down the other—like most of Cornwall, roads in Roseland do not follow a crow's flight—past the village of St. Just-in-Roseland. Here we stopped to revisit a church we remembered vividly from a visit ten years before, possibly the most beautifully sited parish church in England. The medieval (thirteenth- and fifteenth-century) church of St. Just-in-Roseland lies on the water, nestled into a gentle wooded hill that slopes down to a silted mirrorlike tidal creek. Behind the church, palms, hydrangeas, fuchsias, and many other semitropical trees and flowering shrubs grow so richly that they almost obscure the graves. Since our last visit, the gardens—for this churchyard is much more than a cemetery—had expanded into a new section with two ornamental pools. (We also noted a new large parking lot, sized for tour buses.) Although by mid-June many of the azaleas and rhododendrons were almost finished blooming, the churchyard was still a jungle of greenery and color, a living metaphor of resurrection.

When we arrived in St. Mawes, we went straight to the quay for the ferry to Falmouth. It had just left. This time we took the necessary tea break at Broomer's, an unpretentious cafe that provided a generous bowl of rhubarb and gooseberry fruit crumble with a spoonful of clotted cream. A sunny place with white walls and white bamboo chairs, Broomer's does a side business in packaged homemade Christmas puddings. According to a notice on the wall, its chef had trained at the Savoy in London. St. Mawes was obviously quite up-to-date.

Back at the quay, we boarded the *Adrian Gilbert*, bigger than the midget ferry to Place but still only a converted fishing boat. It whisked us to Falmouth in twenty minutes. After the briefest scrutiny of quayside Falmouth, which seemed rather bleak—charity shops, purveyors of cheap goods, empty storefronts—we hopped aboard a small cruising boat for a two-hour excursion up the Fal. Despite the sunshine, the boat was only half filled, so we sat almost by ourselves on the front deck, watching the heavily wooded banks of the river slide by and sleepily listening to the captain's meandering commentary.

Although the Fal no longer serves the shipping trade it once did, its sheltered anchorage—up to eighty feet deep—still held a surprising number of large ships. They seemed marooned there, tethered out of sight of the ocean, lost in a green wilderness. Only a few crew members appeared on the decks of these ships, either hanging about or working at some desultory task. One rusty, forlorn-looking vessel, an old refrigerator ship, awaited a cargo that might never come. Another merchant ship was flying a red flag; that meant, our captain reported, its owners hadn't paid their crew—rather like Hester's famous A, I thought, a flag that flaunted the owner's sin— so the ship was not permitted to leave the harbor. Two Croatian ships, their paint badly peeling, could not go home until the Bosnian war was settled. They had already been waiting, the captain added, a long while.

But war seemed very far away that peaceful afternoon on the Fal. Small sailboats and modest yachts were beached or anchored on back stretches of the river. A few sailed slowly by us, barely moving in the light, sunny breeze. Snuggled into a little dip in the river and half camouflaged by trees, Smuggler's Inn, a historic pub, offered boat moorings and waterside seats to the lucky patrons who had managed to find their way here either via the river or along the almost unmarked lanes behind the King Harry Ferry.

High above the river, looking down past green slopes mown by sheep, the imposing classic colonnade of Trelissick House commanded one deep bay of the river. Farther on, set back on another hilltop, another grand house presided over a deer park. Our captain said the manor belonged to the Viscount Falmouth. Most names in this part of Roseland—the King Harry Ferry, Smuggler's Inn, the Viscount Falmouth—sounded to me as if they'd been plagiarized

from an impossibly romantic novel. I was glad I didn't know anything about the viscount, who might well have been a balding
middle-aged businessman; in my ignorance I could happily imagine
him to be a dashing cavalier.

Since the tide was too low to go farther toward Truro, our boat
turned around before reaching that inland port. After silt and
mining wastes eventually clogged the Truro River, the town's main
quay was filled in. Anyone stopping in that busy administrative
center today, perhaps to see its cathedral or eighteenth-century
houses, would never know that it was once a vital link to the sea.

Although I dozed a bit as we drifted downstream, I remembered,
as we passed Trelissick again, that we needed to spend some time at
its famous garden. Next day—this one drizzly and misty—we arrived
at Trelissick in late morning, a few minutes after crossing on the
King Harry Ferry, whose entry road leads right past Trelissick's
gates. Most of Cornwall's grand gardens are either on the sea or on a
tidal estuary. Trengwainton, near Penzance, has stunning views over
Mount's Bay; the steeply terraced gardens of St. Michael's Mount
are on an island in the bay; Glendurgan and Trebah, both deep
flowering valleys, run down to the Helford estuary; Caerhays
Castle's fabled collection of magnolias, rhododendrons, azaleas, and
camellias cover a hillside that is set just out of sight of a tiny sandy
cove. Trelissick looks out on the Fal just as it opens into Carrick
Roads and surges toward the sea.

Like these other Cornish gardens, Trelissick is at its best in April
and May, when the spring-flowering shrubs almost overflow with
flowers. But on a wet rainy day in June, Trelissick had its own attraction. A woodland walk winds through its vast park, bounded by the
Fal on three sides, and directed by a National Trust brochure, we
decided to take our umbrellas and follow it.

For two hours, canopied by trees as well as our brollies, we walked
on one of the footpaths at which the English excel. Wide, unobtrusively tended, with a mulched surface keeping mud at bay, the path
let us pass unhindered through wet woods and shrubs without plas-
tering our legs with leaves and grasses. I like not having to blaze a

trail, so rather than watching my feet, I can glance around me instead.

Our path led away from the house, across the brow of the grazed and open park, where we could see, shining below, the route along the estuary where we had floated so dreamily yesterday. Veering away from the main drive, we passed through a formal plantation of trees and in front of a little one-story neoclassical lodge, built in 1823, looking rather like a secret temple in the woods. (It is now, like our Lieutenant's Quarter, a National Trust holiday cottage.)

After crossing the ferry road, we turned steeply downward, into Namphillow Wood, a dense thicket of oak, beech, and Scots pine. Beside us a little brook, bordered by ferns, rippled through old watercress beds and hurried downhill. Although the rain sometimes fell in heavy bursts, the leaves overhead were interlaced so intricately that we mostly heard, rather than felt, a gentle patter high above us.

At the foot of the hill, we had reached the head of Lamouth Creek, a shallow estuary of mud flats merging into sedges and seaweed. A detour took us on a short loop along the creekside to Roundwood Quay, a promontory with earthworks left over from an Iron Age fort and ruined wharves from an eighteenth-century boom in tin and copper. Ships were built here as late as the 1870s, and, pushing aside the scrub brush, we looked (in vain) for the remains of a sawpit still in the middle of the quay. Now Roundwood, isolated and overgrown, has almost completely returned to the encroaching woods.

But we could easily look from Roundwood onto the Fal, where the huge oceangoing ships we had passed yesterday looked even more incongruous when glimpsed from this neglected quay. Retracing our steps along the creek, we turned at its head and followed the other bank back to the Fal. The path then led us in and out of more woods—among them, oak, sycamore, ash, sweet chestnut, and larch—carpeted with ferns. When, just below Trelissick House, the woods gave way, we were so captured by the stunning views down the widening estuary that we sat on a bench for a while to look across the mist-shrouded water toward the sea.

Later that night, as we took our usual amble from our cottage around St. Anthony Head, I looked back up the estuary, whose farther shores were now cloaked in darkness. Here on the Roseland Peninsula it was impossible to ignore Cornwall's complex and intimate relationship with the ocean. For almost our entire walk at Trelissick, we had never really left the water—a little brook, Lamouth Creek, the River Fal, and finally Carrick Roads, whose rainy blackness was almost complete.

Remote as our watery retreat often seemed, the Lieutenant's Quarter was also a surprisingly convenient base for excursions into other parts of southwestern Cornwall. Although I was reluctant to leave the water, we didn't have to. When we drove to the bustling market town of Penzance, with its colorful Morrab Subtropical Garden, a municipal Victorian treasure with ponds, ornamental fountain, and bandstand bedecked with wrought-iron curlicues, we also sauntered the entire length of a fine seaside promenade. At St. Ives, a popular resort and art colony, we checked out its beaches and part of the coastal path (see Chapter 13, "The Barbara Hepworth Museum at St. Ives"). Exploring in another direction, we found ourselves alone on the sands just outside Veryan. There we stopped for a long, luxurious lunch at the Nare Hotel, whose yellow-curtained, festive dining room looks out on an utterly unspoiled stretch of coast. Near Mevagissey, when we discovered the Lost Gardens of Heligan (see Chapter 22), we could just catch a glimmer of the bay from a high hill in this restored Victorian paradise.

When, at the end of our week, we had to leave the Lieutenant's Quarter, we took one last tour around the tip of our headland. The sun was again glinting on the water, and a freighter we hadn't seen before was slowly moving from the Falmouth dockyards toward the open sea. The white lighthouse seemed almost dazzlingly bright in the morning sun, but beyond, up the estuary, the shore was still a dark shady green. I thought of the paths we hadn't yet taken—from

St. Just-in-Roseland along the estuary to St. Mawes, from Creek Stephen Point to the crumbled remains of Dingerein Castle, down a lane past Philleigh into the woods. My map of the Roseland Peninsula was covered with enticing dotted lines we hadn't followed. But on a morning like this, it was easy to believe that all would be waiting when we came back.

A Few Floating Facts

The Lieutenant's Quarter is one of more than two hundred holiday cottages rented by the National Trust by the week (and, off season, for shorter periods). An illustrated color catalogue of these properties is available at very low cost; in England, ask at any National Trust shop or contact the Holiday Cottage Booking Office, P.O. Box 536, Melksham, Wiltshire SN12 8SX. You can also call direct at 0122-579-1199 or fax inquiries to 0122-579-0617.

The Royal Oak Foundation is the U.S. affiliate of the National Trust. For further information, write, call, or fax: The Royal Oak Foundation, 285 West Broadway, New York, New York 10013. Telephone (212) 966-6565, fax (212) 966-6619.

For a full discussion of rental cottages, from how to find them to how to assess catalogue descriptions, see "How to Be Your Own Travel Agent" in England As You Like It.

16

Searching for the Golden Apples: The Isle of Mull

*E*verybody talked about Skye. Almost nobody mentioned Mull. As I delved into guidebooks about Scotland, I wondered why. On the map, Mull looked almost as large, with its own set of Celtic offshore islands: Inch Kenneth, Staffa, Little Colonsay, Ulva, Treshnish, and, of course, Iona, the "cradle of Christianity," whose church was founded by evangelizing St. Columba in 563 A. D. Like Skye, Mull's deeply indented coastline sheltered sea lochs and rose into mountains, and it, too, was marked by only the tiniest dots for towns.

Other than Iona, Mull didn't seem to be famous for anything. Skye was. The well-known "Skye Boat Song" celebrated Bonnie Prince Charlie's escape to the island in 1745. ("Carry the lad that's born to be king / Over the sea to Skye.") Cruises stopped at Skye. Day tours from Glasgow and Inverness advertised quick breaks to Skye. At Armadale, the Clan Donald Centre attracted ancestor-hungry MacDonalds from all over the world. Skye was busy and important enough for a new (and controversial) bridge connecting Skye irretrievably to the mainland.

But the more I learned about Skye, the more I yearned to go to Mull. I liked what the map told me about Mull's undisturbed landscape. The rare comments I found about Mull were fervently appreciative of its remote wild beauty. It was like wanting to meet a popular girl's shy sister, someone of whom a few discerning people said, "Ah, Mull. Yes, indeed. You must get to know Mull."

It had taken me years to plan a trip to the Hebrides. When I was an avid young reader, I used to confuse the word with the Hesperides in Greek mythology—Juno's trusted handmaidens who jealously guarded her golden apples in an enchanted garden, a place eventually known as the Islands of the Blessed. These islands, the myth said, were at the remotest end of the western world. Even when I understood that they were rocky islands off the coast of northern Scotland, whose treeless slopes and salt-washed shores did not promise any golden apples (or even very much sun), I thought of them with a sense of mystery. Isolated from the mainland Highlands, which themselves seemed dauntingly unapproachable, the home of the Hebrides promised their own kind of stark magic.

But for a long time, I didn't want to make the effort—the arduous drive to a distant Scottish port, the complications of ferry schedules and reservations, the uncertain attractions of a week on an unknown island. And then, gradually, as James and I traveled more and farther throughout Britain, the Hebrides began to seem less intimidating. If we flew to Glasgow, we could easily drive in a few hours to Oban, the main base for the Caledonian-MacBrayne ferries. The Scottish Tourist Board sent an illustrated folder of self-catering (kitchen-equipped) cottages on Mull. One, a low stone farmhouse, was tucked below a heather-covered hill between the sea and a long, curving sea loch. The photograph showed nothing around the house but unkempt grass, hill, and sky. Making a phone call, I discovered it was available for a week in September. The shy sister was going to accept our date.

Almost as soon as we left Glasgow, we found ourselves on a road that seemed to beckon us toward the Hebrides. It led along the wooded shores of Loch Lomond, still surprisingly pristine, despite the lake's proximity to Glasgow, and then through shadowy gray-green glens, past moorland and stony pastures, beneath lowering stony hills, and beside burns and an occasional gleaming loch. In Oban, a small but busy town with the cheerful brusque animation that seems peculiar to seaports, we waited in line for the ferry, and I peered across the water toward Mull. Heavy gray clouds, lightening over the sea to a thick whitish mist, obscured Mull into a looming dark shape on the horizon. The trip to Craignure, our port of destination in Mull, was only an hour's slow steaming across the water, but it was long enough for me to savor the excitement of a short sea voyage. The mainland gradually disappeared behind us. Although a light rain was falling, many passengers, like us, still sat on deck, huddled under umbrellas or parkas. All faces turned eagerly toward the hills and mountains before us. Their cloud-softened outlines receded backward in layers, like stage settings jutting out of the wings, until the farthest and faintest disappeared entirely in the mist.

Short as it was, our journey made us feel like mariners. Gulls followed from Oban, and one, an experienced forager, soon flew so close that it hung motionless over the deck. A resourceful passenger rummaged for a cracker and held it gingerly out over the deck rail. Hesitating only a moment, the gull dived in a blinding whirr of white wings. Snatching the tidbit, it settled immediately above the deck again, hovering as if cushioned on the brisk sea breeze. Soon, as more passengers flocked to the rail with offerings, the gull began performing a graceful and intricate ballet, swooping, turning, whirling, and somersaulting a few feet over our heads. Moments later, a school of porpoises suddenly leaped out of the water just ahead of the ship, diving back and forth in exuberant accompaniment. Mull had already begun to work its magic.

As we moved along the edge of the island, passing a gloomily romantic stone castle on a spit of land, I saw only a very few houses. They were almost lost in endless rolling dark green hills and mountains, a coast that rose to barren peaks, looking as if someone—a giant kindergartener—had pummeled, kneaded, and molded the recalcitrant landscape into mossy lumps. Washed in a gray rain, Mull was rather forbidding—but also austerely beautiful.

On our half-hour drive to our cottage, Mull's remoteness began to penetrate my consciousness, slowly but thoroughly, as if the cool rain were seeping into my skin. One main road runs from Craignure north to Tobermory, Mull's largest town (population 700), and south, then west, across the Ross of Mull to Fionnphort, the port of departure for Iona. Tour buses to Iona roll off the ferry at Craignure and rumble along this road, and a few speed north to Tobermory. But on the other Mull roads—and there aren't many—cars and trucks edge along a single lane, punctuated with frequent pulling-off places for passing. As soon as we left the main road, we found ourselves jouncing along over a bumpy, rocky track, barely wide enough for our compact car, gingerly rounding blind corners and sometimes veering past deep ravines. James had to drive so slowly that a trotting horse could have easily overtaken us.

Thinking of my guidebooks' blithe recommendations for touring around Mull, I rapidly began to revise my plans for the week. We would not be heading out for many long drives. But when I saw Barrachandroman, the farmhouse that would be our holiday cottage, I knew at once that I would not, in fact, often want to leave. Barrachandroman sits just off the shore of the west end of Loch Spelve, a five-mile-long loch whose waters flow in from the sea through a narrow passage about four miles from our house. The shingle and pebble shore of Loch Spelve is almost empty, except for a sprinkling of cottages near Croggan, a bygone fishing hamlet with an abandoned pier. Otters live along the shores of Loch Spelve, and salmon leap ceaselessly from the watery pens of a fishery on the far side of the lake. Just beyond Barrachandroman, a much smaller freshwater lake, Loch Uisg, nestles between the road and hills. The road trickles to an end at Lochbuie, another tiny hamlet—perhaps four or five houses—at the head of another, even broader, sea loch.

So if we wanted to explore, we would not have to go far from our front door. Most days we remained happily within a few miles of our house. For one favorite walk, we drove three miles to Croggan, parked at he end of an overgrown unpaved lane, and hiked around the tip of our little peninsula and along its seashore. Scrub and bracken-covered high hills—so stark and lonely I thought of them as mountains—separated us from Barrachandroman. My map indicated their Gaelic names, as well as those of other landmarks, in a faint italic script; studying it, I felt we might as well be on the moon: *Port nan Crullach SgarLeathan, Port na Maice Duibhe, Maol Ban, Creag nam Fitheach, Cruach na h'Airighe, Coill a' Bhealaich Mhoir.*

Although our walk only lasted two hours, we felt so removed from the ordinary world that I was startled when I strode over a low dune and found myself almost nose to nose with a large reddish-brown beast adorned with long curling horns and shaggy locks that fell over its eyes. Several other Highland cattle—actually very gentle and pacific creatures—were grazing on the tufts of seagrass around the edge of a little bay. They mooed in protest and shambled away from us. I could not imagine how they had found their way here or who tended them.

As we followed first a rough track and then a footpath next to the sea, we could look across the Firth of Lorn, a sweep of sea between Mull and the mainland, to misty blue shapes we could never quite identify. Was that another island, perhaps Seil or Luing or the Garvellachs? Or simply the hills behind Oban? In the Hebrides, hauntingly blue islands wreathed in mist seemed to shimmer on every horizon. What I remember most about that walk—and our other walks on Mull—is how peaceful it was. Besides the occasional cry of a seabird, we could only hear water lapping on the shore and sometimes splashing down a rocky bed in a hillside burn.

Because most of Mull was intensely quiet, we learned to listen carefully for distinctive sounds. When a rare car or motor scooter rattled down the road, we could hear it miles away. One afternoon, when we took our landlord's rickety outboard onto the dark surface of Loch Spelve, we heard a distant plaintive cry, soon turning into a tremulous bleating chorus, above our sluggishly chugging motor. James cut the motor. Spilling down the far hillside, just opposite our boat, was a huge flock of sheep. As they hurried across the steep slope, they formed a stream that wavered, turned, broke apart, and blended together once more. By squinting hard, we could just make out two black-and-white dogs, who crouched so low they were almost indistinguishable in the grass. When a man with a whistle signaled with his arms or blew high sharp commands, the dogs burst up and darted around the flowing sheep. As more and more sheep trotted onto the road, several other men and two more dogs urged them into a surging line.

For half an hour we sat, drifting in the boat, as the energetic sheepdogs dashed up and down the hill, retrieved straying sheep, and pushed them purposefully down the road. When all the sheep were off the hill, the line seemed at least half a mile long. Although we had sometimes watched one or two sheepdogs moving a small flock, we had never seen a such a large-scale operation, one that required constant attention and skill from both dogs and handlers. It was a superlative show for which we had grandstand seats.

We also caught the second act. Next morning, encouraged by our landlord and his wife, who knew the owner of the flock, we walked to a neighboring farm where the six hundred sheep had all been penned. Climbing a short way up the hill behind the farm, we sat cross-legged in the heather and watched, fascinated, as the sheep were manhandled through chutes, rapidly sheared, heaved into a pool of medicinal sheep-dip, prodded with a long broom until they briefly submerged, and then sloshily marked with identifying dye. Afterward, the farmer invited us into one of the sheds so that we could see his stored pile of fleeces, heaped so high they looked like woolly haystacks. The coarse wool of this particular breed brought him little money; most of his sheep were raised for meat. That night we could hear, even at a distance, the frantic crying of the market lambs, who had been separated for the first time from their mothers. I was just as glad we did not have to see the final scene.

Although watching sheep being moved off a hill was one of our most exciting events on Mull, we did sample some of the island's more conventional tourist attractions. They, too, were quiet. At Torosay Castle, only a few miles up the coast, we wandered lazily through a Victorian baronial mansion, surprisingly unpretentious, filled with a disarming miscellany of family artifacts, including mementos, photographs, and maps of one intrepid member's trip around the world. Outside the house, we roamed all the paths in a large and handsome garden, whose twin gazebos on a high terrace looked out toward the sea and the shadowy tower of Duarte Castle.

Duarte, the doughty headland fortress we'd seen from the Oban boat, dates from the thirteenth century, although it was eventually ruined, then restored in 1912. The traditional home of the chief of the MacLean clan, Duarte attracts far-flung MacLeans, as Armadale in Skye does MacDonalds. Since the late chief was also Chief Scout of the Boy Scouts, Duarte offers exhibitions on the history of Scouting, but its most rewarding displays are outside. There, from its barren promontory, the castle offers spectacular views of sea, sky, clouds, and mountains, which, on a rainy or misty day, all seem to melt together into a watery blue-gray. On a really clear day, I thought I might be able to see to the very end of the Hebrides.

Tobermory, Mull's "capital," a charming and lively port, also provides views, as well as groceries, fancy chocolates, handknit sweaters, and other staples of Scottish tourist towns. From the road above the town, we looked down upon a harbor surrounded by terraced houses washed in bright colors—reds, yellows, blues, greens—that seem to sparkle with good humor. (Although unhappy people doubtless live in some of these houses, I would have to be convinced.) Sailboats and fishing boats gently rocked at anchor a few yards from these houses, and a Caledonian-MacBrayne car ferry was just nudging its way next to its mooring dock. Although we could have dawdled in Tobermory, the sun was shining and the seacoast beckoned. So we meandered for an hour down a woodland path that began near the harbor, past bushes laden with ripe juicy blackberries, along the side of a high cliff to a lonely lighthouse that jutted out into the sea.

On the way home from Tobermory that day, we followed directions from a local tourist pamphlet that promised to take us on one of "the top five walks in North Mull." This proud phrase tells a lot about Mull. In London, guidebooks ranking the city's top attractions include palaces, great museums, grand parks, and splendid churches. In Mull, such a list features walks. (Note that this particular list only covered North Mull; South Mull, an hour's drive away, had its own array.) With a scant week on the island, we only had time to sample a few from the more than twenty itineraries suggested by various helpful guidebooks. Some of these itineraries were strenuous, covering ten or twelve miles over uneven hilly terrain, and others, like our stroll to the Tobermory lighthouse, were easy, asking a leisurely hour or two on level well-marked paths.

Our "top five" walk was indeed at the top. It required an hour's climb up a low worn mountain, 'S Airde Ben, to a volcanic crater now filled by a small lovely loch. Parking at a ruined cottage by the side of the road from Tobermory to Dervaig, we followed a sheep track up the hill, up and up and up. Sometimes the track, barely discernible where the grass was beaten down, dissolved into other tracks, and although we were in no danger of getting lost—the hill was all tussocky moorland, with its only trees off to one side—we were not always sure how to avoid boggy spots and thorny patches or where to step next. Mostly we followed a burn next to the main sheep track. Even when we could not see the running water, we could hear it, splashing and gurgling beneath a small jungle of bracken.

The climb was hard enough so that when we finally arrived at a rock cairn that marked the peak, I sank gratefully down on the thin rock-strewn grass. Other cairns indicated a circular route around the small mountaintop loch, which shone like a dark blue sapphire, but I did not want to move. From the peak, we could look inland over distant scattered forests, deep valleys, and farther mountains, and then, turning toward the sea, we could see the sparkling blue water of far-off bays and more peaks rising beyond. The sky was filled with white clouds that looked themselves like drifting mountains. Although I knew a road lay far, far below us, I could not really believe at that moment that anyone else was moving anywhere on Mull.

Although our week held other low-key adventures—following confusing squiggles on a map to a thoroughly hidden ancient stone circle, nervously edging our way along the interior staircase of a ruined castle tower, watching concerned villagers along a neighboring estuary trying to rescue an injured dolphin—I think back most often to our short time on 'S Airde Ben. In its isolation, sense of tranquillity, and astonishing beauty, that mountaintop held for me the essence of Mull. If the Hebrides were to guard the Golden Apples, I thought, that is where I would find them.

17

The Unexpected Romance of Anglesey

Sometimes I choose a destination partly by its intriguing name—a lunch stop in Chewton Mendip, for example, rather than nearby Radstock; Monk's Gate instead of Horsham; High Newton-by-the-Sea near Snook Point, not Wooler. When we consider a week's stay, I am also influenced not only by its name but by how remote our flat or cottage seems and what promising walks surround it. When I discovered an available rental at Clegir Mawr, an old restored stone farmhouse located near the coastal path at Church Bay, outside Holyhead on the western border of Anglesey, an island in farthest northwestern Wales, it sounded irresistible.

What I didn't know—for I knew almost nothing about Anglesey when we snapped up that week in July—was that Clegir Mawr would be a gateway to some of the most unspoiled and romantic beaches I'd ever seen. On forays from our perch above Church Bay, we also explored prehistoric sites, stones, and assorted ruins; ancient churches; and a grand mansion whose most famous exhibit is a wooden leg. Full of surprises, our week on Anglesey even included a circus.

Anglesey itself has a plain but evocative name with an ancient ring: Angles, Jutes, Saxons, as if it might be almost a separate kingdom of its own. In Welsh, it is known as "Mon Mam Cymru," or "Anglesey, the Mother of Wales," since in centuries past the fertile fields of this low-lying land provided sustenance to the mountainous areas of inland Wales.

When I studied Anglesey on my map, I could see that it was surprisingly large, about the size of southern Cornwall, but not very populated. Its scattered villages were awash in blank white spaces. Holyhead (population 14,000), the largest town and a ferry port for Dublin, was almost marooned on Holy Island, a little island of its own. Only one main road, the A5, cut straight across Anglesey to Holyhead, where it appeared to run abruptly into the sea.

To get to Anglesey, starting from Gatwick, we would need to drive all the way up to the Midlands and then through the Welsh Borders to northern Wales. At Bangor, we would cross one of two bridges over the Menai Strait into Anglesey. Anglesey was nowhere near the popular tourist haunts of the Cotswolds, Lake District, Yorkshire, or, in the other direction, Devon, Dorset, and the fishing ports of Cornwall. Unless someone wanted to go to Ireland, Anglesey didn't seem to be on a route to anywhere.

At first I was afraid that maybe it was undiscovered for good reason. At the entrance to the island, we had paused at Llanfairpwll, whose official name, the longest in Britain—Llanfairpwllgwyngyllgogerychwrndrobwllllantysiliogogogoch—is a famous tourist lure. But Llanfairpwll's main attraction, aside from its name, is a huge retail woolen outlet of James Pringle, selling blankets, sweaters, souvenirs, and the kind of fudge that someone must make in a Tourist Central factory and distribute to every British gift shop.

As we continued across the island toward Holyhead and the turnoff to Clegir Mawr, I looked around with some apprehension. Although I had realized from my reading that the interior countryside was farmland, quite unlike the dramatic mountains of Snowdonia we had just left, I was a little disappointed by the flat and even rather monotonous landscape along the A5. (This was to remain my least favorite drive in Anglesey.)

But I stopped worrying about monotony as soon as we left the A5. What I now worried about was whether we would ever discover

Clegir Mawr at all. Usually the National Trust, whose cottage we were renting, includes highly detailed, accurate instructions about how to reach their holiday properties. We had no trouble turning onto the quiet A5025 toward Llanfachreath and Llanfaethlu and then onto the even quieter narrow lane past Rhydwyn—though I was definitely out of practice in rapidly pronouncing Welsh names, as in "No, not the turn to Llandeusant or Stryd y Facsen, we don't want to end up in Mynydd Mechell"—but after passing the turnoff to Church Bay, we found ourselves on what seemed like a private drive to a dead end.

Following our printed instructions, we were creeping—so slowly that our car muttered and almost stalled—along a bumpy, rocky, barely visible track that led just below the curving crest of a hill. Grass grew high and wild between the two rutted lines of the track, as if no one had driven over it for years. Ahead and to our left, below a steep drop, we could see uninhabited fields and pastures, stretching to the sea, a mile or so away. To our right the hill rose just high enough so we couldn't see over it, nor could we see what lay beyond each sudden bend in the road. Dusk was beginning to darken the track, and Clegir Mawr was nowhere in sight.

The track grew even narrower and wilder. As we rounded each curve, I held my breath, as if the track might simply plunge into space—or disappear entirely. Even James, who is always optimistic, became dismayed. "Nobody would have a cottage back here. I mean, *nobody.* I'd turn around," he confessed, "but I don't know where." After one unexpected twist that sent us lurching down an unnerving dip, he saw ahead a slight widening of the roadbed, just wide enough so that he could slowly do an inch-by-inch U-turn. Back we thudded and jounced, all the way to the junction of the narrow lane with this almost indecipherable track.

While I read and reread the baffling instructions, we repeated this maneuver three times. Each time we painstakingly U-turned at the tiny widened space and grimly returned to the junction, looking with a certain desperation for some clue or signal we might have missed. Now it was almost dark. We would soon have to give up and hope we could find a room for the night in Holyhead. On our third try, just before beginning his U-turn, James said, "What the hell," and drove forward instead. Moments later, after one more unsettling curve in the road, we suddenly found ourselves in front of a low whitewashed farmhouse, until now entirely hidden from view. We were so startled that James killed the engine. The car stopped. We had arrived at Clegir Mawr.

There was certainly nothing dull about the setting of Clegir Mawr. The old stone cottage was sunk deep into a sloping hillside that looked toward a broad wash of fields and sea. Dots of sheep flecked the distant pastures. Although Holyhead was only a few miles away, from our front door we could see only one other farmhouse, whose fields spilled over into the sea. We could not easily walk to the water, but we felt as if it were almost at our front door.

Old stone cottages may seem romantic—in a Cotswold village, bedecked with thatched roof and climbing roses, they are a staple of English postcards—but they are not always quite as cozy as they look. An unassuming, plain, thick-walled farmhouse, Clegir Mawr was rather dark and damp. (A thoughtfully placed new skylight in the upstairs bedroom, however, made our retreat there quite tolerable.) Nor were its low ceilings intended for a six-foot tenant. After the first day, James began keeping his broad-rimmed rainhat on the bedside table. When he got up at night to go to the bathroom, he grabbed the hat. "Okay, maybe I look funny," he said when I giggled, watching his pajama-clad figure rise groggily from the bed and crush his hat onto his head, "but this hat is going to save whatever brains I've got left." Peering through the moonlit darkness, I saw the bedroom doorframe strike an inch of waterproofed canvas. James staggered slightly, but moved valiantly on.

The sense of remoteness that surrounded Clegir Mawr was part of the atmosphere that enveloped much of Anglesey. Many places on the island seemed hard to find, as if they were removed from the rush of ordinary life or still caught in the past. Angelsey's footpaths, for example, were often roughshod cousins of those in other parts of Britain. Near Church Bay, when we tried to follow a dotted line on our Pathfinder map that should have been the coastal path, we found our way choked with burning weed before the path itself simply disappeared. Another tantalizing path, near Clegir Mawr, was supposed to take us to a cave called Ogof Lowry. Climbing fences, opening and closing gates, walking along the edge of plowed fields, we searched everywhere for the way to Ogof Lowry. But it was as impossible to find as if it had been the cave of Ali Baba.

Quietly, but unmistakably, Anglesey kept defeating my expectations. Whenever I expected it to be like Cornwall, say, or Devon, or Northumberland—with well-marked coastal paths, quaint well-kept villages, enticing restaurants recommended by the *Good Food Guide*, dozens of stunning gardens open to the public—I was frustrated. Anglesey was different. It had a spirit and feeling of its own, best discovered by chance or fate.

We had our first real glimpse of that spirit on the day we drove to Beaumaris. This little town (population 2,100) was once Angelsey's chief port, and today it is a charming enclave of restored half-timbered Tudor buildings (like the Ye Olde Bull's Head Inn), Victorian and Edwardian terraces, a yacht-filled little harbor, and a massive yet stately thirteenth-century castle. But we best remember Beaumaris as our route to Penmon Priory.

In our travels around Britain, we are often drawn to monastic ruins, the remnants of Henry VIII's fierce attack on Catholic institutions. Medieval monasteries and priories were usually built on sites of great beauty, commanding a deep green valley, sheltering in the bend of a wooded river, or, like Penmon, looking proudly out to sea. (At Penmon, the sea was confined in the Menai Strait.) Most of these ruins still have an extraordinary ambience. Although they always make me feel that the age of faith departed a very long time ago, they offer a brief glimpse into the heart of silence.

Penmon Priory was only three miles from Beaumaris, but an off-and-on rain, falling lightly, discouraged us from a long walk. Instead we piloted our car slowly inland among narrow lanes, heading toward the tip of the peninsula until we could veer back toward the shore, park the car, scramble for half an hour along the vast shingle beach that stretches from Beaumaris, and arrive at the priory on foot.

Penmon, my guidebooks agreed, was one of Anglesey's holiest spots, traditionally the site of a Celtic monastery established around 540 by St. Seiriol. In the twelfth century, the present church was begun; in the thirteenth, a reorganized community of Augustinian priors added a range of monastic buildings. As we approached from the beach, we saw a complex of austere gray-stone structures, enclosed within high ivy-covered stone walls. One large building, the former canons' dining hall and dormitory, was roofless.

The church was locked, but two smaller buildings were open. One, a part-brick chamber, protected St. Seiriol's Well, a dark, still pool once thought to hold healing powers. Holy wells can be found in many parts of Britain, in use until the very recent past. I half-expected to see someone hobbling down the little path to the stone bench outside and take a seat to wait his turn at dabbling in the cold water.

The other building sharply reminded me of how, over the centuries, even the holiest places often become inextricably entwined with everyday life. Not far from the monastic buildings was a handsome, square dovecote with a vaulted dome roof, built around 1600 by the Bulkeleys, a local family who eventually acquired the church and its lands. Inside the dovecote, we could look up to an open cupola through which birds once flew in and out. A stone pillar with corbelled steps stood in the middle of the floor, enabling a servant to set a revolving ladder against the pillar and climb up to collect eggs from the one thousand nests in the high walls. During the long winter months, doves and pigeons also would have provided a critical source of fresh meat, so this impressive dovecote represented quite an enterprise.

Aside from a few birds flitting high above us, the dovecote was deserted. As we walked slowly back along the shingle beach toward our car, the Penmon buildings loomed behind us, now even darker and grayer as the rain grew heavier. I remembered from my guidebook that they were now technically part of a deer park, since the

Bulkeleys had turned Penmon into a walled deer preserve in the eighteenth century. A sixth-century saint, a twelfth-century church, a thirteenth-century monastery, a seventeenth-century dovecote, an eighteenth-century park: Penmon was like a timeline one could grasp and follow, hand over hand, back into the past.

In a way, Penmon unobtrusively prepared us for our other excursions into Anglesey's astonishingly long history. That history went back far beyond the Celts. All over the island we saw reminders of its earliest and little-understood civilizations: standing stones, passage graves, burial chambers. Although marked on our detailed Landranger map, they were never surrounded by any fanfare. When we searched out Bryn Celli Ddu ("The Mound in the Dark Grove"), a burial chamber that is the best-known prehistoric monument on the island, we discovered a grassy mound, rather like a small knobby hill, in the middle of a cleared field. (The "dark grove" had long disappeared.) It was encircled by a partially filled-in ditch and a ring of stones. Peering into its closed-off entrance, we could see a long dark passage. That was all.

What seemed so strange about Bryn Celli Ddu was how it simply appeared in the middle of a flat agricultural landscape. The road ran right by it, and it was part of a very ordinary farm. Aside from a few discreet signs and plaques, it demanded no attention. It was just there: mysterious, intriguing, silent.

In case anyone wants to know what *can* be known about such ancient sites, Cadw, or Welsh Historic Monuments, issues an explanatory guidebook for Anglesey. But even Cadw does not have many answers. What is anyone to make of this? "The excavations (at Bryn Celli Ddu) revealed a pit in which a fire had been lit and a human ear-bone placed at the bottom." Whose? Why? Why not two ear bones? No one knows.

Some of Anglesey's historic monuments were less baffling. At Din Lligwy, we walked through fields and a wood to reach a ruined dry-stone settlement that dated probably to the first and second centuries. This tiny walled village—it covered only half an acre— seemed reassuringly familiar. We could cross stone doorsteps and enter circular stone huts whose foundations, and even walls, were still partly intact. The huts, both houses and workshops, all opened sociably into a common courtyard. Because we could so easily envision some kind of daily life here, this second-century remnant seemed almost less distant in time than Penmon's thirteenth-century monastery.

Just a short walk from Din Lligwy, we paused at the ruined church of Hen Capel Lligwy, begun in the twelfth century and rebuilt in the fourteenth. (Centuries seem to pass with giddy swiftness in Anglesey.) It was a simple, unadorned structure, whose roofless gables pointed starkly up to the sky. But it looked over a dazzling view, past green meadows with grazing sheep, a few windblown trees at the crest of the hill, and then miles of sandy beach, sea, and sky at Lligwy Bay.

Sea views are never far away on Anglesey. When we decided to investigate Barclodiad y Gawres Burial Chamber, a huge reconstructed Neolithic mound, we found ourselves on a spectacular path that took us along rocky cliffs just above the ocean at Trecastell Bay. The path was more impressive, as I remember, than the rather too neatly restored tomb. Cadw's guidebook somewhat smugly reports that from examining the tiny bones in a sort of stew poured over a fire in the chamber, "we know [the stew] contained frog, toad, snake, mouse, hare, eel, wrasse and whiting." But what was the stew used for? Did anyone actually eat it? Cadw is forced to leave those frog and toad bones rattling in the visitor's imagination.

The relic from Anglesey's past I remember most vividly had no suggestive details for visitors to ponder, no explanatory plaques, indeed very little advertised history at all. In one guidebook I'd seen a stampsize picture of the ancient Church of St. Cwyfan, a shadowy outline on top of a very small walled island. Medieval churches on the sea are very special places. So one rare sunny day, on our way somewhere else, we took a spur-of-the-moment detour to try to find this church.

Turning off our road at Aberffraw, we followed a long, meandering, single-track lane past an occasional desolate-looking farmhouse and sparse fields to a small rocky cove. It felt so out-of-the-way that we were astonished to find a group of scattered teenagers there, wading in the shallows, poking under rocks, brandishing magnifying glasses, and writing in notebooks. They were on an excursion to gather specimens for a project in marine biology, one of them told us. As we watched them calling to one another, splashing about, laughing, and later sinking noisily onto the shore and opening their lunch bags, I thought that Anglesey must be an enviable place to go to school.

To reach the Church of St. Cwyfan, we had to pick our way very carefully over a narrow peninsula of rocks strewn with slippery seaweed. The causeway, only uncovered at low tide, was almost like a giant's pile of stepping-stones. At the end of this strip of rocks, marooned in the water, the little walled island looked rather like a high parapet that the giant's child might have raised in an afternoon. The island was only just big enough to hold the tiny church.

When we clambered up the stone steps hewn out of the parapet, I saw that all the windows of the church were broken. It was sad to think of its being abandoned for my guidebook had said that although this particular building, a plain, rugged, hutlike rectangle, dated back to the twelfth century (restored in 1893), the site had been used for worship for five hundred years before that. On rainy, blustery, or stormy days, people must have had to struggle very hard to reach this sea-tossed bit of land. When the winter storms were really severe, I could picture how the waves must have crashed over the stone walls.

But the church was not quite as abandoned as it seemed. Inside its stripped sanctuary was a homely wooden table that evidently still served as an altar. On the table was a simple wooden cross, and in front of it, carefully arranged, were a small bouquet of faded wildflowers, a bunch of tall seagrasses, and some shells and pebbles neatly laid out in the shape of another cross.

Not all our time on Anglesey was spent searching out abandoned or ruined medieval churches by the sea, or investigating prehistoric Celtic or Roman monuments. Anglesey has several other vaunted tourist attractions, including Beaumaris Castle, one of Edward III's most magnificent outposts; Anglesey Sea Zoo; and Plas Newydd, the grandest house on Anglesey, the family seat of the Marquesses of Anglesey. We peered dutifully and rather quickly at the first two but wandered at length through the rooms and gardens of the latter.

Now owned by the National Trust, Plas Newydd is an eighteenth-century mansion, part classical in style and part neo-Gothic, set on the shores of the Menai Strait. During our week on Anglesey, I kept repeating, like a mantra, wherever we went, "The views here would be incredible if only the clouds (or rain, or mist) would lift." Staring across the strait from the grounds of Plas Newydd, where the snow-capped mountains of Snowdonia would be silhouetted against the sky if I could only see them, I tried my mantra. It didn't work.

Perhaps partly because the Marquess of Anglesey and his family still occupy part of the house, Plas Newydd felt like a home, not a museum, whose well-lit rooms and sumptuous furnishings looked surprisingly comfortable. But what set Plas Newydd apart was a certain agreeable eccentricity. For a brief time in the 1930s, the house had a kind of resident artist. Rex Whistler, born in 1905 and killed in 1944 in Normandy, was a great family friend, and not only is part of Plas Newydd devoted to an exhibition of his work, but Whistler turned its once-staid dining room into a theatrical piece of art. (Rex Whistler is not to be confused with the painter James McNeill Whistler, famous for his so-called Whistler's Mother.)

A celebrated stage designer, Whistler painted a flamboyant trompe l'oeil mural on a fifty-eight-foot canvas, which was then glued to the dining room walls. The mural is a high-spirited pastiche of motifs, mostly chosen from architecture, ships, and the Snowdonia mountains visible (when one's mantra works) from the window. An architectural buff can spot, for example, the steeple of St. Martin-in-the-Fields, Trajan's Column, the Round Tower at Windsor, and a Roman church, all occupying the same imaginary landscape. Humorous asides—family in-jokes—abound, like the French bulldogs and a pug who belonged to Lady Anglesey's daughters. My favorite touch was an unobtrusive set of wet footprints padding up the steps from the sea—suggesting, as the house's brochure points out, "that the seagod himself had joined the family at the dinner table."

More theatre was provided in Plas Newydd by the fifth marquess, known as "Toppy" or the "Dancing Marquess," who died a bankrupt in Monte Carlo at the age of thirty. At the turn of the century, Toppy, who loved the theatre, turned the family chapel into a private theatre, dressed himself up for various gaudy roles, and squandered a fortune on jewels and furs. A wall of photographs celebrates this highly idiosyncratic marquess. In one, perched nonchalantly on a column, he wears a broad straw picture hat, a full-sleeved silky shirt with a long knot of pearls, striped mid-length pants, and polished dancing slippers.

Even the most staid exhibits at Plas Newydd, like those in the Cavalry Museum, turned out to have a touch of the bizarre. The First Marquess (1768–1854) was a companion of the Duke of Wellington. At the Battle of Waterloo, he reportedly said to the duke, "By God, sir, I've lost my leg!" Wellington's famous reply was, "By God, sir, so you have!" In the Cavalry Museum, one can view a sprig of willow from the tree under whose shade the leg was buried with military honors. But the pride of the exhibit is one of the artificial limbs designed for the marquess, the world's first articulated wooden leg, still known as a type called "the Anglesey leg." (This is the kind of bemusing information I always think might someday come in handy.)

Since rain, mist, and thick clouds hid so much of Anglesey during our stay, when early-morning sunshine did sparkle through our bedroom skylight, we hurried through breakfast and headed for the beach. Anglesey's little ports, seaside villages, and vast sandy beaches attract so few visitors, even in July, we often had long stretches of sea and sky all to ourselves. (The Labour Party might hold its convention in Blackpool, but never in Benllech.)

On the late morning when James and I drove in first gear down a precipitous road and emerged on Traeth-coch (Red Wharf Bay), my first thought was that I had never seen such an expanse of gleaming, inviting sand. The beach was so long and so wide, more than ten square miles at low tide, I had to squint to catch a glint of bright blue ocean at its far edge. Shining ribbons of water, left by the retreating tide, laced the golden sand.

The sun was hot, the sand was irresistible, and in minutes James and I were both dangling our shoes in our hands. For more than an hour we paddled barefoot in the shallows, letting the surprisingly warm water slosh up to our ankles. The shallows seemed to stretch out for miles. We sometimes had to detour around dark barnacle-covered rocks that broke the sweep of sand, and we forded a few wandering, deep channels that suddenly appeared before our feet, but mostly we just walked on and on in a kind of sun-induced daze.

As we approached Benllech—with a modest population of 3,000, it is considered one of Anglesey's busiest resorts—a few children were happily flailing about in waist-high water, and some bright beach umbrellas arose from the sand like a sprinkle of bright flowers. The beach did not look at all crowded. Looking up at the headlands enclosing the wide bay, I could see fields and pastures only as a blur of green, striped and patched with woods in a darker green. Any signs of civilization simply melted away into all this green and blue.

If I had to pick a favorite beach on Anglesey, it would probably be the one at Llanddwyn, near a spot sacred to the patron saint of lovers. Like many other wonderful places on this reclusive island, Llanddwyn Bay hides itself from public view. From Nwbwrch (Newborough), we looked for signs to Newborough Forest, a pine plantation whose regimented trees offer a kind of plainclothes disguise to the stunning beach and peninsula that lie beyond them. Once we emerged from the rather boring piney blackness of the forest, we found ourselves in a large parking lot. This, too, seemed unpromising.

But as soon as we walked through a ripple of dunes, we were on a hard-packed sandy beach that, like Red Wharf's, seemed almost impossibly long and wide. The dunes were part of Newborough Warren, a nature reserve of 1,500 acres, where rabbits still peep out of their burrows in the protected low, sandy hills. For once we could also appreciate Anglesey's famed views. In brilliant sunshine we looked across the water to the jagged peaks of Snowdonia, softened by distant blue haze. With their shadowy forms and crenelated outlines, they might have been an abstract stage set, a dramatic background for the much more muted, subtle scenery of Anglesey.

As the sandy beach curved around the bay, it led toward a little peninsula crowned by a white lighthouse. James and I began walking toward the peninsula, very slowly, so we could try to take in the panoramic views. A few people must have been somewhere on the beach that afternoon, but I cannot remember them. My snapshots show only tumbled dunes, a dizzying sheen of sand, a white line of gently breaking water, and a backdrop of blue mountains.

When the beach ended, we then followed a path along the narrow rocky spine of the peninsula, through seagrasses and wildflowers, past little coves and smaller strips of sand. A sleek sailboat was moored in one cove. On one side, we looked back at the long, sheltered beach, and on the other, we could see the rolling breakers of Malltraeth Bay. The vistas of sand and water were so beguiling that we finally sank down on a grassy patch and sat, just looking. A soft breeze blew in from the sea, ruffling our hair and making me turn up the collar on my light jacket. Then we lay back, put our hats over our faces, and let the sun lull us into a short nap.

When, a little later, we bestirred ourselves to continue slowly along the lighthouse path, we stopped again to ponder the ruins of a Tudor church with both a large Latin and a Celtic cross. The church and crosses marked the peninsula (known somewhat misleadingly as Llanddwyn Island) as a holy site, where St. Dwynwen once founded a chapel. She is traditionally revered by Welsh lovers, who sometimes exchange cards on St. Dwynwen's Day, January 25, rather than Valentine's Day.

But St. Dwynwen's story sounded rather chilling to me. Dwynwen ("Dwyn the Pure") was supposedly a beautiful princess in twelfth-century Wales. She was deeply in love with a young man named Maelon, but her father had sworn she would marry someone else. So dutiful Dwynwen prayed for release from her love, and an angel obliged, proffering her an enchanted potion. The potion not only destroyed her passion but also turned poor Maelon into a block of ice. Then, rather handily given three subsequent wishes, Dwynwen arranged to have Maelon thawed out, secured her freedom from marriage to anyone, and requested that she should become the patron saint of lovers.

That was like Anglesey, I thought. You read that a certain place is sacred to romance, and then you find that its tutelary saint froze her lover and turned her back on marriage. So much for preconceptions. But Llanddwyn Island itself was certainly no disappointment. I had found it magical, the kind of place where, on a glorious sunny July afternoon, you could curl up next to your dozing husband in a little nest of dune grass, catch a whiff of salt in a lingering sea breeze, listen to waves breaking on a deserted beach, and think how blessed you really are.

Anywhere but Anglesey, it might be a long way from a saint's island to a circus tent. But on the afternoon following our visit to Llanddwyn, we were in ringside seats under a canvas tent, among excited children, balloons, and pink spun-sugar cones, while we all watched trained seals balance beach balls on their noses. Although I plan many of our days, I think of our afternoon at the Chipperfield Circus as part of traveler's luck (or Anglesey's magic). One day, driving by the Anglesey Showground near Mona, I noticed a tent and circus posters. So off we went.

Although many years ago I took my young daughter to a mammoth three-ring circus in a Minneapolis auditorium, I had not sat under a big top in a grassy field since I was a very little girl. The scale of this small circus was just right. We were only a few feet from the ring, and the lively four-person orchestra belting out amplified show tunes filled the tent with music. A team of superb young acrobats balanced and somersaulted, and in another act, they reappeared and climbed to trapezes. A pretty girl in spangles rode one of her parading Arabians and then, later in the bill, swung in a ring high above us. The dapper ringmaster, in a spiffy tuxedo, kept up a seamless running commentary that sounded as if he'd memorized all the old circus movies ever made.

Trainers showed off not only performing seals but also African elephants and, in a tour de force of light whip-flicking, five roaring tigers. I had never been so close to Bengal tigers—they were confined in a collapsible barred cage with a huge net suspended over it that could be dropped in case of emergency. (The various riggings of the tent, changed in a twinkling for different acts, were almost as fascinating as the acts.) All around us, small children, their mouths open, stared in awe and clapped wildly. As a child, I never questioned such a use of wild animals. Now, caught up in the thrills and gaiety of the circus, I must shamefacedly report that I applauded, too.

The rain had stopped by the time we left the tent for home. Half an hour later, as we bumped our way along the overgrown track to Clegir Mawr, tigers, spangles, and spun sugar seemed to belong to a different world. Below us, a distant farmer was moving his sheep from one field to another. In the still evening air we could hear a faint bleating. Beyond the field a fog was closing down over the sea like a gauze curtain. "And tomorrow?" James asked. "What shall we do tomorrow?" I shook my head. I wasn't sure. Anglesey would provide its own surprises.

A FEW FLOATING FACTS

For information on how to rent Clegir Mawr, and more than two hundred other holiday cottages owned by the National Trust, see the note at the end of Chapter 15, "A Beacon on the Cornish Coast."

IV

*Beyond Piccadilly:
Favorite Places*

18

A Modernist Castle in Dartmoor

Anyone brought up on fairy tales has a weakness for castles. When James and I travel around Britain, I often ask him to make unlikely detours so we can visit one. While some, like Arundel, Chiddingstone, or Alnwick, are still lavishly furnished homes, many more are vacant shells or shattered heaps of stone. Since James is a modernist architect, he is less interested in tramping over grassy ruins than in exploring extant buildings. But when we discovered Castle Drogo, near Drewsteignton at the edge of Dartmoor in Devon, we found a castle we could both love.

Hidden at the end of a long moorland drive and approached only by a series of narrow, winding, and high-hedged lanes, Castle Drogo is the last grand castle built in England. It is not, however, a moldering medieval ruin. Completed in 1930, after twenty years of construction, Castle Drogo is a modern masterpiece designed by Edwin Lutyens (1869–1944), who is often considered the greatest of English twentieth-century architects.

We first came to Castle Drogo several years ago mainly to visit its celebrated gardens, awarded two stars—the highest rating—in our trusted *Good Gardens Guide*. But when we saw the austere, monumental walls of the granite castle rising above the Dartmoor skyline, we realized we had much more than a great garden to explore. Each subsequent visit to Castle Drogo has increased our acquaintance and pleasure with Lutyens's genius.

Lutyens designed Castle Drogo for Julius Drewe, who made a fortune beginning as a tea importer—his shops helped turn the British market for tea from China to India—and then founding the Home and Colonial Stores. By 1889, when he was only thirty-three, Drewe was able to retire and to fulfill his dream of building a country seat. After some research, he concluded that he was a descendant of a Norman baron whose line had named the twelfth-century parish of Drewsteignton. Julius Drewe wanted a medieval castle in that very parish.

As a visitor approaches the west front of Castle Drogo, Drewe's seriousness of purpose is apparent. This is not a toy castle. The walls are solid granite, up to six feet thick. The two front turrets have jagged parapets with arrow slits, and the door below has an actual portcullis that works, with chains and winches. Above it struts a carved heraldic lion, complete with Latin motto. On either side, the building stretches out, with wings, towers, and more granite walls with impressive mullioned windows, commanding the rocky outcrop on which it stands.

Lutyens once hoped to raise an even more magnificent structure, according to plans and sketches on display at Castle Drogo. In a bravura gesture, he arranged a full-size wooden and tarpaulin mockup (recorded in a 1913 photograph), but his scheme was reduced by two-thirds. Even so, the building took twenty years to complete. As a visitor walks around Castle Drogo today, it is almost impossible to imagine that the castle might have been still more awesome.

Yet despite its scale and panache, Castle Drogo is not a daunting building. Its lines are spare and elegant, a smooth undulation of granite walls whose only ornamentations are the masterfully cut, clean stone and the banks of multipaned windows. The roughly textured blocks of granite glow in sunlight with a mellow color that varies from golden to grayish brown.

Inside, the castle remains a framework of pristine simplicity, with granite walls left unplastered in the main halls, staircases, and most interior spaces. But Lutyens has also managed to create a feeling of airiness, mainly from light flooding through all those mullioned windows. The grand staircase that leads from the front hall down to the dining room is a triumphant processional space between imposing clifflike granite walls, yet an enormous window, breaking the expanse of stone, looks out upon the green wildness of Dartmoor.

Furnished with an eclectic assortment of period furniture, hung with tapestries and carpeted with Persian rugs, the rooms in Castle Drogo are surprisingly livable. Lutyens made sure that the castle would be a welcoming home, from the green-stippled wood paneling and Venetian chandeliers in the drawing room to the glass-fronted cupboards, armchairs, and Bechstein piano in Mrs. Drewe's sitting room.

The first twentieth-century house to be acquired by the National Trust, Castle Drogo is in some ways a furnished museum, showing a vanished way of life, as led seventy or eighty years ago by a wealthy, newly established landowner. (By his death in 1931, Drewe had acquired an estate of 1,500 acres.) Part of the fun in wandering through Drewe's castle is trying to imagine what it might have been like to order tea in the oak-beamed library, in front of its vast fireplace, or take a turn at the ponderous billiard table in the adjoining alcove. I particularly fancied ablutions in the well-lit, mullioned bathroom, in which Lutyens designed stepped granite window seats, handy for towels and robe, or, perhaps, for an intimate if stone-cold bathside chat.

The fittings of Castle Drogo are decidedly not medieval. The shower-bathtub is a late Victorian extravaganza, with five gleaming chrome taps for the bath and an elaborate shower enclosure that sprays from side pinholes as well as from an enormous overhead disk. In the dining room, the table is set with fine china and crystal on damask, underlaid by an odd electric contraption, a cloth with little connections for lighting candlesticks. A guidebook notes that dinner often lasted for two hours. Eyeing the tabletop electric plugs, I thought of all the excitement an inventive, bored child could cause if those hours stretched out too long.

Working in Castle Drogo must have had its compensations, for Lutyens did not stint on the service quarters. The granite-walled kitchen, although on a lower level, is lit by a large circular lantern in its domed roof. Lutyens designed all the furniture—tables, teak drainboards, oak-framed sinks, cupboards, even pastry boards—for kitchen, pantry, scullery, and larder. Unified in their simple but meticulous design, all these rooms (free, in their museumlike state, of any cooking mess or odors) seem more like culinary temples than belowstairs workrooms.

Although it would be easy to idealize life at Castle Drogo, the house holds a poignant reminder that even the Drewes were not entirely fortunate. One small room is a shrine to Adrian, the Drewes' eldest son, who was killed in 1917 in Flanders during World War I. "This kind of family memorial was once common," notes the Castle Drogo brochure, "but today this room is a rare and touching survival." Surrounded by school pictures, athletic souvenirs, and other mementos, a full-length oil portrait of Adrian in uniform dominates the room. He is a sober, slender, and very young man. Facing each other in a silver dual frame are pictures of Adrian and an unnamed beautiful young woman, who, a National Trust volunteer told me, had been his fiancée.

If the past seems memorialized inside Castle Drogo, its gardens, in which both Lutyens and his old collaborator, famed garden-designer Gertrude Jekyll, had some hand, are vividly alive in the present. On a sunny summer day, they are filled—though seldom crowded—with visitors who move slowly up and down a series of terraced beds and lawns. Crisply trimmed yew hedges and a rigorously straight central path with granite steps give the garden symmetry and formality, allying it to the nearby castle. But the stone-edged perennial borders are bursting with flowers to the point of abandon, mainly old-fashioned favorites like lupines, campanulas, delphiniums, and hollyhocks.

Even the garden has its surprises. At the top of the terraces, an enormous close-clipped croquet lawn, almost abstract in its simplicity, is ringed by a high yew hedge. (Upon application at the National Trust reception center, visitors can arrange to hire equipment and play the most refined croquet game of their lives.)

At the other end of the gardens, another majestic yew hedge, cut like a gate, acts as an entrance into a very different world. A terraced walkway, eventually leading toward the castle, overlooks the wild woods and heathland of the River Teign valley. Stunning views from the castle front terrace (and from many castle windows) open out upon the expanses of Dartmoor and its rocky, open moorland.

Public footpaths and bridleways cross the Castle Drogo estate, with access to most parts encouraged by the National Trust. Each visit James and I plan to spend plenty of time on those paths, but last summer, as always, we only managed a tentative beginning. We still become too absorbed in Castle Drogo itself, a modernist castle with a luxuriously preserved past.

A FEW FLOATING FACTS

Castle Drogo is located five miles south of the A30 Exeter-Okehampton road, near Drewsteignton. It can also be reached by DevonBus 359 from Exeter.

The castle is open from April 1 to October 31, daily except Friday, 11 A.M. to 5:30 P.M., the garden from 10:30 to 5:30. A licensed restaurant is open at the castle from noon to 5:30, and a tearoom on the grounds is open from 10:30 to 5:30. Telephone 0164-743-3306 for further information. Admission is charged.

19

Touring England's Ark

*I*t all began with a secondhand copy of *Down Among the Donkeys*, a memoir whose intriguing title caught my eye in an outdoor London bookstall. Picking up the memoir, I quickly became immersed in Elisabeth Svendsen's lively narrative of her lifelong passion for donkeys, which led eventually to her founding a sanctuary near Sidmouth, Devon, a small coastal resort in England's beguiling West Country. I knew little about donkeys, but I was suddenly curious. A donkey sanctuary? What would it be like?

Since James and I were about to leave London for Cornwall, I consulted my map. The Donkey Sanctuary was not only directly on our route, but it was also within a few hours' drive of the Tamar Otter Park at North Petherwin, Cornwall, and the Cornish Seal Sanctuary at Gweek. We had a tempting opportunity to witness in action one of the most famous English obsessions, their love of animals.

Anyone who travels in England quickly learns how most people feel about animals. When I walk into a crowded pub or even a fancy restaurant, I always look carefully at my feet, lest I tread on the protruding paws or gently waving tail of someone's golden retriever or Jack Russell. As we drive through the countryside, I relish the signs advertising what Americans call a prosaic *cattery*. The English dream up much more alluring labels: OAK MANOR: CAT HOTEL or FERNDALE: CATS' HOLIDAY HOME. Daring or poignant rescues by the

Royal Society for the Prevention of Cruelty to Animals appear in daily newspapers as often as dispatches from a battlefront—which, given the current furor to repeal blood sports like fox hunting, the countryside sometimes resembles.

Since James and I have always cherished our own pets (currently two cats, as yet deprived of visits to a cats' holiday home), we find this English passion quite congenial. Although James, who often brings a needed dose of reality to our travels, wondered whether we might not be wasting time at a children's tourist attraction, perhaps a carnival-like place that offered donkey rides, he, too, was curious.

When we arrived at the Donkey Sanctuary on a damp, cool morning last July, what surprised me first was its splendid location. Occupying the former Slade House Farm, the sanctuary nestles among sloping fields that run down to the sea. Some donkeys drift over green pastures, while others are tended in barns and in special-care facilities. The buildings are spacious and well kept, gardens (donated by benefactors) edge the walkways, and roses even grow over an arbor that leads to the public toilets.

Stopping at the well-stocked information center, we quickly began to learn about donkeys, both in England and abroad. (The sanctuary sets up clinics and mobile treatment centers in many other countries.) When treated well, Ms. Svendsen promises, donkeys are devoted and affectionate pets. So, walking through a pen holding geriatric donkeys, I paid dutiful attention to an inviting sign—DONKEYS LOVE A CUDDLE—and managed my first tentative donkey squeeze.

Since a soaking rain was falling that morning, we only walked by a few of the pastures. They held donkeys of all sizes and colors— smooth, shaggy, white, brown, black, piebald—but did not seem at all crowded. This relative scarcity of donkeys is deceptive. When Svendsen began caring for donkeys—"Why donkeys?" she writes. "I must be asked this by almost everyone I meet and even now I can't really give them a straightforward answer."—she could not have known what lay ahead.

Since its start as an organized charity in 1973, the sanctuary has now taken into care more than 6,000 donkeys, guaranteeing them veterinary care and attention for the rest of their lives. Only about 630 are housed on the 236 acres of Slade House Farm. With a full-time staff of 160, the sanctuary has gradually expanded to a total of nine farms with more than 1,300 acres.

Other donkey havens exist elsewhere in England, but, according to a recent newsletter of the Donkey Sanctuary, this is the largest charity in the United Kingdom dealing specifically with donkeys and mules. It is also probably the best known. We did not personally meet Svendsen (who holds an honorary degree in veterinary medicine, as well as a royal M.B.E., Mistress of the British Empire), but from pictures, video, and publications, not to mention the book that had first caught my attention, we could see that she has the gift of conveying her enthusiasm to a wide public.

Some of the Sidmouth sanctuary's most important work takes place indoors, not just in its fully equipped hospital but also in the facilities of the Slade Centre. There, for twenty years, handicapped children have been encouraged to make friends with specially trained donkeys. The Slade Centre holds a riding ring, a cheerful playroom, and an outdoor play area with brightly colored equipment for these children. Up to two hundred of them can come to the center each week.

Impressed by the scope and determination of Svendsen's enterprise, I found myself lingering in the sanctuary's gift shop so that I could browse among its many offerings, including children's books about donkeys by Svendsen and her second illustrated memoir, *For the Love of Donkeys* (1992). The shop also sells many donkey souvenirs, such as calendars, stationery, coloring books, postcards, Christmas cards, prints, and posters. Like the rest of the sanctuary, the shop is a heartfelt celebration of donkeys.

Finding the Tamar Otter Park requires a certain amount of sleuthing. I first noticed its general location when I was studying a tourist map of Cornwall. On a minor road near North Petherwin, a village northeast of Launceston, Cornwall, the otter park is tucked away in a tranquil, wooded valley next to a stream called Boles-bridge Water. Compact and modest, with only a few structures—on our visit, three breeding enclosures for British otters, two for Asian short-clawed otters, and a tidy visitor center with tearoom—the park is a branch of the larger Otter Trust, a registered charity, at Earsham in Suffolk.

Since the British otter has declined in numbers as the result of modern farming methods and loss of habitat, the Otter Trust hopes to breed enough otters to reintroduce them into the wild in many different parts of England. According to the Trust, otters still thrive in the wild in Devon and Cornwall and a few other places, but a traveler rarely sees these elusive and enchanting creatures. In more than a dozen trips to the West Country, James and I had yet to glimpse a single one.

It does not take long to tour the otter park, but modest size has some advantages. Because the pens were relatively small, we could watch otters from a few feet away. Three European otters, all siblings then a year old, frolicked in the water, rolled on the grass under the bright warm sun, tussled and slid over one another, and finally fell asleep in a heap. But we cherished most our visit to the interior enclosure for British otters, where, standing in a darkened porch, we were able to look down through a glass top and quietly observe, only inches away, a sleeping mother otter curled protectively around her weeks-old cub.

Besides otters, the North Petherwin sanctuary protects several small marshy lakes filled with waterfowl. Screaming peafowl, pheasants, and wallabies also wander the grounds. After duly admiring two peacocks in full display, we left the main cleared area for a long walk into Wild Wood. This section of the park covers some twenty acres of unspoiled woodland, including an abandoned quarry whose walls are now a damp, vine-hung jungle.

Lurking in the dappled shadows along the path were small herds of Chinese water deer, muntjac or barking deer, and fallow deer. We also passed several aviaries for breeding British owls (an introduction that prepared us for a later adventure). Although now accustomed to being surrounded by wildlife, I was nevertheless startled to look up a hillside at three immobile badgers, who, I knew, are ordinarily shy nocturnal animals. It took me several minutes to realize they were carefully painted replicas, placed in the underbrush to indicate the location of a badger "sett."

If the Tamar Otter Park is modest and appealing, the Cornish Seal Sanctuary at Gweek is almost glitzy. Widely advertised as a tourist attraction, the Gweek sanctuary, in a tiny village about six miles from Helston near the tip of England's southwest peninsula, is Europe's largest rescue center for seals. Its site is spectacular, along the wooded banks of the unspoiled Helston River estuary, a haven for yachts and sailboats.

The seal sanctuary proved even harder for us to find than the otter park. Although we carefully followed all the signs, they seemed to lead us in circles. The notice of GWEEK, 5 MILES would be followed every half mile by another sign, also blithely promising GWEEK, 5 MILES, or, more disheartening, GWEEK, 6 MILES. Now part of our family lingo is the line, "Just as easy to get to as Gweek!" But we kept trying—backing up, returning to the last crossroads, muttering, and trying yet another route—and we finally arrived.

After viewing an interpretive center, which included displays about marine life and an audiovisual show, we walked first to the seal hospital. Its gleaming tile cubicles were now almost deserted, because in midsummer seal pups can't be rescued for release onto crowded beaches. Usually as many as thirty pups are taken in each year, treated, and freed, if possible. Those who are severely disabled are provided permanent homes.

Following a shady walk along the estuary, we soon arrived at the most popular part of the sanctuary, the outdoor pools that overlook a broad sweep of the Helston and the rolling green fields beyond. Divided into nursery, rehabilitation, convalescent, and resident sections, the pools are filled with gray seals and enormous sea lions. On the afternoon we visited, several large school parties of excited children were crowding against the fence to watch the antics of the animals as they awaited their feeding.

Although its many visitors, ice cream stalls, tourist tram, and bustling souvenir shop give the seal sanctuary rather the air of an amusement park, the place is clearly run with intense devotion. The keeper who provided a running commentary as she tossed fish to the seals and sea lions mentioned, for example, that resident Rocky, blind from inoperable cataracts, was so lonely that the sanctuary searched worldwide and eventually imported two appropriate female companions, Ursa and Papper, all the way from Cape Cod.

Notice boards, which advertise donors who "sponsor" specific animals, provide other evidence of such concern. In front of one pen, a sign explained: "Magnus is our largest male, and he is also the most disagreeable. . . . Jenny is our steadiest and strongest female and therefore seemed the ideal grey seal to keep Magnus company." Both Magnus and Jenny remained soundly asleep, eyes closed and flippers up, despite all the hubbub around them, perhaps attesting to the success of this careful matchmaking. Other notice boards explained the seals' and sea lions' histories, ailments, and current status.

After leaving the seal sanctuary, we thought we had completed our tour of these modern British arks. But several days later, on a side road not far from Lanhydrock House near Bodmin, we noticed a tacked-up sign directing us to SCREECH OWL SANCTUARY. Turning down a narrow, rough drive, we quickly found ourselves at Rew Farm, a haven for owls started in 1991. The sanctuary did not harbor screech owls, a North American subspecies, but it carried the serendipitous name of the owners, Tom and Carolyn Screech.

Registered as a charitable trust in May 1993, the owl sanctuary was an informal, homespun affair, with voluntary helpers and a handful of somewhat makeshift cages. (Since our visit, the sanctuary has moved to new and larger quarters at Trewin Farm, Gossmoor, St. Columb, not far from Bodmin.) Three large owls were tethered on a bit of lawn. But passion was present here, too. Clive, a young man donating his time to the sanctuary, showed us around (we were the only visitors) and introduced us to the owls, like Charlie, a "rather crochety" European eagle owl.

As he talked, a little eight-inch Athene Noctua owl, a special pet of Clive's, clung to his sweater. We also met, among others, Indiana, a Bengal eagle owl; Rupert, a rare Siberian eagle owl; and Donald, a gray-faced tawny owl from Scotland, who somehow smuggled himself into a helicopter there, landed at Culdrose Air Force Base in Cornwall, hit a rotor blade, and broke his leg, a fracture so severe he can never hunt in the wild again.

According to Clive, the sanctuary routinely deals with tawny owls who are missing a leg, an eye, or part of a wing. They are injured, he explained, because they hunt by sound; diving upon their prey, while honing in on just the right frequency, they are temporarily blind and neither see nor hear approaching cars. Neighbors also bring disabled jackdaws, crows, pigeons, and even buzzards to the farm for help.

Besides collecting unusual owls and tending injured ones, the Screech Owl Sanctuary has the beginnings of a breeding program. Another volunteer took us into a shed so we could glimpse several three-week-old barn owls hatched in an incubator. It was hard to imagine that these tiny cream-colored balls of fluff would someday become as impressive as, say, Charlie, who moments before had spread his wings for us in a whirring flash of power.

When we reluctantly left the Screech Owl Sanctuary that afternoon, I hoped I would remember the incredibly soft plumage of a tame owl I'd been allowed to stroke. I knew I would not forget the devoted work and single-minded focus of all the sanctuaries, comforting havens of preservation in a world too prone instead to wanton destruction.

A FEW FLOATING FACTS

Although it would be possible to visit these animal sanctuaries by a combination of public transport and taxi or walking (train or bus to the nearest large town, then either taxi or a local bus), I recommend a rental car for anyone on a schedule. (See "How to Be Your Own Travel Agent" in England As You Like It *for extensive advice on car rentals in En-*

gland.) *Buses to small towns like Gweek are intermittent, and taxis are
expensive.*

*The Donkey Sanctuary, Slade House Farm, Sidmouth, Devon, is
open every day of the year, 9 A.M. to dusk. Admission is free. Telephone
0139-557-8222. A picnic area is available in the car park; a kiosk there
sells ice cream, drinks, and snacks in season.*

*The Tamar Otter Park, North Petherwin, near Launceston, Corn-
wall, is open daily, 10:30 A.M. to 6 P.M. from April 1 to October 1.
Admission is charged. Telephone 01566-785646. Light lunches, teas,
and other refreshments are available in the tearoom.*

*The Cornish Seal Sanctuary at Gweek, Cornwall, is open from
9 A.M. every day (except Christmas). Admission is charged. Telephone
0132-622-1361. A cafeteria serves snacks; an open-air barbecue offers
burgers and hot dogs.*

*The Screech Owl Sanctuary at Trewin Farm, Gossmoor, St. Columb,
near Indian Queens, Cornwall, is open 10 A.M. to 6 P.M. seven days
a week. Admission is free, but donations are welcome. Phone 0172-
686-0182.*

20

A Fresh Wind at
Groombridge Place

S tanding in front of the wide moat at Groombridge Place, a
handsome seventeenth-century manor near Tunbridge Wells,
I stopped to admire the reflection of mellow redbrick walls and
chimney stacks in the dark, mirrorlike water. I had paused in front
of the Priest's House, a small gabled extension jutting into the moat.
Glancing up at its second-floor window, I suddenly gave a startled
cry. One of the leaded casements was open, and staring out at me
was a huge gray face—at least twice the size of a human one—
impassive and disconcertingly blind.

In a moment, I realized that the disembodied, half-obscured face
looming out of the darkness belonged to a monumental stone head.
I had not noticed a small notice board just a few feet from me, one
of several that unobtrusively turn up here and there at Groombridge. The sign revealed that the Priest's House, a former chapel,
was now dedicated to the goddess Diana and her peacocks. Diana, I
saw, was keeping an ominous silent watch on visitors.

Her peacocks, I quickly discovered, were not so silent. They
seemed to be everywhere, strutting, preening, sometimes spreading
their flamboyant plumage, and frequently screeching from unseen
cover with unnerving effect. Their eerie cries added just the right
touch to the goings-on at Groombridge, recently transformed, with
more than a whiff of English whimsy, into Groombridge Place Gardens and Enchanted Forest. (An earlier Enchanted Forest, the fic-

tional home of Winnie-the-Pooh, is only a few miles away, in Ashdown Forest near Hartfield, A. A. Milne's former home. (See "Ashdown Forest: Pooh Country" in *England As You Like It*.)

Most country houses in England open to tourists exude an air of grandeur, complacency, even a certain pomposity. They seem to be deliberately frozen in the past. Groombridge, which has as venerable a heritage as any—dating back originally to a thirteenth-century castle, of which now only the moat remains—is quite different. It is a fascinating work of art in progress.

Although its current owner, Andrew de Candole, who came here only in 1992, hopes to open the house (currently under restoration) to the public, he is now concentrating on turning its surroundings, both gardens and woodland, into a combination of historic formal gardens, park, and fanciful pleasure grounds.

Mr. de Candole is making no small plans. A "Millennium Project" at Groombridge promises to provide a showcase for the best work of British garden designers, including Myles Challis, Ivan Hicks, and others. Other attractions at Groombridge include a branch of the Raptor Centre, a sanctuary for birds of prey, which offers a display of specially trained birds at rest and in flight, as well as daylong courses.

When James and I arrived at Groombridge just as it opened for its second year, we first emerged into the Drunken Garden, so named for the oddly twisted topiary that stand like misshapen sentinels on a green lawn. No one seems to know just why these trees acquired their lurching forms. According to a Groombridge gardener, they may once have been formal topiary whose trimming was long neglected until their original shapes were lost. Their effect, accidental as it may have been, is uncanny.

The Drunken Garden is also part of the brooding backdrop of Arthur Conan Doyle's mystery, *The Valley of Fear*, in which Sherlock Holmes finds an important clue dropped in Groombridge's opaque moat. "As I looked at the deep-set windows and the long sweep of the dull-covered, water-lapped front," says Dr. Watson, "I felt that no more fitting scene could be set for such a tragedy. . . . I took a stroll in the curious old-world garden which flanked the house. Rows of very ancient yew trees cut into strange designs girded it round."

Groombridge's subtly mysterious atmosphere also attracted the filmmaker Peter Greenaway, who used it as the seventeenth-century setting for *The Draughtsman's Contract* (1982), a murky and disturbing thriller starring Janet Suzman and Anthony Higgins. (Videotapes are sold at the gift shop, but British VHS does not correspond to ours; once home, we had to jettison the tape, but we easily rented another instead.)

Groombridge had many unsettling moments. In the midst of the Parterre Garden, whose intricate knots of newly planted box were only inches high, a man and a woman lounged casually on a stone bench. Glimpsed out of the corner of my eye, they looked somehow a little disconcerting. When I turned to look more closely, I realized that they were larger-than-life twig sculptures. They seemed as much at home in this curious garden as its ancient elements—for instance, the only remaining apple tree from Elizabethan times, which had a surprising green mistletoe springing from its bare gnarled branches. The mistletoe, we learned, had been grafted onto the apple tree in Victorian times.

Not far from the twiggy couple, another couple—this one very much alive—was poised over a giant marble black-and-white chessboard sunk into the lawn. Moving from square to square, they were just completing a game played with enormous wooden chessmen. As the young man lifted a knee-high castle and removed it from the board, he smiled triumphantly at the young woman. She grimaced and laughed. The game, he told us, had been going on for two hours. Minutes later, we saw them walk off, arms around each other, heading toward the Secret Garden—a small space hidden from view behind tall hedges.

The formal walled gardens near the house are only the beginning of many enchantments at Groombridge Place. A long walk leads along a canal behind the house, past newly planted estate vineyards, to a series of stepped pools below a centuries-old spring. (In the summer season, a small motorized boat ferries passengers along the canal.) Once used for smelting iron ore, the pools were buried and forgotten for hundreds of years. Now the watercourse is gradually being uncovered and developed. Following the stream downhill on a zigzagging path, visitors can walk past iris and primrose, crossing the pools on stepping-stones and listening to the music of the rippling water.

At the top of the hill lies the Enchanted Forest, a woodland with paths we did not have time to explore that late afternoon. But the entrance to the forest was seductive. What seemed like dozens of wind chimes hung in the surrounding trees, softly ringing in a pleasing contrapuntal harmony. It sounded like a chorus of distant woodland voices, beckoning us in.

Here, at the edge of the Enchanted Forest, I was caught once more by the unexpected. Gazing idly around at the surrounding trees, I found myself staring at another enigmatic stone face—this one embedded in the trunk of a large tree. The bark had been only partially cut away, hiding part of the face and one eye. The effect was riveting, as if an expressionless giant were imprisoned inside the trunk, staring out.

As we walked slowly back to the manor and our parked car, we stopped several times at benches placed along the hillside. The view over the blooming Kent countryside was bucolic, past the new vineyard, across fields to the canal, beyond pastures to the River Grom and scattered woods. Clouds of hazy white blossoms from wild hawthorn hung in the distant air.

This, I thought, is the traditional view of England, a heritage in which Groombridge Place Gardens certainly intends to preserve a distinguished place, with its restored walled gardens, protected ancient trees, close-cut formal lawns, and tranquil medieval moat. But another perspective was also possible. Behind us, a stone face peeped eerily from a tree trunk, while wind chimes played overhead; not far away, a man and woman made of twigs sat casually on the manor lawn; a young couple moved gaily among giant chessmen; a startling Diana guarded her moat. I liked this Groombridge Place Gardens, too.

A FEW FLOATING FACTS

Groombridge Place Gardens (telephone 0189-286-3999) is open 10 A.M. to 6 P.M. daily. Admission is charged. It is located on the B2110, just off the A264, four miles southwest of Royal Tunbridge Wells and nine miles east of East Grinstead, about fifteen miles from Gatwick Airport. It is about a seventy-five-minute drive from London.

21

At Home in Cloth Fair

As a longtime London visitor who revels in the city's hand-some residential squares, spacious green parks, and bustling shopping streets, I never thought I'd find myself in love with a London neighborhood bounded by a hospital, a high-rise complex, and a wholesale meat market. But for several years now, James and I have eagerly returned for stays of a week or two to a rented flat in Cloth Fair, a tiny hidden street not far from St. Paul's Cathedral. Here, in the oldest part of London, we have explored corners of the city many tourists never see.

We were lured to the City, the mainly financial sector of London, by an unusual chance to stay in a distinctive flat formerly owned by a poet and lover of architecture. Sir John Betjeman (1906–1984), once poet laureate and also known for his enthusiastic appraisals of England's architectural heritage, lived for many years at 43 Cloth Fair.

This short but fascinating street has a long history. A few yards away sprawls St. Bartholomew's Hospital, a venerable mishmash of buildings, courtyards, and pedestrian precincts. "Bart's," as Londoners affectionately call their oldest hospital—fierce protests greeted the Tories' recent decision to close it—was once part of the medieval Priory and Hospital of St. Bartholomew.

The priory held the right to stage an annual fair on the feast of their namesake, and by Elizabethan times this fair was one of the great events of London. (It is vividly depicted in Ben Jonson's rollicking comedy, *Bartholomew Fair* [1614], still occasionally performed.) Although the fair eventually attracted many different participants, the first were members of the nearby cloth trade. So Cloth Fair was named for the site where the fair was originally held.

Betjeman's former flat is part of a "terrace," a British term for several connected dwellings—in this case, houses built over shops. The Landmark Trust bought the terrace, including Nos. 39 to 45 Cloth Fair, in 1970. Landmark is a charitable organization that rescues small historic buildings, restores them, and then rents them out as holiday flats or cottages by the week (or for "short breaks" of a few days in the off season). Because the Cloth Fair buildings enclose the only house in the City supposedly dating from before the Great Fire of London (1666), it is a special prize in their collection.

Since the seventeenth century, the vicinity of Cloth Fair has dramatically changed. But entering the street—not an easy matter, requiring an unexpected and very sharp turn from whizzing Long Lane into a narrow one-way passage—is like returning, however briefly, to an earlier, slower-paced London. Few cars venture into Cloth Fair. Short as it is, it still shelters several pubs and a wine bar, attractive residential flats above dignified offices, and an ancient church and graveyard. The street has, the Landmark handbook approvingly notes, "a lingering feel of how the whole City of London once was before it was destroyed by money, fire and war—a place where long-established institutions, trades, houses, and markets were mingled together, all rather too close to each other."

The church of St. Bartholomew-the-Great, one of the few churches in the City to escape the Great Fire and considered the oldest in London, sets the quiet tone for the whole street. From our window we look into its small churchyard, with patches of lawn and clumps of bright flowers among old weathered stones. At night loiterers and drunks do sometimes congregate among its wooden benches, and—a regrettable sign of the times—on our last visit we sadly noticed that one night vandals had overturned all the gravestones. But the church still conveys a powerful presence.

Sometimes we attend one of its regular services, and, entering from its original portal around the corner in West Smithfield, we pass under a medieval half-timbered gatehouse with leaded windows into the churchyard and then into the much-restored church itself. Its Norman choir remains, restrained and massive, along with bits from later centuries, like the stone tracery of fourteenth-century windows.

Like many centuries-old churches, St. Bartholomew's forcibly reminds its worshippers of a traditional religious theme: the brevity of life amid the eternity of time. One recent Palm Sunday James and I joined a handful of worshippers and solemnly marched with the choir around the nave as everyone sang and waved palm fronds. The gray stone walls and floor oozed damp and age, the pale light from the high windows did little to brighten the dark March morning, and, despite the celebratory procession, we felt as if we were indeed properly preparing for the approaching Good Friday.

Just outside the portal of St. Bartholomew's lies another reminder of mortality, a tiny fenced square called West Smithfield, surrounded by swirling traffic. If the parklike square attracts any notice at all, is probably due to the surprising number of taxis parked around it day and night. (Beneath the square is an underground toilet, open twenty-four hours a day, so many taxi drivers head here for their breaks.) But this was once a notorious and terrifying place. In the Middle Ages, Smithfield, which derives its name from "smooth field," was one of London's main execution sites. Here, at the then rural edges of the city, excited crowds gathered to relish the spectacle of public burnings and hangings. Among those executed at this spot were the famous "Smithfield martyrs" who had the misfortune to be tenacious Protestants under a Catholic sovereign.

If I am tempted to forget "All flesh is grass," I need only walk across the street. Smithfield Market, formally known as the London Central Meat Market, is not exactly gloomy, but it is certainly grisly. Now that Covent Garden, Billingsgate, Spitalfields, and Leadenhall have all been redeveloped, only Smithfield still provides the hustle and hurly-burly of the old open London markets.

At least once every stay at Cloth Fair, James—who was brought up in the heart of Minnesota farming country—rises early to take a look at the meat market. During the night, as mammoth refrigerated trailer-trucks roll in from all over Britain and the Continent, we sometimes hear their heavy rumbling outside our window. Much of the market's activity takes place in predawn darkness. At five A.M., the market opens, and by seven or so, when James arrives, it is already winding down.

From the outside, the Smithfield Market is a grand Victorian structure with elaborate ironwork and glass-roofed halls, and its stone and brick exterior walls are extravagantly ornamented with arches, pilasters, rosettes, and curlicues. Recently repainted, the market's accent colors—gold, teal blue, scarlet, purple—are startlingly gay. It could be a concert hall, a dance pavilion, or a museum.

But inside the operating market, the colors are quite different. Workers are dressed all in white, their jackets and aprons spattered with bright red blood. They hurry back and forth, shouting and calling to one another with friendly dispatch. Innumerable rows of carcasses—a duller red streaked with cream-colored fat—hang in a series of stalls that line the long hall. White enameled overhead lights shine onto gleaming metallic tables and knives, also splashed with blood. If the Smithfield Market were a museum, it would be full of Breughels.

Once we turn east from Cloth Fair, our neighborhood takes on a very different dimension of cosmopolitanism and culture. A few minutes' walk down Long Lane, the Barbican looms, a modern concrete behemoth of residential high-rises ("tower blocks") and low-rises, connected by a series of terraces, courtyards, stairways, and tunnels. Built mainly in the 1960s and finally completed in 1982, the Barbican is either, depending on one's view, a masterpiece of urban planning or an inhumane monstrosity.

We have become quite fond of the Barbican. Its vast public courtyards, reached by stairways from street level, are landscaped with shrubs, flower beds, and benches. Few people ever seem to use these open spaces. When we emerge from the stairway onto an empty courtyard, we are in an eerily quiet and seemingly uninhabited world, and I have to resist the urge to run and shout and wait for echoes.

Once we descend again into the Barbican Centre (well-marked signs lead to a myriad of entrances and exits), we are in the heart of London's high-profile culture. The center is literally stacked with the arts. Its ten floors include a large concert hall that houses the London Symphony Orchestra, two theatres where the Royal Shakespeare Company performs during its increasingly short London season, movie theatres, a roomy art gallery, a library, and various auditoriums.

Given its daunting size and unabashed modernity, the Barbican Centre is also an unexpectedly welcoming place to hang out. Several restaurants and cafeterias provide meals and refreshments, which we sometimes take outside to the awning-shaded tables on a plaza overlooking a two-acre ornamental lake and fountains. In sunny weather, we bask in the sound of cascading water, look up curiously at the hundreds of windows and terraces in the surrounding apartment blocks, and admire the view of St. Giles Without Cripplegate across the lake. This sixteenth-century church, now incongruously confined within the Barbican complex, has a memorable past: among others, Oliver Cromwell was married there and the poet John Milton is buried inside.

When it rains, we can visit the Barbican Conservatory. Surprisingly unknown, this is a huge indoor garden on several levels, with towering palm trees, bougainvillea, ponds with exotic fish, an aviary, and countless tropical and desert flowers. (Check out the Swiss cheese plant and a saguaro cactus named Fred, a gift from Salt Lake City.) Its opening hours vary; a token admission is charged.

At the end of an afternoon, especially when we are tired from sight-seeing and walking, we often stroll over to the Barbican for one of its free concerts. In its monthly calendar, these are listed as

"Performance Platforms." Except on Mondays and Tuesdays, "platforms" take place either at lunchtime, between twelve-thirty and two P.M., or between five-thirty or six and seven P.M. Avid concert-goers can pile on one performance after another by attending a platform concert, hurrying through the cafeteria, and then seating themselves just in time for a seven-thirty P.M. curtain.

But when we arrive at the Barbican, we usually stop rushing. If we're early enough to find seats, we sink blissfully into one of the cushiony sofas or chairs scattered around the cavernous foyer. (At crowded platforms, some people have to sit on the carpet.) On a raised stage along one wall, soloists or small groups perform Bach, jazz, folk, big-band music. One afternoon it might be the Princeton Tigerlilies, another Chetham's School of Music Ensembles, or the Jive Aces, or a guitar duo. People saunter casually through the foyer, sometimes oblivious to the music, and others on nearby sofas chat in low voices, sip their cocktails, or eat their sandwiches. Between numbers, a few get up and leave, and sometimes we do, too. Platforms are very laid-back events.

Good music abounds around Cloth Fair. Despite the City's reputation as a commercial preserve, its churches and halls offer a number of concerts. Just outside our door, St. Bartholomew-the-Great often schedules free organ recitals. A short walk away, other City churches, like St. Anne and St. Agnes in Gresham Street, sponsor wonderful free lunchtime music—the Isis Trio playing Haydn, for example, or the City University Chamber Choir singing Bach, Debussy, and Monteverdi. (Listings are available at the City tourist information center across from St. Paul's Cathedral.) St. Paul's itself is the grandest of concert spaces; its outdoor notice board announces regular organ recitals.

Although we do not see it from our windows, St. Paul's Cathedral dominates our neighborhood. Its famous dome no longer rises commandingly above the City as it once did. Ugly postwar office blocks now crowd around it and clutter the skyline. But everyone who knows anything at all about London knows St. Paul's is still there. It is an implicit part of the landscape—arguably the heart of the traditional city—just as the Empire State Building and Rockefeller Center are somehow integral to New York.

We pass St. Paul's every day. When we come and go almost anywhere, we take a bus from beneath its magnificent shadow. The shadow itself is full of shadows: niches, loggias, columns, porticoes, Sir Christopher Wren's masterful variations on Baroque themes. It is our landmark—"No, that's east of St. Paul's"; "Just set us down at St. Paul's"; "We'll meet you on the steps of St. Paul's"—and our point of reference. "Cloth Fair is just north of St. Paul's," we explain to puzzled friends who've been to London, and immediately they know where we live.

Our first night in London, before going to bed, James and I always walk the few blocks from Cloth Fair to Paternoster Square, cross its deserted plaza (pretending not to notice the few transients huddled inside their sleeping bags), and stand in the floodlit darkness in front of a silent, sleeping St. Paul's. Looking up at the proud dome, floating imperturbably in the night sky, I breathe a sigh of acknowledgment and relief. Nothing is permanent, but St. Paul's comes close.

Crowds surround St. Paul during daylight hours, and inside the aisles are clogged with tour groups. But, like most of London, St. Paul's has its quiet secrets. The Saturday morning ten A.M. choral matins is perhaps not exactly a secret. But in an era when churchgoers seem a vanishing breed, at least in England, the idea of actually attending a service at St. Paul's doesn't seem to occur to many tourists. If it does, they don't usually think of Saturday morning.

A choral matins, a service almost entirely sung by a highly trained choir of young boys, is a wonderful way to experience a cathedral. Last spring, on a cool, rainy Saturday, we apologetically jostled our way to the front of the line waiting to pay admission into St. Paul's. "We're here for matins," I said to the guard. He nodded, beckoned us in, and pointed us toward a few people—perhaps thirty or less—who were seated just below the great dome. There, while the tour groups waited behind the ropes, we sat for perhaps an hour, absolutely caught up by the high, clear voices that led us through a traditional Anglican service of soaring prayer and praise.

St. Paul's is our gateway to another integral part of London, the Thames. From St. Paul's, we cross the street and head south, past several office buildings, until eventually unexpected stairs lead down to a riverside pedestrian walkway. This path, Paul's Walk, continues to the Blackfriars Bridge and then onto the Victoria Embankment. It is usually remarkably quiet—noisy traffic is diverted above—and it offers unobstructed views of the surging gray river (see Chapter 14, "New Views on an Ancient River").

Sometimes, when I'm extolling the pleasures of life around Cloth Fair, London visitors who have seldom ventured beyond Blooms- bury, Holborn, or Fleet Street are skeptical. They ask if we don't miss the parks, museums, restaurants, and shopping in the West End. I seldom have time enough to tell them what lies within a short walking distance of our flat. Parks? The City is filled with jewellike gardens, some of them—St. Dunstan-in-the-East Church Garden, for example, in the flowering ruins of a Wren church—so tucked away among office buildings that they are known only to locals (or to those, like us, who happen to discover them, either by chance or by using the *Good Gardens Guide*).

Museums? Among the newer and most imaginative in London, the Museum of London lies a few blocks from Cloth Fair. The museum, illustrating the city's entire history with lavish displays, multimedia shows, and whole reconstructed buildings, is in turn part of the London Wall Walk. This paved walk circles high above the City, with stairs leading down to the Barbican, Guildhall, and other important sites, including sections of the old Roman wall.

Although Harrods is admittedly far away in Knightsbridge, we do plenty of heavy-duty shopping only three blocks from Cloth Fair— in a Safeway supermarket on Whitecross Street. Not only do we treat ourselves to delicious yogurts, cheese, lamb chops, fresh salmon, fancy lettuce, new potatoes, crumpets, bramble jam, and other English staples (at prices sharply below Harrods Food Halls), I even pick up my souvenirs there—quintessentially British biscuits, shortbreads, chocolate, jams, soaps (see "A Supermarket of Souvenirs" in *England As You Like It*).

An outlet of Crank's, the popular natural-foods restaurant and bakery, sells fresh whole-grain bread on the other side of Smithfield Market. Dillon's, London's biggest chain of bookstores, has a tiny branch in the Barbican. A newsagent a few yards from our door sells morning papers and fresh-cut sandwiches. Books, bread, the London *Times*—what more could we want?

Although the City is not known for its fine restaurants, all those well-heeled merchant bankers have to eat somewhere. Cloth Fair's pubs, wine bar, and eateries offer informal dining as good (or bad) as anywhere in London, but upscale restaurants continue to open and thrive in the neighborhood. Rudland & Stubbs, which specializes in fresh fish, draws discreetly well-tailored suits to its lunchtime tables in a dark, utilitarian room in Greenhill's Rents, around the corner from Smithfield Market. (The working-class aura is strictly for show; prices are quite aristocratic.)

Stephen Bull's Bistro, on St. John Street, a few minutes' north from Smithfield Market, attracts the sort of jaded gourmets who warm to escabeche of red mullet with spiced aubergine or deep-fried sardines in chickpea batter with saffron dressing. A recent competitor on St. John Street, the restaurant St. John, draws the same kind of clientele, perhaps even more modish. Its chilly black-and-white minimalist interior is a showcase for trendy versions of very down-to-earth dishes like pigs' cheek with stuffed duck's neck and sausages, boiled bacon collar and peas, and grilled ox tongue with potato.

Trendy as Stephen Bull's, or St. John are, possible harbingers of a newly fashionable atmosphere around Cloth Fair, they are unlikely to change the neighborhood very much. St. Paul's will remain; so will St. Bartholomew-the-Great, Smithfield Market, the Barbican, the London Wall, and the whole complex of ancient and modern structures that comprise the City. Best of all, appealing Cloth Fair itself, with its secluded street of shops, offices, and historic houses, will continue to welcome us to an out-of-the-way part of London that the milling crowds in Oxford Street, Piccadilly, and Trafalgar Square will never know.

A Few Floating Facts

The Landmark Trust rents two flats in the same building in Cloth Fair; one sleeps two, the other sleeps four. For rental information, contact the Landmark Trust, Maidenhead, Berkshire SL6 3SW; telephone 0162-882-5925 or fax 0162-882-5417. Or try the U.S. office at RR1, P.O. Box 510, Brattleboro, VT 05301; telephone 802-254-6868.

For more information on the Landmark Trust and its rental properties throughout England, Scotland, and Wales, see "How To Be Your Own Travel Agent" in England As You Like It.

22

The Lost Gardens of Heligan

*I*magine a great Victorian garden surrounding a seventeenth-century manor house near the sea in Cornwall. Picture its pleasure grounds, its massed rhododendrons, rare specimen trees and shrubs from exotic climes—palms, tree ferns, bamboo—and its dazzling walled flower gardens. Add elaborate glasshouses and cold frames, espaliered fruit trees, and even an unusual pineapple pit, everything an established Victorian estate with a wealthy family, its guests, and a large staff might need to feed itself in style.

Now, with a chill any fervent gardener will feel, imagine that this treasured place, developed over several generations, is suddenly abandoned. In 1914, most of the staff goes off to war. The family vacates the house, to return only briefly after the war. Eventually the house is sold and turned into flats. No one is left to care for this complex and exceedingly large (close to two hundred acres) set of gardens.

For almost seventy years, everything lies untouched. Laurel hedges run wild, forming impenetrable walls. Brambles thrive in the moist, mild, semitropical climate. Trees, dying or crashing in storms, lie where they fall. Other trees self-set everywhere. Before long, decaying plant material, compost, mud, and muck layer much of the garden. Boundaries and paths disappear, and then even the garden itself vanishes.

Then, in 1990, three men—John Willis, who as a direct male

descendant of the original Tremayne family had just inherited the estate; his friend Tim Smit, a former archaeologist turned successful songwriter and rock producer; and Smit's friend John Nelson, a talented builder—decide to explore the garden. Hacking their way through brambles and undergrowth with machetes, they glimpse at first only the tops of palm trees waving above riotous vegetation. But what they eventually find is so tantalizing—the remnants of an authentic and unchanged Victorian garden, with many plants and trees still alive, if almost buried—that they decide to rescue it.

Although Heligan is now the site of the largest garden restoration in Europe, not many American tourists know about it. I found it only by chance—or, perhaps, like Heligan's rescuers, by something more than chance. Sipping prelunch sherry in the lounge of a seafront hotel near Veryan, Cornwall, James and I began chatting with a vacationing British couple. When they learned of our love of gardens, the woman exclaimed at once, "Have you been to the Lost Gardens of Heligan yet? No? It's an absolute must! And it's so close! Why, if you're not doing something else after lunch, you could drive there in twenty minutes!"

What garden lover could resist the idea of a lost garden? It suggests, among other seductive possibilities, a secret Eden waiting to be discovered. After lunch, as we threaded our way among narrow Cornish lanes and followed a few scattered signs toward a vague notation on the map, I wondered what Heligan would be like. "Restoration" sounded a little ominous, implying a museumlike quality, tidiness, scholarly notecards. I hoped it wouldn't turn out to be dull.

But as soon as I walked under the thick overarching rhododendrons that form a dark and leafy entrance to the Lost Gardens of Heligan, I knew I needn't have worried. From the formal sweep of Flora's Green, a sweeping lawn edged with giant rhododendrons; along a twisting, romantic ravine among mossy rocks and ferns, with deliberately uneven boulders underfoot; past an enchanting Italian garden with gazebo and lily pool, I was enthralled as I wandered through Heligan's dramatic contrasts.

After the Melon Yard, with its newly restored glasshouses, I admired the vast (1.8-acre) vegetable gardens. In early spring, most plants were only beginning to sprout, but, after studying an almost dreamlike sketch of future plans posted in front of the new furrows, I could easily visualize lush but disciplined ranks of sea kale, potatoes, onions, leeks, asparagus, beans, and more.

Near Heligan's bee boles, a wall of vaulted recesses used for moveable beehives, stands the Crystal Grotto, a dark cave whose roof is studded with set crystals, meant to reflect the light of candles on summer evenings. Part of Heligan's allure is this unusual juxtaposition of utility and beauty.

Beyond the walled flower garden, with its eighty-two-foot peach house newly repaired, is Heligan's most astonishing feature, The Jungle. Suddenly, leaving a placid hillside with views of distant fields and pastures, the path dives downward, into an undulating, tumultuous sea of greenery. Clustered around four descending pools are giant tree ferns—the most extensive collection in Britain—as well as immense stands of bamboo, palm trees, rhododendrons, and three trees that are the largest known (Pinus thumbergii, Cedrela sinensis, and Podocarpus totara). A boardwalk winds among all this opulent foliage, carrying one deeper and deeper into green shadows.

Everywhere in Heligan are exciting signs of a garden coming to life again: tiny sprigs of ornamental box just set into a new pattern, paving stones half laid in front of a gleaming glasshouse, a cleared hillside newly planted with tree seedlings. Part of the fun is talking to the staff and volunteers who are tackling this daunting task with such enthusiasm. Anyone seems willing to put down a spade and answer a question.

For a comprehensive overview and history of the garden, Tim Smit's conversational brochure is full of fascinating facts. When, for the first time in seventy years, sunlight was able to get at some of the beds, long-dormant seeds from unusual plants began to sprout. By using a metal detector, the team found more than two hundred fifty lead-zinc Victorian plant tags buried belowground. Paths, buried under eighteen inches of loam and ivy, were uncovered by digging down to the hard surface and then peeling back the covering like a carpet. (The salt in sea sand once sprinkled on the paths had kept roots from penetrating.)

When Tim Smit talks about Heligan, even after six years of intense planning, fund-raising, and labor, he sounds as thrilled by the garden as he was the day he discovered it—when he said to himself, "Right, the rest of your life starts here." Now he hopes to add a wildly fantastical garden, one that will, he says with a grin, "pervert nature as far as possible."

Heligan is truly enchanted. With some reluctance—"I don't want to scare anyone away"—Smit tells how, in his early days at the garden, certain bothersome spirits kept appearing, often as guides dressed in timeless gardener's workclothes. These guides would politely escort visitors around, but then they would suddenly, and quite literally, vanish. A less wholesome spirit also lurked near the woodland garden. So eventually Smit called in the bishop of Truro, whose official exorcist duly arrived and dismissed the unwelcome residents.

But plenty of magic remains at Heligan. Anyone who has ever dreamed of discovering a secret garden can now travel to mid-Cornwall and find it, emerging from seventy years of sleep, in a hidden valley above the sea.

A Few Floating Facts

Heligan is located near Pentewan, St. Austell, Cornwall. Telephone 0172-684-4157 or -3566. From St. Austell take the B3273, signposted for Mevagissey. The increasingly popular gardens are open all year daily from 10 A.M. to 4:30 P.M. Admission is charged.

V

The Imperfect Traveler

23

Advice for the Guilty Traveler

I am prone to feeling guilty. Perhaps one reason I love to travel is that once I lock my door, pick up my suitcase, and hurry to the waiting taxi, I leave a lot of guilt behind. Instantly I remove myself from the sight of my reproachfully untidy desk, heaped with correspondence, aging bills, and half-finished manuscripts. I don't have to confront the wrinkled heap of ironing in our spare room. I forget the list, infinitely expanding, stuck on the kitchen counter: pick up cleaning, drop off film, get flu shot, order window blind, return library books, call Tess/Stephanie/George. . . .

Now I only have to deal with the guilt of travel. Ideally, traveling shouldn't involve guilt. It should be purely pleasurable—allowing, of course, for unavoidable minor strains, such as cracking one's molar on an unusually crusty slice of bread, or leaving one's cash-stuffed billfold in a vanished taxicab, or cowering helplessly on a plane, which, two hours over the ocean, has just turned back to Gatwick because the pilot has discovered an inexplicable failure in its electrical system. In none of these situations, I am glad to say, did I feel guilt. (Actually, it was James who left the billfold in the taxi.)

But I still suffer guilt when I travel. Consider, for example, sights unseen. When I was growing up in Ames, Iowa, in the 1950s, European travel—let alone travel to India, China, or Kenya—was rare. The chosen few—missionaries, a honeymooning banker and his bride, a retired couple on a splurge—who made a overseas trip could dine out and show their slides for years afterward. More fortunate than the rest of us, they had a moral obligation to give testimony to high school assemblies, youth groups, and assorted neighbors about the Eiffel Tower, St. Peter's, and the Parthenon.

What I learned from looking at all those tourists' slides (apart from acquiring a loathing for slide shows on any subject) was how lucky anyone was to travel. But those who could had a responsibility to those who couldn't: see it all, and, later, tell about it. (Telling for me eventually became writing.)

Besides this implied responsibility, I just want to see it all, anyway. For weeks before a trip to England, I consult guidebooks, trace routes on maps, make notes of walks, gardens, country houses, and museums. In London, I check shows in art galleries, current plays, and special events. But no matter how realistic I think my planning is, I always find it isn't realistic enough. Everything takes longer, and my energy grows shorter. At the end of a trip, no matter how wonderful, some sights remain unseen.

Sometimes this lapse is unremarked, except for my own backward-looking regret. (Would the view from the top of Ham Hill have been worth the climb? Should we have braved the pelting rain to walk around Iona? Will I ever have tea at Claridge's?) But all too often, friends at home, those who couldn't or didn't go, pierce right to the point. "You mean you didn't take the tour inside Buckingham Palace? You didn't try the maze at Hampton Court? You didn't even get to the British Museum?" Well-traveled friends can be worse. "So did you catch Maggie Smith in *Three Tall Women*? How about African art at the Royal Academy? That fabulous new Conran restaurant?" No, no, I'm afraid not, no.

More awkward than failing to see the proper sights is my persistent—in fact, downright recalcitrant—failure to see the proper people. Seldom do I leave on a trip without one or more friends pushing scraps of paper into my hand: "Since you'll be in Cambridge, you absolutely *must* call Irene. I know you'll simply love her, and I've written to tell her you're coming. So she'll be expecting your call." Sometimes, hoping Irene will be too busy to see me, I wait until the last moment. Sometimes I don't call at all.

Maybe I *would* like Irene. But when I travel, my days are already overfull. I don't usually want the further complications of social arrangements—shall we meet for lunch, tea, or dinner? When, where, who pays? I don't like the rigidity of appointments. I'd rather feel free to follow my whims: leave a museum early, change my mind about a matinee, drop into a Wren church, eat early or late, go home for a nap.

Even if I ignore the unknown Irene, how can I explain to an old friend who lives in a city where I'm stopping for a day or two— whether London or San Francisco or Denver—that I don't actually want to come to her house for dinner? That I'd rather see a performance of *The Tempest*? That I can't even meet her for a long, leisurely lunch because I plan to spend the day in Muir Woods? Of course, if I don't let her know I'm coming, I'm safe. But will she perhaps find out from someone? From my Christmas letter?

I even stew about postcards. "Be sure to send me a postcard," friends and family cry cheerily as they wave us off. I nod glumly. I hate sending postcards. I don't mind the cost—though a single card plus postage from London runs at least a dollar—but I sigh at all the time they take. Buy the cards, laboriously hand-write repetitive notes, look up addresses, locate post office, stand in line, affix stamps and stickers. Besides, I always forget someone important. One trip I misplaced my address list—I can't imagine how this happened—and returned home, happily guilt-free, long before those pesky postcards would have arrived anyway.

Besides sins of omission, I am also vulnerable to occasional pangs about self-indulgence. Although I plan our trips carefully, I am still sometimes overwhelmed with the undeniable costs. An inflated three-digit figure for one night, maybe twelve hours, in a nice— nice, but not wonderful—hotel? How long will it take to earn the price of this tasty dinner—tasty, but not memorable—in the hotel's dining room?

At dinner, however, I usually brood less on money than on dessert. Since I rarely eat out at home, I regard a trip as an excuse—indeed, as a mandate—to treat myself. A treat means dessert: not fresh fruit or sherbet, but Dessert. Chocolate gâteau with raspberry coulis, floating island, lemon meringue pie, sherry trifle. *That* kind of dessert.

What follows, besides late-night indigestion, is, of course, guilt. For weeks before the trip, I've sprayed my toast with fake butter, munched carrots, and nibbled on apples. Now I'm sure I won't be able to zip my jeans in the morning. After a week or two on the road, my jeans *do* feel tighter. Just in case, I stop looking in mirrors. Sternly I pledge myself upon return to a disciplined regimen. But, contemplating the bleak future, I decide to sample the charlotte russe that night.

The only kind of guilt I'm getting better at deflecting is frequent flyers' guilt. In the past few years, James and I have traveled often enough to excite a certain envy. For years as a relative stay-at-home, I felt it myself. I understand and sympathize.

But I can tell I'm getting hardened. Now, when I call my daughter, a struggling young artist in New York, I wait until the end of the conversation before I slip in quickly, "By the way, I don't know if I told you, James and I are going to Northumberland in April." I pause a moment for her long, mournful wail—she'd like to go anyplace, anytime—and gently remind her that her day will come. Then I hang up quickly.

When anyone asks me when and where we're planning our next trip, I used to glance at my toes and mumble. Now I just look my inquisitor in the eye and answer. Last week, mailing a package at my corner postal substation, I admitted to Dawn, the friendly young woman at the counter, that next week we'd be going to London. Making a wry face, she said, "I hate you." Then she smiled. As I smiled back, I barely felt a twinge of guilt.

24

Strategies for the Sneaky Shopper

"We're not going to be doing any *shopping* on this trip, are we?" asks James warily. Alert for signs of feigned innocence, he gives me a suspicious sidelong glance. "What do you mean, shopping?" I answer indignantly. "Did I say anything about shopping? Of course I haven't planned any shopping." This is quite true. A sneaky shopper doesn't plan. What happens simply happens.

This ritual exchange can occur, for example, when I have suggested, very casually, a leisurely Saturday morning excursion to London's Portobello Road street market. ("Picturesque," I point out, "and definitely a tourist attraction. We'd be going to look, not to *buy* anything.") Or it can pop up on a rainy afternoon in a Cotswolds village, when I wonder aloud if we shouldn't stop for tea on a main street lined with half-timbered, flower-decked store fronts. ("Don't you need a little pick-me-up? That place looks as if it would have fresh hot scones.") It surfaces abruptly at the moment I cross the courtyard of a historic country house toward a National Trust shop. ("Postcards, dear. I'm just going to get a few postcards.")

If you travel alone, you can shop whenever and however long you want. No one peers over your shoulder, asking, "Do we really *need* that?" or "Where in the world would you put that?" or, just when you've found exactly what you were looking for, "Are you ready to go now?" But if you travel with a nonshopping but otherwise delightful companion, who cheerfully drives along the murderous M25, who carries your bulging suitcase to a third-floor room without complaint, and who frequently provides far-out clues to your clipped *Times* crossword puzzle, you need to develop a few strategies.

Except for those rare occasions when James and I head in different directions for several hours—not always easy, for instance, in a Cotswolds village—I have realized I will never be able to poke aimlessly about in shops. Actually, I buy very little. (James is quite right; we don't need anything.) I worry about materialism (mine in particular, everybody's in general). I think about Thoreau.

But I do love to browse and to bring home a memento or two— souvenir, after all, is literally translated from the French *to remember*—especially if it is fairly small, quirky, and colorful. Looking at a pink stuffed flamingo pajama-bag, now draped over our bedroom chair, I think of the charming village of Lynmouth, Devon, where I found it. When I arrange a few lilies-of-the-valley in a splashily blue patterned vase, I remember a rainy day in a pottery shop on a remote bay in southwestern Ireland. When I open an elegant umbrella covered with pink roses, I am transported to an out-of-the-way street corner in Paris.

So I do occasionally want to shop—just a little, now and then. My first strategy is the fast dash. As James and I are strolling along a shopping street, I cast a quick calculating eye on the windows. If I see something I like—really like, passionately like, instantly know I want—I wait until we've walked just a little farther. At a spot where James can occupy himself briefly, a newsstand, say, or an architectural extravaganza, I stop, touch him on the arm, and say, quite suddenly, as if the thought had just occurred to me, "James, would you wait here for a moment? I forgot something. I'll be right back."

Before James can reply, I'm off at a fast trot, credit card already in hand. In seconds I'm inside the shop. I'd already cased it; I knew it was almost empty. "That rainbow-striped shirt in the window? Do you have it in a medium? Here's my card. Don't bother to fold it, just stuff it in a bag." When, breathless, I return, James looks at my bag, rolls his eyes, but knows better than to ask.

When coping with sizes, however, this can be a chancy maneuver. The errand ploy is safer. Back at our flat or hotel, I generously offer to run out for a little while to get a newspaper, a bottle of sherry, a box of crackers, stamps. On the way, of course, I can duck into a store or two. Later, if James inquires quizzically, "So how far did you have to go for that loaf of bread?" I shake my head wisely. "Quite far," I say. "You'd be surprised."

When subterfuge is impossible, I often have success with a bold frontal approach. Since I'm the travel planner, when I argue that a particular place has cultural significance, I speak with authority. "Everyone has heard of Harrods Food Halls," I announce smoothly. "It's a place where you can see a duchess in tweeds and pearls buying her smoked salmon, brace of pheasants, or foie gras." If we've missed the elusive duchess at Harrods, she may well lurk among the aristocratically blended teas at Fortnum & Mason. "We ought to look at the famous picnic hampers there," I assure James. "Right out of one of Dorothy Sayers's Peter Wimsey novels. You know, Edward Petherbridge on PBS *Mystery!*" As for the Burlington Arcade, just off Piccadilly, with its flashily uniformed beadle, who would want to miss this important Regency survival from an earlier gilded age? Once in Harrods, Fortnum, or the arcade, as any shopper knows, the trap quickly closes.

If a cultural argument fails, I try an esthetic one. Since I'm married to an architect, I appeal to his professional pride. "I've read that someone, you'd know the name, I just can't remember who, has designed a spectacular interior on a shop here on the King's Road. I think the design won a prize. Was it for Jaeger? Or Janet Reger? We'll look as we walk along." I sometimes even dangle a deviously practical suggestion: "Wouldn't you like to whisk through the new branch of Conran's? I know you've been looking for some ideas for that house you're working on. And didn't you want a present for that client you really liked?"

Since England abounds in charity shops, which resemble semipermanent rummage sales, I am not above an appeal to both baser and higher instincts at once. "Why don't I just dash into this little shop for a minute or two? That Royal Doulton candlestick in the window is really a vintage piece. You can barely notice that little jagged chip on its edge. No, it doesn't matter that it's not a pair. It's a fantastic bargain at a pound, and besides, just think of where the money is going. Did I ever tell you what Oxfam does?"

But the most unassailable argument is simply "Here we are!" When fate has decreed that a wandering, unplanned walk through the back streets of London leads you past an intriguing antiques shop, an invitingly dusty secondhand bookstall, or an outdoor street market, one must pay proper attention. If your route lands you in front of an acknowledged hot spot, like Foyle's, a Reject China Shop outlet, or an uncrowded charity shop, all you need to say is: "Look at that! I had no idea that we were so close to Foyle's! Who would have thought that Reject China had a shop on this block? Since we happen to be right here . . ." Nothing, I should point out, prevents a little quiet research before a meandering stroll. A sneaky shopper may not plan, but he or she is always prepared.

25

Travel Time

When I was seventeen, I discovered the magic of travel time. As a freshman at Smith College in Massachusetts, very far from my home in Ames, Iowa, I read in the students' handbook about something called "Travel Time." Both Christmas and Easter vacations at Smith always began at a sternly precise minute—12:05 P.M., as I remember—and failure to register in that last morning class, on what was called an Official Calendar Day, brought dire punishment.

But those few students who lived beyond the Mississippi were eligible for Travel Time. If they could satisfactorily prove to the registrar that their journey took more than forty-eight hours, they were allowed to leave up to two days early. All that first fall I had been desperately homesick, marking off each alien day until I could return to my loved and familiar Midwest. *Two days early?* Incredulous, but hopeful, I read that paragraph in the handbook again. Yes, there it was, in incontrovertible print.

Quickly I figured my train connections. First the Boston and Maine commuter from Northampton to Springfield, then the long-haul New York Central to Chicago, and finally the stop-and-go, rackety ride on the Chicago Northwestern right into the Ames station. At first my total was several hours short, but I judiciously adjusted here and there—after all, trains *were* always late—until I came up with an only slightly padded figure of forty-nine. One more hour than I needed! Suddenly it was as if someone had erased two days from an immutable sentence.

In the world of Travel Time, hours—even days—still mysteriously appear and disappear. Settling down in my airplane seat in Minneapolis, I look at my watch. It is nine P.M., Monday. But in England, where I plan to wake up, in the blink of an instant as I reset my watch, it is now three A.M. on Tuesday. Of course I know, rationally, that those missing hours haven't really been sucked into some black hole, but—especially as I've gotten older—emotionally, I'm not so sure.

Disorienting as it is to lose those six hours, I am even more rattled by the undependability of time during my first few days overseas. Woozy when I am usually alert, and fiercely awake when I would rather be asleep, I feel, quite rightly, as if the hands of my inner clock are wildly spinning. Although I try to live on London time immediately, I cannot help but occasionally remember, "No wonder I want to go back to bed. It's really midnight, not six A.M.!" or "At home, everyone is just sitting down to breakfast. And here I am on my way to a matinee. *Macbeth* before orange juice? Weird!"

Living for a moment simultaneously in two zones, I am suspended somewhere between, or above, them both. Several years ago, a physics professor tried to explain to a group of nonscientists, including me, Einstein's theory of the relativity of time. I did not entirely follow his lecture, but I was delighted by one analogy. If you are sitting on one train and watching another train pass by your window, how can you tell which train is moving? Yes! I'd felt that! And that is how I feel during jet lag. I was not surprised that the analogy involved travel.

Sometimes, during those groggy first days, I remember what another young mother once said to me, many years ago, when we were comparing notes on our lack of sleep. "It's like walking underwater all the time," she remarked, almost in awe. That is what jet lag makes me think of: slowly moving, like an undersea diver in a bubble helmet, through rippling water, green and pellucid, that refracts light and time into unstable, wavy patterns.

Actual time—that is, my sense of actual elapsed time—dramatically changes on trips, too. It took me many years to realize the falsity of a commonly accepted travel equation. On an itinerary, two nights does not really equal two days, three nights does *not* equal three days, and so on. Most travelers arrive at a destination toward the end of a day, and they leave again on a morning. (Hotels frown on departures after noon.) So an itinerary that reads, deceptively, "two nights in London," really only provides one day. "One night in London" allows only a few hours of sightseeing, and "two nights in Bath" leaves a mere day to tour the Pump Room and Roman Baths, attend a service in the abbey, admire the Royal Crescent, pass through the Assembly Rooms and the Museum of Costume, and take a leisurely walk down Pulteney Street, let alone shop or eat or stop for tea.

Impossible for one day? Probably, but many travelers do have the gift of time compression, although I sometimes think it may have been ill-wished by a stay-at-home fairy godmother. On a much-anticipated, expensive trip, it is hard not to want to cram it all in. Especially when James and I visit new places, I always plan more exploration than could possibly fit into one, two, even three weeks. At home, when I have to spend a day dashing about, doing one thing and then another, I become ominously irritable. I love routine, and I treasure long, uninterrupted hours in my own house. But on a trip, I think of time quite differently. It has no set allocations; it offers no routine; it exacts no regular errands or household tasks. Instead, time is open and tempting.

So I rise to its challenge. Each day James and I venture forth, and seldom do we return before suppertime. We see and do so much— even if "doing" is only a long walk on a deserted beach and "seeing" is just a carefully observant walk down a village High Street—that I have to jot down a daily record of our comings and goings. Otherwise, soon after we arrive home, the days and weeks blur together.

Because our travel time is so densely filled, with intense if often quiet experiences, I am always astonished at what has happened—or rather, what has not happened—when we return home. After two weeks of living so vividly, newness in each hour, I feel as if I must have changed in significant ways. We have been gone, I am sure, a very, very long time—even though the calendar may claim we were only away for ten days.

"Where did Jim put the mail?" I ask eagerly, expecting wonderful if unspecified news.

"I think I'll call Dennis or Bill and find out what's been going on at the office," James replies with an offhandedness belied by how quickly he starts to dial.

A few hours later, we sit down at the dinner table and ruefully compare notes. "Anything interesting in the mail?" James asks.

"Not really," I admit, though I pat a small stack of first-class letters, dwarfed by the mountain of throwaways, "but a few things you might want to look at. How about the office? Anything new?" James shakes his head. All that time, I think, we were gone *all that time* and so much happened to us, and back here, time stood still. It couldn't have been the same ten days in Minneapolis that it was in the West Country.

And of course it wasn't. We had been at the bottom of the sea, walking through an entrancing but illusory green light, in Travel Time.

Land's End Is Only
the Beginning. . . .

This is my third book about England, and each time when I've finished, I have felt relieved, a little sad, and very hopeful. I'm relieved because not only have I completed my book, but I have also actually managed to share something about my travels in England (and a little about Scotland and Wales). Before most travelers leave, their friends often say, "Oh, I can hardly wait to hear about your trip. Be sure to call me when you get home so we can have lunch, and you can tell me all about it."

But what happens at that promised lunch? Oh, your friend may indeed ask politely, "Did you have a good time?" or "Did you have good weather?" But you are only expected to give brief replies. If you enthusiastically begin to describe, say, Castle Drogo or the Lost Gardens of Heligan, your friend, despite a determined smile, soon begins to look a little glazed. Then, if you pause for a moment and rummage in a briefcase or purse for your snapshots, you suddenly discover the conversation has swiftly moved on—to family problems, work, politics, new movies, a good book—anything, in fact, but your trip.

So, like most travel writers, I revel in the chance to talk about my trips. Writing these books is like showing all my prized snapshots, except that I use words instead, and if anyone's eyes glaze over, I'm not there to see the book put back on the shelf. "Here," I get to say, "look at this! Isn't that a marvelous view?"

And, besides indulging myself, I can offer to guide someone who wonders how to find a quiet spot for a picnic in London, or take a long walk on a Cornish coastal path, or visit a secret garden in Devon, toward some of the pleasures I've been lucky enough to discover in my travels around the United Kingdom.

But when I finish a book, I'm a little sad, too. Writing about my trips reminds me that they're over; I will never have exactly that experience again. (Sometimes, though, I get so excited when I relive a special day or week that as soon as I type the last sentence of a chapter, I rush downstairs and announce to James, with a sudden sense of urgency, "It's time for us to go back to the Roseland Peninsula!")

Perhaps that touch of sadness has to do with my realization that places and people change. Travelers know this. Perhaps we take those snapshots because we know that even if we return to this precise spot, it will never be exactly the same. (Nor will we.) How long will that secret garden be open? When will others converge upon the picnic spot along the Thames? Will it always be easy to find solitude on the coastal path beyond St. Ives? Now, I want to urge everyone who dreams of going to England, go NOW.

I'm also hopeful. Although I rationally understand that I will never, ever see all of the places I'm curious about, I am also glad that, for me, the pleasures of traveling in the United Kingdom seem inexhaustible. Every time I plan a trip to England, Scotland, or Wales, I make difficult choices. Should it be the winding Cloquet River Valley in Northumberland? I want to walk again on the long sandy beach outside Alnmouth, admire the oak-paneled library at Alnwick Castle, and climb the wooded hills outside Rothbury.

Or should we return to Cloth Fair in London, our cottage near Loch Buie on Mull, or our perch above Church Bay in Anglesey? On the other hand, we've never investigated the medieval churches in Lincolnshire, the famous bookstores in Hay-on-Wye, the Pre-Raphaelite art in Birmingham, the blue hills of Housman's Shropshire, Bess of Hardwick's Tudor mansion or Chatsworth in

Derbyshire, the Maritime Museum in Exeter, the zoo at Port Lympne in Kent, or the Chatham historic docks.

I used to tell myself that someday I would see the British mainland from John O'Groats, at the northern tip of Scotland, to Land's End, at the southern point of Cornwall. Now, many trips later, I have indeed looked out to sea from both of these jumping-off points. I have also visited many places in between. But the more I travel in Britain, the more I want to see. For any reader of this book, I hope that Land's End is also only the beginning.

About the Author

Susan Allen Toth has written for *The New York Times, The Washington Post, Harper's, Victoria, Vogue, McCall's, Travel and Leisure,* and many other publications. Her previous books include *Blooming, Ivy Days, How to Prepare for Your High School Reunion, My Love Affair with England,* and *England As You Like It.* She lives with her husband, James Stageberg, in Minneapolis.